Deborah's teachings and observations are direct and to the point. She does not mince her words to allow the reader to say, "Where is that statement in the Bible?" The reader thirsts for the Scripture regarding the statement and begins his or her quest to desire the truth.

Deborah takes the hungry and thirsty on a journey for the Scripture desiring to know more. She writes with a zest for objectives to be understood and draws the reader to study the Bible to show themselves approved.

Indeed, I can recommend this book for Deborah truly is a today "watchman on the wall."

—Rev. Dr. Hilda F. Brittain
Founder & President of Brittain Ministries, Inc.
Hickory, North Carolina

Jeremiah 4:21 asks, "How long shall I see the standard, and hear the sound of the trumpet?" This question is being asked and is now becoming a battle cry. Dr. Starczewski reveals the answer. Every individual, leader, church, and politician needs to read this book and answer the question "How long"?

—Dr. James D. Craig
Reed to Pillar Ministries
Elkin, North Carolina

Our politicians have forgotten or rejected the fact that America was founded on Christian principles. They have allowed our laws and governmental institutions to stray from godly principles, and have given us a poor substitute in the form of micromanaging the people under innumerable laws, regulations, and watchdogs. Deborah Starczewski's book is a call for us to return to God, and to follow His principles. If we were to do this, we would see an amazing and immediate revival of the American spirit and of our economy. Reading her book will inspire and encourage you.

—Karen Carty
Former President, Iredell County Republican Women
Charlotte, North Carolina

Dr. Deborah Starczewski challenges us to take a stand in America for the Lord Jesus Christ. In order to do so, we must know who we are in Christ. This is something that many Christians have lost sight of in America today. I believe God has positioned Deborah to be a voice for Him as He speaks to her in visions and dreams! Her example of listening to the voice of the Lord is to be commended and is an example to us all!

—Derrick Ross, Lead Pastor
Celebration Church/Lakeville, MN

I recommend *The Midnight Hour: Will America Turn Back to God*? If you want to be stirred—this is a no holds barred, in your face call to repentance. It is timely and exactly the message that is needed in these difficult days. Dr. Starczewski has offered a strong exhortation that is anchored to the hope of Jesus.

—Joe Phillips
Founder of JPM

THE MIDNIGHT HOUR

Will America Turn Back To God?

Dr. Deborah Starczewski

Xulon ELITE

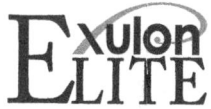

Copyright © 2015 by Dr. Deborah Starczewski

The Midnight Hour
Will America Turn Back to God?
by Dr. Deborah Starczewski

Printed in the United States of America.

ISBN 9781498441667

All rights reserved solely by the author. The author guarantees all contents are original and do not infringe upon the legal rights of any other person or work. No part of this book may be reproduced in any form without the permission of the author. The views expressed in this book are not necessarily those of the publisher.

Editor's note: this book's message arrives in a critical moment for our nation. Throughout the book's development, Dr. Starczewski and I observed confirmations from the Holy Spirit on an almost daily basis and in just about every way imaginable about the timeliness of this message. The spirit realm is stirring profoundly right now. Doctor Starczewski has been a good and faithful steward to capture that stirring and present its various meanings here, for such a time as this.

Unless otherwise indicated, Scripture quotations taken from the English Standard Version (ESV). Copyright © 2001 by Crossway, a publishing ministry of Good News Publishers. Used by permission. All rights reserved.

Scripture quotations taken from the Good News Translation (GNT). Copyright © 1992 American Bible Society. Used by permission. All rights reserved.

Scripture quotations taken from the King James Version (KJV) – public domain

Scripture quotations taken from the New International Version (NIV). Copyright © 1973, 1978, 1984, 2011 by Biblica, Inc.™. Used by permission. All rights reserved.

Scripture quotations taken from the New King James Version (NKJV). Copyright © 1979, 1980, 1982 by Thomas Nelson, Inc. Used by permission. All rights reserved.

Scripture quotations taken from the New Living Translation (NLT). Copyright © 1996, 2004, 2007 by Tyndale House Foundation. Used by permission. All rights reserved.

Scripture quotations taken from the The Living Bible. Copyright © 1971 by Tyndale House Foundation. Used by permission of Tyndale House Publishers Inc., Carol Stream, Illinois 60188. All rights reserved.

www.xulonpress.com

Contents

Preface... xiii
Introduction... xxiii
Foreword #1, by Neal Speight, MD xxv
Foreword #2, by Pastor Bill Ballance.................. xxvii

The Son Of God Shines Brightly 29
The Last Hour On Earth: Two-Minute Warning............ 35
The Light And Fire 38
Put On Strength....................................... 40
The Heart Matters Greatly 42
Prayer Ignites Faith.................................. 44
The Words Of Jesus Are Life 46
America Is In Serious Trouble 49
Ministering Unto The Lord............................. 52
Repentance And Revival................................ 55
Satanic Traps... 57
Manmade Plans: Choosing Family Over God 59
Inquiring Of God...................................... 63
The Enemy 65
Up Close And Personal................................. 67
The Bible... 70
One Nation Under God.................................. 72
Government And Authority.............................. 75
Submit To Government.................................. 77
Your Life Matters 79
Words Matter Greatly 81

vii

The Midnight Hour

The Doctor Knows Best 83
Standing 85
Vision Matters: Saks Fifth Avenue—Windshield Story 88
Weariness And Pain 91
American Idols, Distractions, And Deception 93
Ignite America. 96
Technology Changes Everything 98
Warnings And Confirmations 100
What Flag Or Banner Are You Raising?. 102
Becoming One With God 105
Matters Of The Heart 107
Race To The Finish 109
Hot Pursuit 111
The Titanic 113
Leading, Being Led, And Abiding 117
Pursuit Or Competition. 122
The Gift Of Fully Relying On God: Christmas Beau 124
Ministry In Action. 128
God's Priceless Treasure. 131
A Leap Of Faith 134
God's Emergency Room. 139
Lowering Your Nets 141
No Room In The Inn. 143
A Deeper Walk With God 144
Be A Catalyst For Change. 147
Where Do You Turn? 148
Evil And Suffering 150
Our Response 154
Knowing The Enemy 156
Life Disappointments 158
Valuable Insight 159
Encouraging Yourself In The Lord 160
The Alarm Went Off But No One Was Listening 163
"Tell Them I Love Them". 165
Cruise Ships 168
Get Your Ticket Now 170
Teach Us To Number Our Days 171

Contents

On The Job Training 173
Collapse 177
Committing To The Race 181
Salvation 183
Truth 186
God's Country 189
Shaking 191
Our Divine Roadmap 194
Silence 196
Purpose To Know God In Changing Times 203
Brokenness: The Power Of Surrender To The Holy Spirit 206
Patience Reveals Purpose 213
Choose Life 216
Abiding In Him 218
Blame Game 221
Unity 223
Destruction Within 225
The Body Of Christ 227
Duel 229
True Freedom 231
Circling The Lawn 233
Honor And Respect 235
Divine Discipline 237
Forgiveness 243
Through The Eyes Of A Child 245
Not A Walk In The Park 251
What Kind Of Suit Are You Wearing? 253
Requirements For Revival 255
The Answer: God's Conditions 258
Seek My Face And Turn From Their Wicked Ways 261
Family And The Family Of God 263
Breakthrough 268
Prayer For Rescue From Difficulty,
Hardship, And Destruction 270
Hearing God 272
Turn Aside 273
Inspired By God 275

Deeper Truths	277
The Spirit Leads	279
Attack—Big Surprise	281
What's Next?	285
The Pit Of Bitterness	289
God-Given Dreams	292
The Remedy For Mind Problems	295
Trumpet Or A Trap	297
The Fields Are White With Harvest	299
The Great Divide	302
My Walk	304
Believe God	306
Inquire Of God	313
Thankfulness	315
Resurrection Power	317
When God's Spirit Moves In Your Life	320
The Thief	322
The Holy Spirit—The Power Source	324
The Kingdom Of God Mentality	325
Change	327
The Greatest Teacher—The Holy Spirit	328
Fresh Power—Help When We So Desperately Need It Most	333
Truth Or Consequences	336
Broken Bridges	338
Recovery Of All	341
Marriage And Sexuality	343
Divine Impact	346
Train Your Brain: Take Every Thought Captive	349
Pressing Onward	352
Conscious Choice	356
Praying God's Word	360
Where Is Your Focus?	362
Pursuit Of Excellence	364
City Gates	366
Pressing Onward Comes From A Deep Fire Within That Is Birthed Through Intimacy With God	371

Physical Renewal Is A Necessity 376
Personality Issues And Renewal 379
Hearts Ablaze For God 381
Crisis And Courage 385
Won By One 386
Conclusion 394
The Call To Evangelism 397

Recommended Reading 407
For Further Study 409
Notes 411
About the Author 413
Contact the Author 415
Other books by the author 417

Preface

The following is a dream and vision I was given in early March 2015, long after this book was gone to editing:
I had a white book (open) in my hand and one drop of blood dropped from heaven on it. When it splattered it was white.

The Lord gave me the revelation: Psalm 51:7, "Wash me with hyssop and I will be whiter than snow."

*The open book represents or symbolizes divine revelation and spiritual truth. As an eternal metaphor, books represent the record of lives, genealogies, and the deeds of people. An open book in a dream also invites free access to its knowledge and implies the call to release its information or revelation!

*This is my life verse for Star National Outreach Worldwide (501-C3 Non-profit)

*My life verse for Star Ministries (Publishing and distributing the Word) Knowing God and Making Him Known is John 2:5.

When American turns back to God, she will be washed through repentance. (See 1 John 1:9.)

*God was making it evidently clear we are on time with the release of this new book for America! I sensed through the dream the Lord was revealing His anointing upon the book He had put in my heart to write and publish—for "such a time as this." When God gives you an assignment, it will bring help to others.

Jesus said, "Say not ye, 'There are yet four months, and then cometh harvest?' Behold, I say unto you, Lift up your eyes, and look on the fields; for they are white already to harvest," (John 4:35, KJV).

The number four: the number of world impact by way of the four corners of the earth. Prophetically, the number four represents something with worldwide impact (The rapture of the church will bring about worldwide impact.) Also, it signifies the four compass points—north, south, east, and west—in its intent or effect.

Divine intervention and acts spiritually involving the four winds of creation run the course of the four quarters of the earth. It is a divine command that encompasses humanity and its planet. While seven is the number of global impact, focusing on the continents of the earth, the number four emphasizes the planet within the orb. (See Genesis 2:10; Jeremiah 49:36; Ezekiel 1:8; Daniel 7:6; Zechariah 6:5; Acts 10:11.)

Christ's blood transcends time and space to reach back to heaven, the place of Lucifer's transgression and to Eden to remit its transgression. Jesus Christ's blood remains effective to the end of the age to cover all those born on the earth until then. (See Hebrews 9:10.)

White also is a color that symbolizes triumph, victory in conflict, righteousness, and purity. It also bespeaks holiness and success. (See Revelation 7:9 and 19:14.) Revelation 3:4 says, "Yet you have a few people in Sardis who have not soiled their clothes. They will walk with me, dressed in white, for they are worthy." (See also Rev. 18:19: "Fine linen, bright and clean, was given to her to wear." Fine linen stands for the righteous acts of God's holy people.) Revelation 19:14 says (from the Treasury of Scripture): "And the armies which were in heaven followed him on white horses, clothed in fine linen, white and clean." We are clothed in the righteousness of God in Christ Jesus. Jesus shed His precious blood that we might be washed clean through repentance and redemption for all mankind. White garments represent the righteous acts of the saints of God mentioned in the Book of Revelation, and outfits of glorified saints of God that symbolize their victory in spiritual matters and reward of authority for being victorious.

*(Information for white and book taken from *The Prophet's Dictionary* by Paula A. Price, Ph.D.)

Sit back and breathe! Victory is at hand!

It is time we stand up and do like Cyrus did in the Bible recorded in Ezra 5:13, "However, in the first year of Cyrus king of Babylon,

Preface

King Cyrus issued a decree to rebuild this house of God" (NIV). As born-again Christians, we must choose to turn back to God for cleansing for ourselves as individuals and for this nation to rebuild on the Word of God! We decree and declare that America shall turn back to God in prayer and repentance. We thank God for the shaking that will turn His people back to Him with hearts that are totally sold out to advancing God's kingdom and making corrections in every area for divine alignment.

With what appears as the unraveling of a nation, with a leadership crisis on all levels, we can choose to turn back to God as a nation and believe God for divine re-alignment, divine breakthrough, divine correction, divine delays that are for repositioning us for our destiny, and divine assignments! When you step out in your assignment, God's provision is already there. Our part is to keep moving forward with God. I believe God wants to restore and heal America if she will cry out to Him in this midnight hour we are presently facing. We must choose as individuals to believe God and not allow our emotions to rule our thinking in the face of the extreme adversity and unrest across the globe.

Paul and Silas were in a prison and chose to worship God, even at the midnight hour. God sent a shaking through an earthquake and they broke free from the chains that bound them. God gave them a divine turnaround as the people of God cried out for them and they chose to worship God (see Acts 16:25). What the enemy meant for harm, God turned it!

Deliverance from the Egyptians came at the midnight hour (Exodus 11:4). God desires to move on behalf of America at this midnight hour. Let us stand up and turn back to God as a nation, on behalf of all people.

Ruth changed the heart of her kinsman-redeemer at midnight (Ruth 3:8–9). Like Esther lying at the feet of Boaz, we must return to God and come back under His covering and protection at this midnight hour. Esther chose to come before the King on behalf of her people and brought about the saving of a nation. Esther 9:1–4 reveals the divine turnaround from the plans of their enemy that God gave His people. The Hebraic word *turned* in the *Strong's Concordance* is the number 2015 and means "to overturn, to turn around, to transform and reverse" (Strong's 245b). The year 2015 is the year for America to turn around and turn back to God.

God requires us to turn to Him and stand firm in the midnight hour of turbulent times and changing seasons. Let us pray together for God to frustrate the plans of evil and all ungodly counsel, and believe God for another great awakening for revival of hearts of all mankind.

The church—the Bride of Christ—is arising and taking back the land God gave her. May the church arise and shine, and move from operating in the natural to living empowered by the Holy Spirit. We thank God for increase of boldness for all Christians to stand up and share their testimony of faith in Jesus Christ.

If you are not a Christian, you might be asking, "What difference does it make who Jesus is anyway?" It makes all the difference for all eternity. There is a plan for every person, but we must choose the free gift of salvation by accepting Him as Lord and Savior through repentance and confession.

We are ambassadors for Jesus Christ as believers—born-again Christians. The Good News of the Gospel is a confrontation between God and sinners and we have a Word from the King—and His name is Jesus! It is of utmost priority that we be trained as soldiers in the army of God in how to get people out of bondage and be cleansed by the precious blood of Jesus Christ. This comes through daily surrender to the Holy Spirit, and then living out of His assurance and empowerment.

May America turn back to God as a nation unto Him! But will America turn? Where is this nation headed? God is in control, even in the midst of such turbulent times. God's omnipotent hand moves behind the scenes, working out His plan and purposes. The kingdoms of this present world shall become the Kingdom of the Lord Jesus Christ! The Bible says, "For He must reign till He has put all enemies under His feet" (1 Cor. 15:25, NIV). No matter whether you believe it or not, Jesus Christ is coming back to earth to rule and reign. The Bible also tells us, "To those who eagerly wait for Him He will appear a second time" (Heb. 9:28). So what are we to do right now? Turn to God in prayer. Pray for the President of the United States and all leadership, national, state, local, and your church congregation.

Preface

Whether we agree or not, spiritual warfare is real. In Ephesians 6:12, Paul writes, "For our struggle is not against flesh and blood, but against the rulers, against the authorities, and against the powers of this dark world and against the spiritual forces of evil in the heavenly realms." If you are a follower of Jesus Christ, you have a real enemy who is invisible to the natural eye and who is out to steal, kill, and destroy. Satan hates Jesus, His followers, and righteousness. Paul writes in 2 Corinthians 4, "The god of this age has blinded the minds of unbelievers" (vs. 4). People who have not been born again cannot see or understand things of the spirit. They can't see the glory of God nor understand the Gospel, the Good News of Jesus Christ. Satan wants to silence us to the point of not standing up for righteousness and eventually quitting. We must choose to have bulldog faith in Christ Jesus and stand upon His Word in this last hour!

We must choose to turn back to God in prayer and unity. When we live out of God's Word, we have boldness that makes the enemy mad. We must live fearlessly in the face of evil. The Bible says, "Indeed, the hour is coming when whoever kills you will think he is offering service to God" (John 16:2). We can see it daily in front of our eyes across the globe. Second Timothy 3:12 says, "Indeed, all who desire to live a godly life in Christ Jesus will be persecuted." Revelation 20:4 speaks very clearly about these Last Days in which we live, "Also I saw the souls of those who had been beheaded for the testimony of Jesus and for the word of God...They came to life and reigned with Christ for a thousand years."

We must learn to be confident and take a stand for righteousness! We must be confident in knowing who we are *in Christ* and in *whose we are*—to stand up and not be ashamed of Jesus Christ. The Bible says, "And they overcame him by the blood of the Lamb and by the word of their testimony" (Rev. 12:11, NKJV).

It is way too late to stay on the sidelines, we must have a heart-cry for revival across this nation; for leaders to arise, for equipping of leaders, and for souls to be on fire for God with a passion that ignites a flame in others. Competition has to cease and courage must arise to be men and women of God willing to pay the price to turn back for the lost. God is calling His church to prayer all over America. God is already working in response to the fervent prayers of His people.

God confirms His Word and His message to all who are listening. He did that for me even for this book. Let me share what happened.

The Lord gave me a dream recently where I saw myself in a four-door white sedan, driving down Sunset Avenue. I saw an older man with white hair and white linen clothing. He asked me if I would pull over and stop. I immediately pulled over and this man gently knelt down at the window and said, "Will you preach My Word to bridge the gap between the lost and Me?"

I knew it was the Lord and I woke up. Interestingly enough, a couple weeks later on a Saturday morning, the Holy Spirit prompted me to text a lady in one of my classes. She immediately sent back a text telling me she had a dream about me a couple weeks prior and wanted to tell me. I called her and she began to share that she saw me with this old man with white hair and white linen clothing. She knew in her dream it was Father God. She said we were riding in an ancient-like car and He was driving with me as a passenger. She said she got a little aggravated that we were going so slowly and she chose to pass us. We then pulled over and stopped, and when she turned around to look back at us she saw me with the white-haired man walking hand-in-hand up a rocky hill. She noticed that as we came to a platform and were seated on a front row, we were all holding hands and worshipping together. She said it was light outside, but all of a sudden a great light shone from heaven on us all. Wow, what confirmation of the dream God gave me.

After speaking with her, the Holy Spirit spoke to my heart to add in the silent years between Malachi and Matthew. I did quick research and learned something amazing about Alexander the Great. He had an encounter with God and the Lord opened his eyes to see a man with white hair and dressed in white clothing. As I read the account of how God revealed Himself to Alexander the Great, I knew without a shadow of a doubt that God will again spare Israel—just like He did through the story of what happened with Alexander the Great and the High Priest who came out ahead of the walls to meet him. Alexander promised not to harm Israel. God goes to extreme measures for His people. (This encounter is what moved him to promise not to siege Jerusalem on his way to Syria. Word of the enemy coming was brought to Jerusalem. The High Priest that went out beyond the city walls to meet the enemy read the chapter in Daniel about the little horn. Alexander the Great realized he was the little horn mentioned in the reading—He was warned by God and used by God for the saving of Israel.) Whoever won't stand for Israel won't stand either. We must stand for Israel. We must stand up for righteousness across the nations.

> *I have set watchmen on your walls, O Jerusalem; They shall never hold their peace day or night. You who make mention of the Lord, do not keep silent, And give Him no rest till He establishes And till He makes Jerusalem a praise in the earth.*
> —Isaiah 62:6–7

This also reveals that when we stay close to God, we make greater progress by doing things with God supernaturally, than in any way under our power in the natural. We must learn to depend upon Him. It's time.

It gets even better. Stay close and keep reading. My spiritual daughter who has adopted us as family, Melanie, who has both parents in heaven now, also had a dream. She dreamed we were all driving to New York where I had a very important meeting. She said the man I was to meet with had a very high title and was of great importance, but she did not see who he was. We were all driving to a white house. Melanie told me she was to take all those who came with us to do some sightseeing in New York City.

She was driving and noticed that all the cars had pulled over on the side of the road and the people were looking upward and pointing toward the sky. Melanie pulled over and got out of the vehicle and looked up. She saw the skyline of New York City to the left and saw dark grey clouds spinning everywhere, circling above the Empire State Building. All of a sudden, she saw a lightning bolt come through the center (like the eye of a storm) and hit the top of the Empire State Building. The earth began to quake and shake, while buildings began to crumble and fall.

Next, Melanie got in the car and came back to warn me of what was going on. She ran up the hill and into the white house's foyer. She told me we had to get out of there. Melanie said I grabbed her arms firmly and I said to her, "Shemitah has begun." Melanie responded, "I know," and I said, "Melanie, you know how important this meeting is and I have to stay. Jesus is coming Friday."

The next day, when Melanie shared this dream with me, I went upstairs and turned to a page in a book by Jonathan Cahn named *The Mystery of the Shemitah* and the page I turned to was about the Empire State Building. Wow! The Empire State Building was built during the Great Depression, which was also a Shemitah year, which occurs every seven years according to the Judaic calendar. The Empire State Building stayed empty for quite some time after it opened. I had never read the book on the Shemitah. I had just bought it and when Melanie shared the dream with me, I dashed up the stairs to get it. Neither of us had ever read it.

What is also very interesting is that the name *Friday* means "day of preparation before the Sabbath (which means day of rest)." I shared this in my Sunday morning teaching and a dear lady in the class shared her recollection that either Oral Roberts or his wife had a similar dream many years ago.

God is speaking the same thing to His people. He is warning us of the times and of turning back to Him as a nation.

America is in serious trouble and prevalent unrest is a global problem. It reminds me of the story of the Prodigal Son in Luke 15:11–32. America is much like the prodigal—in a mess. The more Christlike we become, the more we will turn back and look for the lost and hurting like the prodigal son's father. When we turn back for the hurting, God will never forget us. The more we remain like the elder brother, the more we become cheap and selfish, pushing people around in order to stay in a position, and wanting others to pay for everything though it cost us nothing, to the point of loving people to their faces and talking behind their backs. At any given time, we are one of those three people. Who are you in this story? Are you a prodigal, a Pharisee, or a servant?

God is working on us at all times. Thank God He shows us a couple things at a time rather than revealing all that is wrong at once. No one has arrived to perfection in this life. Only Jesus was and is perfect.

Preface

Like the older brother in the story of the prodigal son, will you be eaten up with greed to throw another person under the bus? Are you so comfortable in the house of God that you have lost sight of what really matters for all eternity? Will you stand in unity with other brothers and sisters in the Body of Christ no matter what color, economic status, or position in life they might hold? Will you turn to God and turn back for others in need of God?

Are you standing at a distance and not taking time to get to know the heart of a person and judging them based on what you have heard or think? Have you lost the heart of the Father God and being used as an accuser? Or are you bridging the gap between the lost and hurting and Jesus, pointing them to God? Will you now choose to bridge the gap between the lost and those in need of God? Will you turn? God said in His Word, "I looked for someone among them who would build up the wall and stand before me in the gap on behalf of the land so I would not have to destroy it, but I found no one" (Ezek. 22:30, NIV).

Will you turn back to God in prayer and intercession for all, or be used by the enemy as "the accuser of the brethren?" Hebrews 7:25 says, "…Jesus always lives to make intercession." Satan is called "the accuser of the brethren…who accused them before our God day and night" (Rev. 12:10).

The time of the ultimate confrontation between light and darkness, with battles raging on every front, is at hand. The church was promised the gates of hell would not prevail against her, and she (the Body of Christ) has been given spiritual weapons that will destroy the enemy's strongholds. Yet we must stand up, shake off our differences, link up in unity with our brothers and sisters in the family of God, and be courageous saints who will not retreat, but turn with solid resolve to stand against the greatest darkness of our time—and turn back to God.

Will you choose to stand with God on behalf of someone else, for your neighbors, and for America? Will you turn back to God in prayer and intercession for the lost and hurting? Will you allow the enemy to use you to destroy others? It is a choice. Jesus said, "Truly I say to you, to the extent that you did it to one of these brothers of Mine, even the least of them, you did it to Me" (Matt. 25:40).

When we choose humility over pride, helping rather than hurting, building rather than destroying, we are choosing the foundation of the Kingdom of God over the present kings of the air and their darkness.

Will you turn to God?

Introduction

This is a deep heartfelt cry for America to return to God with her whole heart. Despite the fact that we now live in a nation that has turned to everything but God and that has created laws that legalize sin, we can still *choose* to obey God's truths found in the Bible. It is not the law that actually makes any nation, but rather, it is the hearts of the people who live in that nation.

From the harbingers that we have seen happen to the four blood moons lining up perfectly in the heavens, we must be prepared and ready, watching for the return of Jesus Christ! Souls are at stake and people are in search of hope. Unless someone tells them, how will they know about the hope in Jesus Christ?

Good people don't go to heaven—only people who have *received* Jesus as Lord and Savior spend eternity with Him. Jesus came and forgave the whole world through His death on the cross and resurrection. We must choose to fan the flame in our hearts as individuals by living in God's Word every second of every day, carrying the Word of God to all!

I know personally that God honors His Word. He raised my husband Dan from the dead in 2012 and made Himself known in extreme measures through twenty-five days at Mercy Hospital. The full account is found in *A Leap of Faith: 25 Days at the Mercy Seat* (published in 2013). God goes out of His way to make His holy presence known so we stay aware and encouraged to keep moving forward. The same resurrection power that brought Dan back to life is still available to us today. Had Dan not chosen to go to the hospital, he would not have been in position to receive the miracles and medical assistance God had available for him to receive.

My prayer is that each and every person reading this book will heed the warnings and return to God as one nation under God. Every problem we are facing is the direct result of a spiritual need. It is not a financial, political, or cultural problem. The major concerns and problems arising are evidence of a nation that has turned away from God and is asleep. I pray that you would look to God and choose to take Him at His Word. May God draw you close and reveal Himself to you in greater measure.

We must choose to take back the ground that has been surrendered by the church, given to her by God. The enemy has enslaved many to false religions, addictions, sinful habits, and has waged war against all believers of Jesus Christ to frustrate the plan of God for believers to spread the Gospel. If we choose to continue or cultivate any known sin, we are giving place to the devil and opening a door for him to gain access to other areas as well. Paul said he didn't want us to be ignorant of Satan's devices (see 2 Cor. 2:11). Many Christians are unaware of Satan's tactics and strategies. It is time for believers to arise and *be* the church. I personally believe we are in the final hour and God has stopped time for more people to come to know Him. Will America turn back to God? Will you? God is our only hope.

It is God who opens our eyes and hearts! He is the only One who truly revives. "Lord, send revival to America, to the church, and the nations." God will not bypass the church in order to bring change. The church must wake up, arise, and operate with the keys of the kingdom that she has been given (see Matthew 16:18–19).

> *And I say also unto thee, That thou are Peter, and upon the rock I will build my church; and the gates of hell shall not prevail against it.*
> —Matthew 16:18, KJV

Deborah Starczewski

www.starministriesinc.com

Foreword #1

I believe the world is getting ready to face trials it has not seen since the days of Noah's flood. I'm not one to make predictions, but I will predict the obvious: the safest place to be is in the center of God's will. We will need to hear His voice more clearly than ever before. The centerpiece of human history is the relationship that Christ sacrificed his life for to give us with God the Father. He was obedient to His call and by doing so gave us the right to approach God directly and to live in the power of that divine inheritance. *The Midnight Hour* is the story of Deborah Starczewski and the wisdom she's gleaned in pursuing and obeying God's Word even in the most difficult of trials. Having known Deborah for more than ten years, I have seen God's supernatural anointing in nearly her every circumstance. Time and again the "coincidences" that occur in her life and relationships she develops seem nearly impossible to have happened by chance. She walks clearly in pursuit of her heavenly Father and in the divine inheritance to which we've all been appointed. The message on her heart is an impassioned plea to the Body of Christ to pursue her first love and turn this nation back to the One who granted its freedom, before it is too late. Please take the time to read and study it carefully for we will all need this wisdom and encouragement in the days to come.

—Neal Speight, MD
The Center for Wellness
Matthews, NC
May 2015

Foreword #2

Having lived more than six decades in the United States of America, through the assassination of a president, the impeachment of another, the removal of prayer in schools, the legalizing of aborting unborn children, several wars, and the decline of foundational principles of morality, family values, integrity, and the fear of God it is not surprising to see the state of a nation that once was the world's strongest power crumble from within. When world nations study the American principles to see what made it great, and they do and have, they are also able to see how hedonism, new age thinking, worship of false Gods, and lust for power and wealth has broadened a divide that is destroying America from within.

What can change the path of a nation headed from destruction? American is a nation that has received warnings and awakenings and a nation whose leadership has snubbed these warnings in arrogant pride, while only depending upon self. What has it lacked? No true repentance! With a finger on the pulse of where America stands and on what God is saying to a nation, Deborah Starczewski takes a stand for the healing of a nation and what it will require. Through biblical patterns of truth and revelation, through God given dreams, hope is birthed through the following pages. Deborah not only calls us to have eyes to see, and ears to hear what the Spirit of God is saying to us individually, and as a nation, rather she is calling us to act and act we must!

It has been the privilege of my wife and I to know Deborah, her ministry and the God anointing on her for the last fifteen years. Her heart for God and the spiritual gifts she operates in are a confirmation of demonstration of the Holy Spirit working in her life. I endorse Deborah to you today. Not only is Deborah a woman of God, she is one whose ear is set to hear the voice of God. I believe that the content of this book is timely to the deliverance of America from the sin of its "piped piper" that has led it down a path of deception. The message rings loud for each of us individually and to all collectively. A message from God to a people whose nation He desires to heal that they might be saved.

—Pastor Bill Ballance
Central Assembly of God
Great Falls, Montana

The Son of God Shines Brightly

Like the sun coming and piercing through the clouds, so will Jesus come again! Like the sun piercing the clouds, may the church arise and shine brightly.

The life of God within makes us shine brightly and leaves a sweet smelling fragrance to all we encounter. Jesus sat down at the well in Samaria and met a woman who experienced life change. Her one encounter with Jesus changed her life immediately and the life of an entire city forever.

She came for water at the well at noonday. Rather than leaving with her water pot filled, she left being filled herself—with the Living Water. She met Jesus personally and left with hope, and contagious faith to believe.

She went back to the same place where people ridiculed and criticized her for her past. The crowds saw something different in her and wanted what she had that was different. They saw a hope and excitement in her as she shared about Jesus. (See John chapter 4)

Rather than living with a cloud of doom and despair from what she had walked through, she came to know Jesus. There is great hope for America if we will turn back to God individually and as a nation.

Much like the woman that came to the well at noonday, America must come to God in repentance and transparency with a desire for more of Him. Anyone can get confused. We can all get confused. My friends—America is in a state of confusion.

We learn from the Old Testament when Israel followed God the people were blessed. When they had a king who did not know God, life did not go well. When the Israelites were confused while wandering in the desert, God sent a pillar of fire to lead them by night, and a pillar of cloud to lead them by day. The woman at the well left with the fire of God within her. She became a living vessel for the Spirit of God to flow through to others. America can have the fire again, too!

Jesus was crucified and died, rose from the grave, ascended into heaven, and is now seated at the right hand of the Father God, interceding for us that our faith will not fail. The Holy Spirit came and dwells within us as born-again believers. The fire of the Holy Spirit represents purifying. Like the woman at the well, we must move forward and leave our past behind, symbolized by her water pot she left behind at the feet of Jesus.

The deeper our relationship with God, the greater refreshing that flows out of our heart, the greater purity of heart, the greater abundance, and the high cost of the deeper calling unto God. Deep calls unto deep.

(Read Mark 3: the miracle, the attack, the boat; multitudes followed Him.)

America is a nation that once knew God. We must turn back to God and dig deeper into His Word. We must have a commitment to prepare our hearts as a place of prayer, worship, and adoration unto God. In order for America to prosper as a nation, it demands personal sacrifices and not personal compromise. It will require a commitment to being flexible rather than being caught up in comfort.

Like the woman at the well, we can't live in the past, but rather keep moving forward to develop and maintain our own relationship in Christ. We must allow the Son of God—Jesus Christ—to pierce our hearts with His great love for Him and for America. And for souls across the nations! May we turn back to God, dig deeper in knowing God, and pray for revival.

Like the sun pierces through the clouds on a dreary day, may we be so full of the power and presence of God through the Holy Spirit, that we represent the Son of God to others, to offer them hope and light.

Like Joshua, we must keep moving forward. We must get rid of hindrances and any sin so that we can be fruitful and have much fruit that lasts. We have to grow through reading the Bible and choosing to go deeper in God. There is more. We have to get up off the pews and move forward advancing the Kingdom of God. We do this through obedience to the Word of God.

Digging deeper is more costly. It is a divine gift from God to have the desire birthed within to dig deeper. Like a tree planted beside the waters, we stay planted, receive life from water, sun, and fertilizer, and stand strong so we will have much eternal fruit that lasts forever. We have to live out of the Word of God, read the Word, and learn to abide in Jesus to have a clean vessel and pure heart that hears the voice of God and obeys immediately.

When we dig deeper and turn to God with our whole heart, we have a hunger and thirst for righteousness that never ends. We choose to keep ourselves clean through walking in God's love, keeping short accounts, confessing our sin, and forgiving others. We choose to keep our hearts as an altar for God. We choose to obey God's Word in advance. People who have chosen to obey God's Word will hear from Him.

I went to a conference about seventeen years ago named "Unstopping the Wells" at a church in Maryland. I remember learning we must get rid of all hindrances and unstop wells. (See Genesis 26:12–25.) As for us today, the dirt represents carnality and anything the adversary has thrown in from the past that we must choose to get rid of on purpose. The life source or the well of living water can only flow out of us when we choose to get rid of all hindrances and carnality. We get rid of the dirt through prayer and fasting.

(Read Genesis 12.) God was going to give the land to Abraham, and God keeps His word. After they overcame Jericho and Ai and found sin in the camp, the challenge was to go back to Ai (see Josh. 7–8). They formed their military strategy and never again were they defeated. They built an altar and gave praise to God for giving them the victory. We can learn much in the Bible by applying it to today.

After Abraham arrived in Canaan, the Bible tells us the first place he went to was Sichem (or Shechem). In Shechem he built an altar. The second place he went to was Bethel, and there he also built an altar. Later he left Bethel and went to Egypt, staying in between Bethel and Ai, the place where he first built an altar. Later he went to Hebron and also built an altar. The names of these three places are significant. Schehem (shoulder) represents a place of strength (Genesis 12:6-7). Bethel (the House of God) is the Body of Christ. God wants to raise us up to fulfill His purpose. God's house—living in the Body of Christ is not only a principle to follow, but also a way of life. The name *Hebron* means "fellowship" in the original language and we must learn that we are designed for relationship with God, not religion. We find strength when we return to God in unity with the Body of Christ and in prayer.

We must stop giving excuses (read Rev. 3: God has opened doors that no man or power can shut). We must either walk through the open door and live as though God is Lord of all—or not at all.

We serve because He says so. We must keep working because it is clear—fear the Lord and serve Him with all faithfulness—and throw away all false gods and idols.

We can put being busy, family, comfort, plans we have for our own children, and anything that is not God's plan up as idols. We must learn to trust God and His plans for us, not always our own. We must abandon ourselves to God and choose to worship and serve Him, while helping others along their journey.

When we turn back to God in repentance, He will heal our land. When we turn back to help the hurting, God will never forget. (See 2 Chronicles 7:14)

When we choose to serve the Lord with all of our hearts, worship flows out of our work. We serve the Lord intentionally in all we say and do. We are cleverly disguised as ministers in whatever sphere of influence we find ourselves. The choice is clear, contagious, and precise. We shall serve the Lord!

Jesus said He has prepared a place for us—we just have to receive Him. If we prepare our hearts—a place for Him—we will experience abiding in Jesus. Giving. It's not about money, but souls. It's not about history, but about Jesus and His story that will leave a legacy of lives changed.

If we prepare a place, the people will come. Every single thing we go through in life, no matter how great the adversity or attack, God will give us a platform of praise for Him. We need the power of His presence and a heart that has chosen to obey the Holy Spirit and follows His leading.

Instead of risking another 9/11—let's focus on Genesis 11, and build unity.

Prepare your heart to receive more. Elijah repaired the altars. We must do the same. The Bedouins lived in tents, but were flexible. We must learn to be flexible and be willing to move forward through attacks, past comfort, and past old wounds and hurts to experience God.

In this midnight hour, it is of utmost importance for believers to recognize the enemy and know how to overcome. Without the Word of God and without standing in the position God has given us by faith, there can be no victory over the enemy. We must choose to overcome the world (the people, things, and events) in our heart on purpose. We must learn to forsake the world and learn to have fellowship with God. This comes by learning to abide in Jesus and sharing our testimony. We learn we are stronger than we think we are when we depend upon the power of the Holy Spirit.

In Scripture, the place named Gilgal speaks of overcoming the flesh, while Bethel speaks of overcoming the world (Egypt is represented as the world and bondage to the world). Jericho is dealing with Satan. While many believers understand the battle between the spirit and the flesh, many do not perceive the conflict that rages between us believers and evil spirits. (See Ephesians 6.) In this final hour the evil forces are raging and stirring up conflict and distress in order to hinder and prevent believers from serving the Lord. Such demonic attacks come in the believer's environment, sometimes in thoughts, emotions, physical bodies, and sometimes in their spirits. To overcome the attacks of evil, we must believe in the Word of God's promise, thus putting the enemy to flight and must choose to stand in our heavenly position that Christ has given us.

We must learn to crucify our flesh where our old ways or old flesh must be "rolled away" represented by Gilgal. Genesis 12:9–14 records the descending of Abraham to Egypt. There he built no altar. His communion with the Father God was interrupted, and his heart of consecration was put on the sidelines for a time. What we learn from Genesis 13:3–4 is Abraham had no fellowship with God while he was in Egypt. It was when he returned to Bethel that he once again called on the name of the Lord. America must return to the place of a spiritual Bethel—where she calls upon the name of the Lord again! The last place is the River Jordan where Jesus conquered death and we await the rapture of the church. Jesus is coming back for His Bride—the Body of Christ. Are you ready?

The Last Hour On Earth:
Two-Minute Warning

Is it the End Times or the end of time? What if it was your last hour on earth? What would you be doing? What kind of pace would you be running for last minute preparations if you knew you only had one hour left? But let me warn you, it *is* the last hour. Time is running out; minutes are ticking away. I believe we have reached the midnight hour—we are now a nation in crisis!

"Little children, it is the last hour" (1 John 2:18, NKJV). You may be thinking you have heard this long ago and it still hasn't come. If it was the last hour when John wrote those words, we most certainly know it is now. We may very well be at the two-minute warning on God's timetable. He may have time standing still for more souls to come to know Him and for us as a nation to turn back to Him.

When John wrote those words, he was watching God's clock, not ours. God's timing and our timing are never the same. Sometimes it can feel like life happens at the wire. Choosing to live with eternity in mind puts everything into proper perspective.

Have you ever watched an hourglass running out through the small neck down to the bottom? It goes faster toward the end. Life has sped up and knowledge is continually increasing. Life is drastically changing before our eyes.

No one knows exactly when the end is, but the Bible gives us warnings and signs for those who are watching and waiting for Jesus to return. What we do know is what Jesus said: "But of that day and hour no one knows" (Matt. 24:36). However, we can obviously tell we are close with all the signs of the end time manifesting across the globe. People are in pain and desperate for answers. There are earthquakes, wars and rumors of wars, terrorist's threats, beheadings, and attacks increasing, and famine in many places. But we also have a famine of the Word of God. Souls are at stake for all eternity in the midst of it all.

We are commanded to snatch men and women from the flames of eternal hell by preaching the Gospel and leading others to Jesus Christ. The Gospel is eternal, but we certainly don't have eternity left to preach it. We are to run the race with Christ *now!*

Right now, my new puppy is running laps in the kitchen. He comes to the gate just behind me and sits to watch while I write. It's funny to watch him run while he throws his baton-like toy, with hearts on each end, up in the air. That is how we are to do life as well. We are to run the race of life, fully knowing hearts are at stake for all eternity. We are called as believers in Christ to carry the Gospel and pass the baton of hope to others. We have had enough warning of what we are called to do. We have to move from the pews and sidelines to the frontlines. We are called to occupy till He comes— that means we work hard and spread the Gospel of Jesus Christ to all mankind.

We are all in training for battle. God trains us so we recognize His voice and warnings. New puppies in training give warnings as well. Sometimes, I miss the puppy's two-minute warnings and find puddles (...and other substances...) on the floor. Puppies and dogs will go to the door when they need to go out. They sit and watch for you as their master.

God uses puppies in training to teach us to pay closer attention. We can be active and even productive throughout the day, and yet still miss God's clues. We are called to watch and pray. We are called to build each other up in Christ. We are to watch for the return of Jesus Christ, for that moment is nearly at the door.

In the midst of waiting, we are to build the body of Christ. The Body of Christ is the church as a whole, made up of all believers. We are called to edify and encourage each other.

Are you building others up or tearing them down? Are you praying for yourself and others, or fraying at the ends? Are you depressed, tired, and worn-out from the battles in life? Your mind may be racing, thinking "Is there really a path we should take?" or "Is there some Creator who has placed us here and leaving us for destruction?" The answer is a resounding no!

God loves all mankind. He gave His only Son that all might come to know Him and be saved. Good people don't go to heaven. People who have *received* forgiveness are the ones who spend eternity with God. The whole world has been forgiven, once and for all, through the sacrificial Lamb—Jesus Christ. However, only those who *receive Him* will spend eternity with Him. This means you repent of sin, believe and confess Him as Lord.

The best is yet to come. Eternity will be awesome for those who have received forgiveness! People who know they have been forgiven are thankful people. We must learn to live in worship and thanksgiving for the completed work of Christ Jesus on the cross. *Thanksgiving is the language of faith that pleases God and causes miracles to manifest in your life.*

The Gospel is simple—it is mankind who has made it complex. Salvation is about a relationship with the God of the universe through Jesus Christ His Son. It is not about religion. It is about developing a relationship with Jesus and living out of His Word, the Bible. We are called to be a light to those in darkness and live in the supernatural power of a transformed mind where we live under an open heaven— access to a life of miracles and God's resources here on earth.

The Light And Fire

The church is to be a light to the world. We are to preach the gospel, in season and out of season. We are called to be a witness and lead people to God. We are called to look for the broken and bridge the gap between them and God through sharing the Good News. Yes, the Gospel of Jesus Christ is good news!

Many churches are actively building ministries—but what about people? We are to be out in the world, operating in the power of the Holy Spirit. We are called to exercise our authority in Jesus and shake the doors of hell. God's people are not given "a spirit of fear, but of power and of love and of a sound mind" (2 Tim. 1:7, NKJV). The Holy Spirit gives us boldness and equips us to touch the lives of others. We are all called as ministers, cleverly disguised in whatever sphere of influence we find ourselves and God leads us to.

The fire of the Holy Spirit is real. The embers in a fire in the natural will burn you if you touch them. They are coals of fire. We all need coals of fire to touch our lips and hearts to cleanse and revive us, once again. When we live in the Spirit of God and remain in His Word, our lives will radiate a certain glow of excitement and will influence others to come to know Jesus as well.

The fire of God will cleanse from within when we receive His touch. The fire of God must flow through us like the blood of Jesus flowing through our veins. When we get on fire for God, we will run the race to win our lost generation. We will not be consumed with trivial stuff such as new lights for the lawn, the latest new phone, or even a new theatrical performance. Of course there is nothing wrong with any of those things, but we are called to live with eternity in mind at all times.

When the power of God is operating, the Holy Spirit draws people and they are saved and changed by Him. This happens in the marketplace, on the job, in the malls, in board meetings, in hotels, resorts, and restaurants. I call them divine appointments, set up by God for us to cooperate with Him. It happens twenty-four seven when we look for God and expect to see His hand in everything. We are called to be a light in the darkness and fish for souls each day. We are in the Last Days and the end is coming, whether we believe or not.

The Bible says, "Little children, it is the last hour" (1 John 2:18). I believe God is holding back time and is giving us major warnings. We don't know exactly where we are on God's clock, but we do know by the earthquakes and signs Jesus warned us about that we are closer than most would like to think. Paul said, "Knowing the time, that now it is high time to awake out of sleep; for now our salvation is nearer than when we first believed" (Romans 13:11). We must strengthen ourselves in the Lord.

With the news of people being slaughtered across the globe, it is foolish to think it won't happen on American soil. It is naïve and reveals a choice to live in denial. But we must wake up, arise, and put on strength!

Put On Strength

"Awake, awake! Put on your strength, O ZION" (Isa. 52:1–2). "Awaking" in Scripture has to do with prayer. The Lord Jesus found the apostles sleeping as He awaited His betrayer in Gethsemane, and said, "Watch and pray" (Matt. 26:41), or "stay awake and be alert."

We have been given a command to pray. Jeremiah 10:25 reveals to us that God will judge the prayerlessness of the families of this world who do not call on His name. The Bible instructs us to pray, seek the Lord, shake off lethargy, pay the price, seek God with all our might, choose to love God deeply, and make Him our number one priority. When we obey God and pray, we find that strength will come. We have strength against sin and temptation, and weakness will go. We choose to put on garments of righteousness and sin is not able to touch us. We may walk through a season of hardship and attack, but we still have joy within because we know God is in control.

The unclean and uncircumcised (of heart) will not be a part of us. We will no longer have fellowship with the world. We also won't run to and fro looking for people to pray for us, but rather, we will shake ourselves from the mess of the world and arise to be set free in Christ. We come to know the power of God for ourselves and have relationship with Him throughout the day. We know we can turn to God in prayer any time of day or night.

When we choose to pray and draw close to God, we enter into rest. We find real peace in Jesus and we are loosed from the grip of Satan and sin that tries to come against us. We choose to cultivate godly relationships and stir each other up in faith. Choose to fall in love with Jesus all over again—and then keep yourself stirred up.

Jesus illustrated this to the apostle Peter when He said to Peter, Simon, son of Jonas, lovest thou me more than these? He said unto Him, Yea, Lord; thou knowest that I love thee. He saith unto him, "Feed my lambs" (John 21:15 KJV).

Jesus was asking Peter if He was first place in his life. When Peter said, "Yes," Jesus instructed him: "Feed my lambs." The point Jesus was making here is this: because Peter was called to ministry, Jesus told him to feed His lambs. But for Peter to actually fulfill the call on his life—and for you to fulfill the call on your life whether it is fulltime ministry or another business or occupation—it will be necessary for you to engage your emotional capacity to love God. If you are going to truly fulfill your call, God will have to be your first love. You will have to develop genuine adoration for Him. For some people, it will be a natural affection, but for others it will be something you pursue on purpose. It will provide strength in battle to face the coming days ahead!

When facing major battles in life, it is wise to have others standing with us through the storms in prayer. We encourage each other and know others are walking with us. We know God is real and personally involved in the details of our lives.

As a nation, we must unite in prayer across America, return to our first love—stand up, call a solemn assembly, and pray like our lives depend on it.

The Heart Matters Greatly

We must call this nation back to prayer. The prophet Joel said, "Rend your heart and not your garments...return to the Lord your God...Blow a trumpet in Zion, consecrate a fast, proclaim a solemn assembly" (Joel 2:13, 15, NAS). A solemn assembly was a sacred meeting or gathering calling God's people to return to Him and renew their covenantal relationship with Him in repentance. When we turn back to God as a nation wholeheartedly, we invite Him back into our homes, our churches, our business affairs, our government, and nation. This returning to God invites Him back into every area of our lives.

A solemn assembly only works when hearts are repentant. It comes from deep down inside the heart, not merely an outward show. When my husband found out he had less than a week to live if he didn't have surgery on his heart, he had a choice to make immediately. There was no waiting around thinking about it for days. If we as a nation sit back much longer, with the destruction that is evident, we will continue to lose ground.

The heart matters greatly because you can't live without it properly functioning. If it isn't working, nothing else works either. Blood has to be pumped and flowing properly or parts of the body will die. Blood is the source of life. The walls of the heart and the valves keep the blood on a "one-way street" through the heart and out to the body.

Dr. Mehmet Oz states: "The heart—the engine underneath the hood of your circulatory system—is like the workaholic friend who never takes her vacation days. It's in a constant state of coordinated activity, with not even a quick break for lunch."[1] The heart is actually a muscle made up of four chambers that pump blood through your body, delivering oxygen and nutrients. The process is repeated over and over. I believe you can see for yourself the necessity of a heart that is working properly. America has a heart problem. God says to return to Him with all of our hearts. He is saying for us as a nation and a people to return to Him as our fundamental source of life. He must be the center of our personal lives—we have to get rid of anything that displeases God. We have to get rid of the trash. Ignoring trash will cause a huge problem. God is giving America an invitation to return to Him with her whole heart and He will help us as a nation—once again.

When a government functions as divine authority as opposed to under God's authority, we as Christians must stand up—stand strong upon the Word and pray, and courageously endure, and patiently accept the consequences of obedience to God. Walking with God doesn't make us immune to attack. Satan hates Christians and righteousness; however, we have confidence of victory even in suffering because we will reign with Jesus.

We overcome through the blood of the Lamb and the Word of our testimony. (See Revelation 12:11.)

Prayer Ignites Faith

Prayer changes everything—most of all us. I pray that our hearts and minds might come to the place of understanding where we know that it is possible for God to take all our human weaknesses and failures and transform us by His mighty powers into a new creation if we *"only believe"* (Mark 5:36).

When we choose to focus on God and look to Him we find hope and faith to believe again. Whatever we focus on in life we see. Whatever we focus on becomes bigger. God is a big God—He created all and owns it all. God desires to fill us with the Holy Spirit that the government will rest upon His shoulders. (See Isaiah 9:6.)

We must pray that the hearts of all people in this nation will turn back to God and dare to believe Him. We must choose to take our own leap of faith into the will of God and trust Him for all.

There is deadness in America that needs a touch from God and His resurrection power. It will revive us and give us hope again. We need to examine ourselves and see if we are truly surrendered to God and depending upon His strength—or have we moved to being self-sufficient and lacking the real power of God through prayer? It is easy to believe God's Word, but it is living on an entirely new level to believe His Word (what He says) over a situation. God desires that we come into divine alignment with Him so we can live out of brokenness (which means empty of self), but full of Him. It is God Himself that moves the Word from our heads to our hearts—so it becomes part of the very fabric of our being. Then when a letter arrives, a knock at the door comes, or the phone call comes, reporting bad news, it is the Word of God that rises up and not our emotions. We learn to respond rather than react.

God desires to fill us to overflow so that a ceaseless flow of the river of life will be made evident to others and us. We must come to a place of surrender—where all we want is Jesus and have a passionate desire to please Him in all we say and do. When this happens in believers, we will see great change. Others will notice the change as well. Our heart begins to yearn for God and we are revived and refreshed; a new hope is birthed within to know God is for us and He has a great plan for our lives. This is how revival is sparked and faith grows.

We must not be satisfied with anything less than real change in our own nature through the indwelling presence and power of the Holy Spirit of God. The overflow of a repentant heart brings restoration and life to all. We experience an excitement and zeal about life again and others want to know what it is—the real fellowship with God.

Our fellowship and intimacy with God overflows and brings about reconciliation with others, and also limits the consequences of sin.

> *"If we confess our sins, He is faithful and just to forgive us our sins and to cleanse us from all unrighteousness"*
> —1 John 1:9, NKJV

If there was ever a time we need God to cleanse us from all unrighteousness, it is now. Thank God His Word is alive, up-to-date, relevant truth for us today.

The Words of Jesus Are Life

The words of Jesus are life. If you believe them, you will feel quickened in your spirit man and you will know that nothing is impossible with God. It may look impossible to the natural eye and to those around you, but you will have a knowing deep down in your soul that God has you in the palm of His hand—that He is at work in the minute details of your life and situation. He loves America and the nations. He loves His church. He loves you. He died and rose again for you.

Listen to the words of Jesus: *"With fervent desire..."* (Luke 22:15); *"the hour has come"* (Mark 14:41). What hour? Time was finished and eternity had begun for every soul that was covered by the sacrificial blood of Jesus. God hasn't kept the ending a big secret. He desires that we all see the big picture in life. He wants us to know the end of the story—He wins. From Genesis to Revelation, we know the full story. He has already won the victory.

God also wants us to know the evil that we are witnessing across the globe is not as mighty as it seems on Facebook or the evening news. It looks bad in the natural—but we who have this hope in Jesus, know He is coming back again for those who are born again and have called on His name to receive forgiveness. He is preparing us to rule and reign with Him in His kingdom. What a day that will be when He comes.

Not everyone knows the truth about Jesus. There are many souls that are lost and hurting in the world. Even though America is in trouble, we do have the answer and His name is *Jesus!* Will you choose to stand up for God and share the hope we have in calling on the name of Jesus?

It's not too late. Moses was eighty when he was used by God to deliver the children of Israel. He tried to do life his way, murdered a man, and ended up in the desert for forty years of preparation and training. He was then brought out by God to deliver the Israelites. What would have been an eleven-day trip turned out to be forty years of wandering in the desert to get the bondage out of them. God allowed them to wander because He was more concerned with getting Egypt out of them than getting them out of Egypt. Egypt represents bondage.

Like Moses, God cannot use any of us in a leadership position until we have passed our tests. The great news is when we face something we have never faced before, it is a compliment from God that we have passed the previous test and are moving forward in Him.

"'You *are* My witnesses,' says the Lord. 'And My servant whom I have chosen, That you may know and believe Me. And understand that I *am* He. Before Me there was no God formed, Nor shall there be after Me. I, *even* I, *am* the Lord. And besides Me *there* is no savior'" (Isa. 43:10–11, NKJV).

"Therefore, as God's chosen people, holy and dearly loved, clothe yourselves with compassion, kindness, humility, gentleness and patience" (Col. 3:12, NIV).

God's plan for each of us is nothing short of a new heart. God would want control of your engine if you were a car. We need to allow God to take over the driver's seat of our lives. You are a person, so God wants to change your heart.

We become new creatures in Christ when we are born again. We are not able to fix or change ourselves apart from God. We must move from self-reliance to dependency upon Him by living out of His Word and applying it daily. When we are empowered by the Holy Spirit, we are empowered and equipped to move out to help others.

HEART CHECK
Read Colossians 3:12–17

What will happen to us when we choose to surrender our hearts to God?

What is one specific change you can make in your daily routine to become more like Christ?

Jesus wants us to have a heart like His. There is no better offer. The heart of Jesus was and is pure, peaceful, purposeful, and spiritual. He was always about His Father's business.

America is in Serious Trouble

America is in serious trouble. She has a heart problem as a nation and is in a leadership crisis. From what happened in the Ferguson, Missouri riots, to beheadings that are willfully misrepresented as "workplace violence," and countless abortions and prejudices, America is unraveling like a garment with a loose thread. Division and bullying, life spiraling out of control, and the horrific breaking news reports bring us to a point of noticing—something serious is happening globally. There is unrest across the globe.

Regardless of what political side you choose, it is clear that life as we have known it is spiraling out of control at an unparalleled rate of speed. Everything from family breakdowns, betrayals of all kinds, the immigration crisis—we are fraying instead of praying. So, what lies ahead?

Since a little child, I have heard about people from foreign nations wanting to move to America because of the so-called American Dream. The American Dream is quickly turning into a nightmare. People are stressed, worried, and overwhelmed. It is time that we, as a nation, turn back to God through repentance and prayer. God is America's only hope. May the Lord God bring revival to every heart across the nation—and globe.

In the midst of this chaos across America, we are either in the End Times or at the end of time. Which is it? What is going on? I believe we are at the two-minute warning of the last hour. We are on the verge of the return of Jesus Christ to judge the earth and set up His earthly kingdom. As a nation, America has turned her back on

God and we are experiencing every consequence of that rejection. We must pray for revival.

Revival happens in the heart first. God begins to speak the same message to hearts in different places across the globe, giving them similar vision. When we come together and find that God has put the same thing in our hearts, a flame is sparked within and we are ignited with passion. Passion fuels purpose. Our conversations turn to God's movement within our hearts, no matter the distance in the natural. God connects us with other believers of like passion so that we can run the race together, doing great things *with* God.

Did you catch that?

It is not about doing things *for* God or about competition. It is about doing what God has put in our hearts to do *with* Him. It is about ministering to Him first and spending time in His holy presence. It is about loving to read His Word and waiting on Him in silence with awe and expectation. Then we are moved to action and do what He has put in our hearts to do *with* Him.

Begin to believe God for revival. Let me share words from Charles G. Finney from *Lectures On Revival*: *"Revival stops whenever the church thinks it will. As the instrument God uses to carry on the job, the church is to work from the heart. Nothing is more fatal to spiritual awakening than for its friends to predict it is going to end. Enemies can't stop it by predicting it will fizzle out and come to nothing. But friends of revival must work and pray in faith to carry it on."*[1]

"When a servant of God looks like he or she will probably succeed, Satan uses his agents to try to distract them and frustrate their efforts....A revival of true Christianity is a great work because great interests are involved...Revival involves two infinitely important things: (1) God's glory in His governing of this world and (2) the salvation of men and women."[2]

God has opened the windows of heaven to His church and poured out a blessing. Things that can hinder revival will also aggrieve the Holy Spirit—when they do not feel and recognize their dependence on the Spirit, when the church grows proud or weary, or when the church turns its attention from the things of salvation to philosophize about abstract points, people fall asleep. When the church engages in competition and tries to get converts to leave one church to come to another, or even in smaller settings such as classes, revival is hindered and the church continues attending its own concerns rather than God's business.

The Son of God gave up everything to save sinners. He left heaven and came to earth. Finney states, *"I am surprised that "brokenness" is a stumbling block to some pastors and people who profess to know Christ. They invite Christ's rebuke, "Are you a teacher of Israel, and do not understand these things?" Until some of them know what it is to be broken, they will do little for the spiritual growth of others."*[3]

Brokenness is being empty of self—and filled with God—desiring to know Him and ministering unto Him first and foremost.

Brokenness is where we come to the end of ourselves and learn to depend upon God. It is the place of surrender and at the same time, a place of learning to take a stand in the marketplace by voting scripturally, and by linking hands with those that will join us in the journey following Jesus Christ by advancing His kingdom and not our own. It is a place where we are concerned about others and we don't make them feel condemned. It is the place of operating in God's power and in His amazing love, where people sense the love of God and experience Him as well. It is the place of loving what God loves, and hating what He hates—with no room for compromise. It is the place where we know we are carriers of the Word of God, and bring life to others through sharing our faith and testimony. It is also a place where we allow the Holy Spirit to lead us to bridge the gap between God and people, bringing healing through God's Word and by loving them where they are on their individual journey.

Ministering Unto The Lord

Early in 2014 as I was studying the Bible, a scripture stood out to me: *"Then David said, 'No one may carry the ark of God but the Levites, for the Lord has chosen them to carry the ark of God and to minister before Him forever'"* (1 Chron. 15:2, NKJV). The word *minister* used here means to wait on, to serve, to minister, and to attend. Minister (*sharat*) refers to the task to which the closest servants of God or the king are assigned. The priests and Levites in their ministry in the tabernacle and the temple served God. Examples of significant positions of service to important persons include Joseph to Potiphar (Gen. 39:4), Joshua to Moses (Exodus 33:11), and Elisha to Elijah (1 Kings 19:21). In today's usage the title *ministers* conveys austerity and self-authority, while the scriptural use of the term conveys yieldedness, servanthood, and obedience.[1]

Wisdom counsels us that God's ways are higher than our ways and His thoughts are higher than our thoughts. He knows the best way to do His work. It is not wisdom to undertake to do God's work in our own ways. Employing human wisdom to accomplish God's work can result in frightening consequences.

When we learn to put God first in every area of our lives, we learn to live in truth. One word from God changes everything. When America turns back to God, there is hope. For example, a person who does not know Jesus Christ as Lord and Savior and turns to Him in life to receive Him and the gift of forgiveness has a life-changing encounter.

In this final hour on God's clock that we are living, we are standing in a doorway between earth and heaven—it is called the gift of time here on earth. It is a sounding alarm for America to wake up, arise out of slumber, and turn back to God. Everything in life has changed.

When we learn who God is and whose we are in Christ, everything changes. People matter, our words matter, and how we spend our time matters. We come to a place of adoration, where we live in awe of God. We can experience great joy and unshakable faith when we come to know God as a little child, spending quality time in His Presence, and resolving to be stronger in our walk with Him. Time spent with God and reading His Word is never wasted.

Let's take a look at what the Bible has to teach us.

"Now in the church that was at Antioch there were certain prophets and teachers: Barnabus, Simeon who was called Niger, Lucius of Cyrene, Manaen who had been brought up with Herod the tetrarch, and Saul. As they ministered to the Lord and fasted, the Holy Spirit said, 'Now separate to Me Barnabus and Saul for the work to which I have called them.' Then, having fasted and prayed, and laid hands on them, they sent them away" (Luke 13:1–3, NKJV). Luke shifts the focus of his book to Paul's ministry and the worldwide spread of the church. Paul stopped at key population and cultural centers, and spoke to both Jews and Gentiles. God desires that His church reach new people with the message of hope found in Jesus Christ—the Blessed Hope. The preaching of the gospel will always draw new converts, in spite of opposition, difficulties, and even blatant persecution.

It is time for the church to arise and turn back to God in unified prayer and fasting. Always remember, if God can save you, He can save anybody. He saved Saul of Tarsus and changed his name from Saul to Paul. "Paul" means "a little man" and that was a constant reminder to him that he had to rely on God, not himself. He was equipped and empowered by the Holy Spirit. It takes no more grace to save a Saul of Tarsus, who was persecuting Christians, than to convert you or me.

If God could save Saul, who was persecuting Christians, He can save anyone. Saul was confronted by Jesus Christ on the road to Damascus, and realized what he had been doing was wrong. His encounter with Christ brought conviction in his heart and it led to conversion. After he was converted, Paul experienced communion, consecration (being set apart totally to God), and was commissioned by Jesus as an apostle to preach the good news of the Gospel of Jesus Christ. Paul had been blind, but when He met the light—the Son of God, he experienced a heart change.

We must choose to turn to God, rely on His strength, and take back our land. We must stand upon God's Word for the lost. That is the heart of God.

When we fully come to know God, we live in a state of amazement and awe through every day. We have divine appointments on a daily basis, we see God's hand in details, and we sense His presence. God is waiting on us to be a people who will be fully committed to Him. He desires to show Himself strong on our behalf.

When we are committed and get to know the Lord, we begin to hear His voice and we know it. We hear Him in small details and we watch life unfold just as He has spoken. We live in such a state of time that we must hear God and know His voice. Whether we believe it or not, there is a war raging between good and evil. Let us pray together for revival in our own hearts and for this nation. Get back to prayer in the home first—and may it spread throughout the communities. We must fully commit to God in every area.

The Bible says, "For the eyes of the Lord range throughout the earth to strengthen those whose hearts are fully committed to him" (2 Chron. 16:9, NIV). The King James Version says, "For the eyes of the Lord run to and fro throughout the whole earth, to shew himself strong in the behalf of *them* whose heart *is* perfect toward him."

Repentance And Revival

During the inception of revival, God speaks and connects His people of purpose on purpose. When a solemn assembly was called for in the Bible, it was called by those in leadership for prayer, repentance, and fasting for change. God has a heart for reconciliation and we must never forget that. We must turn back to God through repentance of sin and igniting a passionate pursuit for God's presence.

Repentance of sin also means that we see life the way God sees it. We love what God loves and hate what He hates. We won't compromise in any area when we are fully committed to God. The enemy will tempt you to go down a wrong path, but you have a choice.

It is the smallest of sins that starts to send a person down a path of destruction. Small sins turn into bigger sins. It's like telling a small lie. One small lie turns into a bigger lie. It may be secretly justifying in your mind paying for a dinner through the organization you work for, yet you know in your heart it is personal. It may be a trip you go on and you lie about it just to have the company you work for to pay for it. It may be taking money from your employer and you justify it in your mind because you *feel* they don't pay you adequately. Whatever the secret sin is—it is really not a secret. God sees and knows all. And justifying the sin is another trap of the enemy to destroy you and your future. When any person begins to justify sin, they are off course and headed for destruction. It is a spiritual problem—a heart in need of surgery by God.

A plane or boat that goes off course will not end up at its correct destination. This is why it is imperative that we make small corrections and never ignore the promptings of the Holy Spirit.

When anyone ignores the promptings, the heart becomes hardened. Anything you give yourself over to other than Jesus Christ will eventually destroy you.

Satanic Traps

If the enemy can't get to you, he will set a trap with a business partner who betrays you, or even a family betrayal. He will try to take you out through an affair, business deception, casual sins, depression, distractions, elevated position that drives a person to competition, and ultimately failure. Satan uses the love of money and sexual immorality as two of his main traps to destroy people.

God sends warnings and people to warn us to keep us from destruction. If we choose to ignore the warnings, we end up with consequences to those choices. *We must choose to pursue truth.* Since our actions flow from our thoughts, we need minds that are filled with the truth found in God's Word. If we don't read the Bible, we can't expect to live holy if we still think the way we did before we received forgiveness.

According to Paul, unbelievers live "in the futility of their mind, being darkened in their understanding, excluded from the life of God because of the ignorance that is in them" (Rom. 6:17–18). Since we live in the world and are surrounded by wrong thinking, it will rub off on us if we don't choose to cleanse ourselves daily and renew our minds with God's Word. When we choose to *anchor* ourselves with biblical principles and apply them to our lives personally, we are empowered by the Spirit of God and can resist temptation to return to the old man nature, our old sinful ways.

When we live in God's Word, we become sensitive to sin and recognize the enemy's tactics. The Holy Spirit warns and convicts us when a particular activity does not line up with God's ways. God warns us to stay away from anything that does not fit our position of righteousness in Jesus Christ.

Before we were saved, we could play in the dirt and not feel too bad about it at all. But after being born again and having experienced personal salvation, sin makes us uncomfortable. This is the power of the Holy Spirit to convict.

We can't play around with sin and justify even the smallest of sin. I have heard people say it's getting too strict when it comes to justifying things a little off course, and that even God will understand if they live with their boyfriend or girlfriend outside of marriage. People justify all types of sin. God will not change His Word for anyone.

When a parent refuses to correct a child, the parent is enabling bad behavior. It is giving a signal to the child that they can get away with it and that it is OK. But it is not OK! Instead of excusing sin, we must confess, repent, and choose to obey the Lord. Playing around with sin brings about destruction. God sends warnings for our protection and we have all fallen short in some area.

Manmade Plans: Choosing Family Over God

Scripture provides us with examples of how one injustice leads to another and everyone involved suffers destruction and disgrace. In 2 Samuel 13 we read where one of David's sons, Amnon, lusted after his half-sister Tamar and raped her. She was no longer a virgin, she experienced disgrace at the hand of family, and no one would want to marry her. Her brother Absalom found out about it and took her in to live with him, while remaining silent for a time. David became furious when he learned of what happened, but never took any punitive action. He allowed his love for his son to overshadow the right thing to do, which would have been to have Amnon arrested and punished for rape and incest with Tamar, his half-sister.

This was in direct violation of God's commandments. Tamar's father, King David, knew the law and chose to ignore it. Absalom was filled with rage, resentment, and revenge. Absalom made arrangements to have Amnon killed by a servant while attending a party at his house some two years later. He plotted murder in revenge and fled the country as a refugee from his father's kingdom for three years. Time passed and David had lost both of his sons and was living in grief.

David's servant Joab knew how David's heart longed to be with his son again and devised a plan for his safe return. Joab was probably not moved as much by restoration of the family as he was by political reasons—he stooped so low to use deception and trickery to get what he desperately wanted.

Joab schemed and sent for a wise woman from Tekoa to tell a story to David about another such case of injustice in hopes of softening his heart toward his son Absalom. The story she told was applicable to David's own situation. Her words convinced King David to reconsider by saying, "God does not take away a life; but He devised means, so that His banished ones are not expelled from Him" (2 Sam. 14:14, NKJV). "The word of the lord the king will now be comforting; for as the angel of God, so *is* my lord the king in discerning good and evil. And may the Lord your God be with you'" (v. 17, NKJV).

Apparently, this woman from Tekoa sounded wise and reasonable, however she misinterpreted God's Word and used deception and flattery to influence King David. The Bible makes it clear in Exodus 20:13 and lists the sixth commandment, "You shall not murder." David's son, Absalom, had murdered Amnon and what he did was punishable by death according to Exodus 21:12–14. God does not take life without reason, but if a man commits murder he forfeits his right to life. God gives us the gift of discernment by His Holy Spirit for us to make wise decisions; and not to angels to decide.

David took this woman's worldly advice and chose wrongly. He sent for Absalom to return to Jerusalem, but was not permitted to see David's face again nor enter his house. King David was torn in his heart between love and anger over his son's actions. Absalom was neither arrested nor punished for his criminal activity. King David made another horrific mistake in judgment and permitted a crime to go unpunished because it was a member of his own family. The right thing to do would have been for King David to recuse himself as judge and provide a trial by other authorities in his kingdom. At this point, he could have trusted God to provide a fair and impartial hearing for his son who had committed a crime.

The Bible tells us that Absalom returned to Jerusalem and after two years of waiting, he demanded to see his father David. "Now then, I want to see the king's face, and if I am guilty of anything, let him put me to death." Absalom showed no sign of repentance and wanted to be totally released. He must have thought his father was weak and would not put him to death. He saw the weakness in King David when he did nothing after Amnon raped Tamar.

Manmade Plans: Choosing Family Over God

Absalom had an outward show when he went in to see the king as "he bowed down with his face to the ground. And the king kissed Absalom" (2 Sam. 14:32). King David forgave his son, while totally ignoring the need for a heart of repentance and justice. He was more concerned with reconciliation of his royal family than righteous judgment. David had a conflict of interest and didn't have the authority to pardon his son.

Reflect back with me for a moment to the curse that Nathan pronounced on him years earlier for his sin with Bathsheba. (See 2 Samuel 11; 2 Samuel 12:26–31.) David had chosen to stay behind rather than go out to battle. Because David was out of position and chose something that was not his for the taking, he sinned against God in several ways. Again, because he chose worldly wisdom and lacked spiritual insight and godly leadership, his mistakes led to the fulfillment of the curse in 2 Samuel 12:10–12, "This is what the Lord says: 'Out of your own household I am going to bring calamity upon you" (NIV).

The people saw restoration and reconciliation between the king and his son. Absalom used this outward display to steal the hearts of the men of Israel away from his own father. He sought to destroy his own father's kingdom. *This is like Satan today—he seeks to destroy all the righteous and the Kingdom of God!*

Look at what the Bible tells us: "Moreover Absalom would say, 'Oh, that I were made judge in the land, and everyone who has a suit or cause would come to me; then I would give him justice'" (2 Sam. 15:4, NKJV). Absalom wanted his father's kingdom and in the course of four years, he persuaded many among the tribes of Israel to pronounce him as the new king in Hebron and to overthrow his own father King David. His plan of demise brought about more followers and he increased through his conspiracy.

David was forced to flee Jerusalem to escape from his own son Absalom and to spare the lives of innocent people if war broke out within the city walls. David stayed behind, but sent his troops onward to wage war with Absalom and commanded his men to spare his son's life.

Talk about sowing and reaping in life! Absalom was riding his mule through the forest when his hair was caught in the branches of a large oak tree. His mule kept going and he was left hanging in midair. The abundance of hair was a symbol of his egotism, pride, and destruction. (Reminds me of Judas in the New Testament as well.) What I found to be very interesting was how Absalom hung himself on his own mule. He had a beautiful, thick head of hair and was handsome in appearance like his father. On the other hand, his heart was full of conspiracy and deceit. He sought man's favor and used political cunning to gain it, but it cost him his life.

Joab found him and plunged three javelins into Absalom's heart. David wept after he heard the news and grieved over the death of his son.

The lives of both David and Absalom give real examples of ungodly leadership and disobedience to God's commandments. We also see what happens when leaders fail to carry out justice and choose worldly and misguided advice with no regard or discernment of God's will. Actually, this story is of far greater importance than the story of David and Bathsheba, as it was mild in comparison to his lack of loyalty to God and his adamant favoritism with his own family time and time again.

Even though David was a man after God's own heart, he was a man that was confused and conflicted when it came down to dealing with family issues. He did what he thought was right in his own eyes when it came to his personal family.

*(Notation: see www.tolr.org–Tree of Life Ministries)

Inquiring of God

We learn a highly valuable lesson from David's youth. He prayed and inquired of the Lord on numerous occasions prior to making decisions. (See 1 Sam. 23:2 or 30:8.) He was committed to God and desperately wanted to honor God, to do God's will, and wanted to know that God was leading him to do the right thing.

What happened to King David? What changed in David's life that caused him to lean on his own understanding in his later years? Obedience to God's Word, use of wisdom and discernment were tossed by the wayside and replaced with worldly understanding. Somehow in his later years after he became king, he chose to lean on natural thinking and due to the bloodshed during his forty years as king, he was not allowed to build the temple for God. Too much sin was on his hands and the assignment was given to his son, Solomon, to complete. If only David had chosen to follow his own advice in his later years. When his time of passing drew near, pay attention to his instructions to Solomon in 1 Kings 2:2: "Observe what the Lord your God requires: walk in his ways, and keep his decrees and commands, his laws and requirements…so that you may prosper in all you do and wherever you go and that the Lord may keep his promise to me: 'If your descendants watch how they live, and if they walk faithfully before me with all their heart and soul, you will never fail to have a man on the throne of Israel.'"

What can we learn as a nation?

Hopefully, we can learn from these mistakes and be better leaders in the Kingdom of God today. One final passage concerning David and his last words: "The Spirit of the Lord spoke by me, and His word was on my tongue. The God of Israel said, 'The Rock of Israel spoke to me: "He who rules over men must be just, ruling in the fear of God. And he shall be like the light of the morning when the sun rises, a morning without clouds, like the tender grass springing out of the earth, by clear shining after rain"'" (2 Sam. 23:2–4). Dear God, send us your grace to be godly leaders, both men and women of God that reflect your glory in all the earth.

Adam chose wrong in the Garden of Eden in the beginning. David and his sons made wrong choices. We can learn much from heeding the warnings found in the Word of God. There was hope for those who made wrong choices in the Bible, and there is still hope for us today—if we choose to return to God!

The Enemy

The enemy is very real whether you believe it or not. When my uncle passed away from a massive heart attack, I was in hopes of having the manuscript for this book edited, but another divine delay caused me to have valuable information of current events to add so all could see what is in our face right now. ISIS overtook Yemen as I heard on the news January 20, 2015—the same day of the State of the Union address. Like Amnon raped his own half-sister Tamar, we have allowed the enemy within America to rape this land. We have allowed the enemy to cross over borders and walk into this nation. We have broken down walls and border problems. No one person is to blame.

My mother and I were driving to another city and I noticed a new building up on a hill and thought the name was strange: "Rapers." It was a large metal building as I noticed it positioned up on a hill behind a mall as we were headed to meet family for dinner. I thought about how we have allowed the enemy to rape America—through abortions, sexual immorality, moral decline and decay, new laws that legalize sin, corruption, and the list goes on. As I began to study the meaning of the name *Yemen*, what I learned was that the original old name was Sheba. David fell when he took Bathsheba for his own. He also did not hold Amnon responsible and have him arrested for the rape and incest of his daughter, Tamar. Her other brother Absalom watched and became enraged as bitterness filled his heart. You know the rest of the story which also serves to give us a picture of America today—the enemy in our face. We must stand up and take back this nation.

If we don't deal with the enemy and stop trying to be politically correct, while befriending the enemy ourselves, we will be destroyed. It is foolish and naïve to think that what is happening in Yemen won't happen here in America if we don't stand up and return to God.

God is making it evidently clear as we hear the reports across the news and media. We can't play with fire and not expect to get burned. We cannot allow the enemy to infiltrate our camp, and not expect to have casualties. Wake up America! Wake up, arise and take back the land. Repent and return to God before it is too late. Repent means to turn to God for His perspective for all of life! America must turn back to God.

Up Close and Personal

In the beginning in the Book of Genesis you will notice what happened in the Garden of Eden, and you can see a pattern throughout Scripture of the same. Adam was not tending the garden and the enemy deceived Eve. The enemy was in the garden. Did Adam not see it? Did he choose to eat of the same fruit because Eve did? God gave him warning and he made a choice. Then Adam hid from God rather than repenting.

God sends warnings and calls us to repent for reconciliation prior to announcing judgment. The Bible tells us God is swift to spare, if we will come to Him and ask Him for a new heart and new spirit as His divine path to seeing hope restored to a nation, a people, and individual lives transformed. (See Ezekiel 18:30–31.) God does not want us to be a distant people. He is a close and personal God and desires that all come to know Him through intimate relationship. It is not about religion. It is about personal relationship and getting to know God. It is about walking with God in our daily life—according to His ways. God sent His Son Jesus that we might be saved. He was born in a manger in Bethlehem. It all started in the Middle East and it will end in the Middle East. While there is still time as we know it, we must turn back to God as a nation.

Did you know that if we turn back to God He is able and willing to turn the mess we have made in America into a message of hope? Any person or any nation that turns to God can find hope again. Will America turn?

We must get on the same page with God as a nation and repent, seeking His face and not His hand. Our solutions will not be found in the White House or in another new president. Our solutions are found in God and His house.

God's house is His house. Salvation through Jesus Christ is simple, clear, and concise. The message is real. Religion has muddled the story and tried to complicate it with rituals. It is not about rituals. It is about a personal relationship with Jesus Christ and not about religion. It is about having a heart change. You hate sin and love God.

It is not about competition, envy, jealousy, division, strife, or being above anyone else in life. It doesn't matter where you reside, what kind of car you have or don't have, what label of clothing you wear, how much wealth you *think* you have acquired in life, or anything else that becomes idolatry in your life because God owns it all. *It's all about Jesus and souls. It's about building His Kingdom and not our own. This world is passing away. God desires that we know Him—up close and personally!*

We must return to God with our whole heart. God takes delight in blessing his children. Like the little girl that survived a plane crash in Kentucky, we must get out in the woods and fields and find help. This little seven-year old girl found her way through the briars and fields to a man's house. It was like an angel of the Lord led her there on a perfect path. She had scratches all over and her little body was bruised and torn from the wreckage and walk through the woods. She told the man that found her at the door of his home that her mommy and daddy were both dead and the plane was upside down. He was overwhelmed with tears.

Are you moved to tears over someone else's crash in life? Or, do you sit back and make jokes or laugh about it? Do you talk negatively about others walking through tough times? Do you think it could never happen to you?

I believe God sees America like this account of what happened recently. America is upside down and has had several crashes—not just one. Will we walk out of the wreckage and seek help? Like the man at the door, I believe Jesus weeps over this nation. He loves the whole world and wants us to know Him—the Blessed Hope.

When we turn to God, He is there waiting on us all along. He responds to us with love. How we respond to other people's problems reveals what is in our own hearts. Do you respond with a heart of

Up Close and Personal

compassion? Do you live in a house yet never take notice to others around you? Do you ignore other people that matter to God and hide out with your own family and well laid plans for your personal life?

Do you surround yourself with people who can do things for you? Do you only want people around you that need you so you can be in a position of control? Do you ever do anything that really costs you?

Has your heart grown cold to the world and Word of God? This little girl lost her family and was tattered and torn. She lost her family in one crash. Would you have had the fortitude to get out and look for someone else alive in all that debris, or would you have given up? If that little girl can do it, so can we.

There are people dying in the fields, people feel like they are alone in the woods due to horrific betrayal and circumstances, families are torn apart, children have betrayed those who raised them, and people are desperate to find someone alive with hope. I have great news for you. God is alive. He is not dead. The message of Jesus Christ is real and He is alive. Jesus came to earth to redeem all mankind. He is now seated at the right hand of the Father and interceding for us that our faith would not fail.

Satan is after your faith. Don't let him have it and don't give in to his ruthless tactics. Fight for your family and turn back to God with your whole heart. Pray your family into the Kingdom of God. Pray for your enemies and those who have spitefully used you. Look for God and expect to see His hand in the intimate details of life, for He cares deeply for you.

Forgive all! It's not worth it. Take a fresh look at the life of Joseph in the Book of Genesis. He was falsely accused, wrongly imprisoned, ignored, and maligned. They meant it for evil, but God mean it for good.

First Samuel 16:7 says, "...man looks on the outward appearance, but God looks upon the heart." Every individual must learn to take the time to get to know a person's heart and stop passing judgment. There is something you don't know in every situation. There is one book that is alive, up-to-date and relevant—that is always true and has the answer for every problem you and I will ever face in life. It is up close and personal. It is God's Word—the Bible.

The Bible

The Bible is the key that holds the answers to life. It is a divine roadmap and basic instructions before leaving earth. This book has come down through the ages and has passed through many hands, not to mention surviving attacks of every kind, but is still up-to-date and relevant for all mankind. People may laugh at you when they find out you love God and the Bible, but guess where they turn when they have a crisis? You got it. They call and ask for prayer. We must pray for America to turn back to God.

On September 11, 2001, this is exactly what happened. America was in crisis and for about three weeks, churches were filled and prayer was happening across the land. Then life went back to normal.

But what is normal?

Life is not normal. America has created laws that legalize sin, taken out monuments that have anything to do with Christianity and God, and have made it evidently clear that some people think they do not really need God. *The enemy has infiltrated our camp.*

Satan hates God and all Christians. He hates righteousness and is against Christ. He wants to drag you under his rule through sin and unrighteousness.

You can make a choice. You can make a difference. I want to make something crystal clear to you today. If you are born again by the Spirit of God, you have received forgiveness from God through Jesus Christ and you are holy. Instead of viewing yourself as some worthless sinner saved by God's grace, recognize who you are in Christ and whose you are! You are God's child. You are His priceless treasure. You are a saint who has been created in the righteousness and holiness of Jesus Christ. It is high time to start acting like it. God has given you everything you need for a life of godliness. (Read 2 Peter 1:3.)

No one is capable of living a holy life without being first declared righteous by God. Jesus Christ is the only person who has ever lived a perfectly holy life. He took all sin and it was nailed to His cross. (See Colossians 2:13–14.) He gives us His perfect robe of righteousness in exchange or in the place of sin. (See 2 Corinthians 5:21.)

If you are not born again and are reading this book, all you have to do is repent of your sins, believe in Jesus, and receive His gift of salvation. You can pray this prayer as the Spirit leads:

Father God, I come to You as a sinner and I admit and confess my need for Jesus as my Savior. I confess I have sinned against You in word, thought, and in my actions. Forgive me for all my sin, and teach me to live in right relationship with You. I receive the gift of salvation right now. Thank You for saving me. Help me to live a life that is pleasing to You. In Jesus' name, amen.

If you just prayed that prayer, you are now born again through Jesus Christ. People around you will notice the change and will also be drawn to Jesus. Find a local church and get connected with other believers. Start reading the Bible. Choose to live and walk in newness of life because you live under God's authority! Live out of His Word—the Bible, under His authority!

As believers in Christ, we can live in freedom. Begin to pray for America and the nation's leaders. Make a list and put names on it that also need to be saved. You can make a difference through prayer. If God saved me, he can save anybody. If God can save you, He can save anybody. God can reach the very one you may think is unreachable. God can do what we think is impossible! Turn back to God in prayer and repentance for America, for family, friends, and for enemies.

One Nation Under God

We have to choose to take back our land. It all begins with a change of heart. There is not much that is free in life. As a matter of fact, the only thing that is totally free is God's grace. God's grace is free, but if you are going to be saved, *you* must pray. If you desire to be delivered from alcohol, *you* must desire it. If *you* want the Holy Spirit to sanctify and teach you, *you* must have the desire to live holy. If God is going to heal you, *you* must use your own faith to receive it. We have to use our faith, actions, attitudes, and words in order to receive.

God's design for us as Christians is to function under His rule—running everything by His Word. America was born out of a desire for independence from the tyranny of England. True freedom really comes when we learn to move from self-reliance to dependence upon God. If America is going to experience godly change, *we* must do something. Every person must get involved in making it happen. God provides grace, but *you* and I must partner with God!

God told Joshua, *"...arise, go over this Jordan, thou, and all this people, unto the land which I do give to them, even to the children of Israel."* He went on to say, *"Every place that the sole of your foot shall tread upon, that have I given unto you, as I said unto Moses"* (Josh. 1:3, KJV).

As long as we sit on the sidelines and do nothing, we won't see our nation under God's blessing. Every person has to get up, move forward, and start walking under God's authority to bring about godly change.

God has given us the freedom to choose whether we will be under His authority or not. The Bible reveals to us that God only promises to bless the people who recognize His authority. (Read Psalm 33:12.) The dominant influence since the inception of America was the Christian faith due to our forefathers and the church.

What does freedom mean here in America? Freedom really means we get to control our own personal choice. Choice can be a frightening thing when you see people making wrong choices that bring about disaster and even horrific consequences for other innocent people. Consequences for the choice of not being under God's authority are showing themselves quickly across the globe.

God is the ultimate authority. He rules by endorsing our personal choices that line up with His Word. He also rules by allowing the consequences of our decisions that go against Him. We learn from the Word of God that, "The Lord has established His throne in the heavens, and His sovereignty rules over all" (Ps. 103:19, NAS).

When any person or nation usurps God's authority, chaos ensues. There is one God and one eternal authority. Here on earth, while there is only one God, there are multiple rulers in positions of authority to rule. Paul tells us to be in subjection to the governing authorities. (See Romans 13:1.) No one can really be a great leader until he or she first learns to be *under* authority.

(Reflect for a moment on what happened at the Tower of Babel when mankind tried to unite to reach God in heaven. See Genesis 11:1–9, NKJV).

> *Now the whole earth had one language and one speech. And it came to pass, as they journeyed from the east, that they found a plain in the land of Shinar, and they dwelt there. Then they said to one another, "Come let us make bricks and bake them thoroughly." They had brick and stone, and they had asphalt for mortar. And they said, "Come, let us build ourselves a city, and a tower whose top is in the heavens; let us make a name for ourselves, lest we be scattered abroad over the face of the whole earth." But the Lord came down to see the city and the tower which*

the sons of men had built. And the Lord said, "Indeed the people are one and they all have one language, and this is what they begin to do; now nothing that they propose to do will be withheld from them. Come, let US go down and there confuse their language, that they may not understand one another's speech." So the Lord scattered them abroad over the face of all the earth.

When people are united they can do anything. The problem is that mankind wants his own rule rather than living according to God's rule. God set divine order in government for our protection and blessing.

"It is impossible to rightly govern a nation without God and the Bible"—George Washington

Government and Authority

In our current government, we have division of power so that checks and balances are in place for our protection against dictatorship and evils arising. America's Founding Fathers separated the judicial from the legislative and the executive branches of government. Human government has been established to reflect the same pattern in heaven with the trinity. I call this a natural manifestation here on earth. God is unified in His purpose and made evident in the Trinity (the Father God, the Son Jesus Christ, and the Holy Spirit). The Trinity of God is unified in purpose but diversified in their responsibilities as well.

Division of power is biblical and is the optimal way for proper authority. Let me give an example. If you drive up to a stoplight and the light is out, in most cases, before long a police officer will be on the scene to direct traffic. You will go when he raises his hand and motions for you to come forward. You will also stop when he signals you to do so.

In the same way, civil government is set in place to create and maintain safety and for our ultimate protection. It is designed to establish order in society. God is a god of order. Civil government is not to replace family and the church. It is created to support and establish order.

When civil government starts contradicting the other two institutions of government (family and church), we experience problems. We are experiencing this here in America right now. Civil government is not to dictate the purposes of the church.

Let's take a look at what the Bible tells us: *"Therefore whoever resists authority has opposed the ordinance of God; and they who have opposed will receive condemnation upon themselves. For rulers are not a cause of fear for good behavior, but for evil"* (Rom. 13:2–3, NAS). Scripture outlines what is supposed to happen according to God. We are to be under God, and civil government is to promote wellbeing and good, while protecting the citizens from evil. God is the ultimate rule of authority. When any nation usurps His authority, chaos ensues. When a nation lives under God's authority, we can flourish as a people.

Submit to Government

> *"Let every soul be subject to the governing authorities. For there is no authority except from God, and the authorities that exist are appointed by God. Therefore whoever resists the authority resists the ordinance of God, and those who resist will bring judgment on themselves. For rulers are not a terror to good works, but to evil. Do you want to be unafraid of authority? Do what is good, and you will have praise from the same. For he is God's minister to you for good. But if you do evil, be afraid; for he does not bear the sword in vain; for he is God's minister, an avenger to execute wrath on him who practices evil"* (Rom. 13:1–4, NKJV).

We learn from these verses that when a government oversteps what is found here, it ends up resisting and neglecting God's divine plan. The Bible says if anyone will not work, neither shall he eat (2 Thess. 3:10, NKJV). It is not talking about a person who is unable to work, but one who won't. Welfare checks given to people who won't work is teaching irresponsibility. It is not God's plan to turn to the government to pay for a person's laziness and unwillingness to work, while taxing others to cover the expense.

Any civil government that becomes overextended limits personal freedoms of individuals to pursue their divine calling unto God. It also restricts their God-given ability to contribute to the economic world around them. When small corrections are not made, we have major problems down the road. And we are now well down that road in America.

It is the civil government's responsibility to remove coercion, deception, and fraud from the marketplace, but it is not to control it. It is also not to go on witch-hunts and toss nets out that take innocent people down with the guilty. Unfortunately, that is what sometimes happens right here in America.

The Bible gives us insight concerning what is happening across the world and here in America. The enemy of our souls wants control. Satan knows his time is short and wants to take as many with him as he can. The enemy can infiltrate the minds of godless leaders.

Look at what happened to Judas. When a person is bought by a bribe, like Judas in the Bible, to cover self, or to save their so-called status in life with materialism, he will reap an eternal harvest—just like Judas. He walked with Jesus but apparently lost focus and was overtaken by the enemy. The enemy wants control. It can happen to anyone—so we must live in God's Word.

Any central control by the government is a foreshadowing of what will come in the near future. It is revealing where this nation is headed—where centralized government control of trade and the marketplace is the economic system of the Antichrist. (See Revelation 13:17.) We are witnessing this happening quickly right now—all against God.

You might be thinking, "What on earth can I do as one person?" Keep reading! You will find out that your life matters and God has created each individual with a divine purpose. It is our choice whether we step into it or not.

Your Life Matters

Your life matters greatly to God. You might be thinking in the midst of all this world change, "What am I supposed to do with my life?" God never promised happiness, but he did promise a plan—and a great plan: *"For I know the thoughts that I think toward you, says the Lord, thoughts of peace and not of evil, to give you a future and a hope"* (Jer. 29:11, NKJV). Your question is not a hard one when you turn to the Creator of the universe, God Himself. One thing you will learn is that comfort and doing what God has put in your heart to do sometimes are diametrically opposed. Satan will oppose you and try to distract you from your life purpose in God.

Finding God's will for your life is easier than you've ever thought. People make it difficult. Living out of God's Word and doing what He has created you to do brings about contagious joy. It creates a passion for purpose from deep within that keeps you moving forward. It brings more joy than you have ever imagined.

Joy comes from within. Happiness is based on external circumstances. Even in the midst of chaos, you can experience real joy because of a personal relationship with Jesus Christ. He has equipped you to do great things with Him.

You have everything you need to do what God has called you to do *with* Him. When you step out, the pieces of the beautiful tapestry, or what might seem like a detailed puzzle will begin to come together. So, it is time for you to stop making excuses, and to step out and change history. You are called to fish 24/7. What? Yes, you read that correctly. We have been created to fish for souls. We are cleverly designed to be about our Father's business. His business is souls—and building His kingdom. Every person matters to God.

We are called by God to fish for souls. The church is to affect the world—not be infected by the world. We are to be a light and influence for Christ Jesus!

Just like God has good thoughts over you and says good things about His kids, we are called to do the same. This doesn't mean we ignore sin, however we choose to confront sin in love and help lift others out of the miry clay. The world seems dark with sin but I have great news. Jesus is the light of the world. He came for all mankind. He gave His life that we might live for all eternity with Him.

Words Matter Greatly

We have a responsibility to spread good words for those around us to hear. And we have a responsibility to repeat only the words we want to become part of our hearts as well. We have a responsibility to share the good news of the Gospel. We must not ignore what is happening across the nation and globe, and truly turn back to God as a nation. We must choose to decree and declare God's Word over America, our lives, our families, and our circumstances.

We must choose our words wisely because words matter greatly in life and eternity. Take a look at this:

> *You brood of snakes! How could evil men like you speak what is good and right? For whatever is in your heart determines what you say. A good person produces good words from a good heart, and an evil person produces evil words from an evil heart. And I tell you this; that you must give an account on judgment day of every idle word you speak. The words you say now reflect your fate then; either, you will be justified by them or you will be condemned.*
> —Matthew 12:34–37, NLT

You may not think words matter in the larger scheme of life, but they do. When a small child hears a parent say something, he or she begins to repeat the same words. Toddlers learn from their parents. Kids hear other kids at school say things over and over again. Whatever you hear and watch actually gets into your heart. That is why it is vital to be very careful of what you allow entrance into your heart and mind.

> "Above all else, guard your heart, for it effects everything you do." [Hebrew for, "from it flow the springs of life."]
> —Proverbs 4:23, NLT

What we say matters. Reflect on the facts about the Hudson River where Captain "Sully" Sullenberger landed the plane in a moment of decision at a point of crisis—Hudson means "a place of landing." America has been blessed as being called "One Nation Under God." Do we need any more warning that we must turn back to God?

The Doctor Knows Best

Have you ever gotten sick and gone to the doctor? Of course, you have. When I was a kid, I remember going to the doctor and he would always ask me to stick out my tongue. I also remember the strong fragrance of that room. It was the cleanest odor I have ever smelled.

Our tongues reveal when we are sick. So do our words. The Bible says:

> *Death and life are in the power of the tongue. And those who love it will eat its fruit.*
> —Proverbs 18:21, NKJV

When you have problems in life, where do you turn? Do you blame God? Do you blame others? Stop and think for a moment—have you obeyed God's instructions? Do you read the Bible and pray? Do you attend a Bible-believing church? Are there sinful habits that you know God is revealing that you need to get rid of in your personal life?

God wants us all to lead people to Jesus Christ and be so much like Him that others can't resist Him in us. Jesus is the "Great Physician." He is the best doctor for all of life. He always knows best.

> *Do not merely listen to the Word, and so deceive yourselves. Do what it says.*
> —James 1:22, NIV

And remember, it is a message to obey, not just to listen to. If you don't obey, you are only fooling yourself. For if you just listen and don't obey; it is like looking at your face in a mirror but doing nothing to improve your appearance. You see yourself, walk away, and forget what you look like. But if you keep looking steadily into God's perfect law—the law that sets you free—and if you do what it says and don't forget what you heard, then God will bless you for doing it.
—James 1:22–25, NLT

Standing

Words matter. Taking a stand matters just as much. Someone had to stand up to provide an open door for Joseph in the Bible. (See Genesis 41:9–40. The chief cupbearer remembered Joseph and chose to tell Pharaoh of Joseph's gift of dream interpretation.) We have to choose to stand up in excellence. God wants us to be like Joseph—his commitment to excellence regardless of circumstances provided him an audience with the Pharaoh. When Pharaoh could not solve a troubling dream he had, Joseph was summoned because the butler remembered Joseph's interpretation from his time in prison.

The butler chose to stand up and seized an opportunity to be a witness. He began by admitting he had messed up in life, and we all have failed as well. The butler chose to tell Pharaoh what he knew. He had met a Hebrew in prison who had done something for him. He believed in his heart that Joseph was real. He was so sure of the authenticity of Joseph that he knew he could not go wrong by telling Pharaoh about him.

One thing I have noticed is that most of the people who have come against me in some form or fashion usually end up calling me for prayer. Watch out for when the enemy tries to get you offended at someone. God sends people to help us and the devil wants us to miss opportunities. Sometimes the greatest blessing comes in the most unexpected people.

Pharaoh chose to call on Joseph and it was done by faith alone. Pharaoh took the word of the butler. Pharaoh told Joseph all that was on his heart. He told him of the dream and how it troubled him. He asked Joseph if he knew what it meant. Joseph answered, *"It is not in me: God shall give Pharaoh an answer of peace"* (Genesis 41:16). Jesus said, *"...Verily, verily I say unto you, The Son can do nothing of himself, but what he seeth the Father do: for what things soever he doeth, these also doeth the Son likewise"* (John 5:19, KJV). *"I can of mine own self do nothing..."* (John 5:30).

Like the dream of Pharaoh with the good years and years of famine, it seems America has had the so-called *American Dream* but presently is experiencing years of famine or a dream that has turned into a *nightmare*. Regardless of the crisis in America, regardless of the season you find yourself in right now; you can choose to believe in God's favor over you. I have found that God's favor shows up in the most unexplainable ways, at the strangest times, and at the wire—at the last minute. God's timing is never ours. I know from personal experience that we can each find ourselves in a place that seems tight or restricting, sometimes through no fault of our own. God wants us to learn the life lesson of keeping faith in Him and living over our circumstances.

If you are experiencing attack, don't tell people you are *under* attack. You may be experiencing real attack and walking through it, but if you are under God's authority and have your faith in Him, you are not *under* attack. You must choose to stand upon God's Word over your particular situation no matter how you feel. I imagine Joseph did not feel excited about being thrown in a pit, ending up in prison due to being falsely accused, or being left in prison because the butler did not remember him at first—even after Joseph helped him.

Genesis holds the key to many life questions if you will take the time to read about Joseph and how he found favor with God in a time when a nation was in crisis. We are at that place again in history. America is that nation. Like Joseph, we must keep our hope in God, and learn to expect divine favor from God at all times. God is constant and never changes. Times change, clocks move, but God is still the same!

As a nation, we must wake up out of lethargy, arise and really pray, and expect God to show us favor—even in this last hour. We actually live in the greatest time for God to bring about revival of hearts and to this nation. We must not allow the news and reality of the current circumstances to dictate or diminish our expectation for God's divine favor.

Never allow a lack of finances to control your heart and spirit. In the same token, you must not allow abundance and blessing to cause you to forget God either. It would be like saying that God loves you because you find a parking place close to the restaurant. Does that mean if you have to park at a distance that God doesn't love you? The mind must be renewed through the Word of God in order to overcome living by your feelings and wrong thinking. God loves us and that is truth. It is not based on what we do or don't do, not on what we have or don't have, and certainly not what we are walking through in life—but the simple truth that God sent His Son Jesus to redeem all mankind.

If you are walking through a season of cancer, tribulation, depression, or maybe attack against your family or business, does that mean God doesn't love you? Absolutely not! God's love is *not* based on our circumstances. He loves us unconditionally. He loves us too much to leave us the way we are and teaches us to mature in Him. He wants us to think before we speak. He wants us to respond the way Jesus would instead of reacting in negative ways.

Stop and think about what you say before you release words. Just because thoughts come through the mind does not mean they need to come across the lips. Every person must learn to rise above thoughts, negative accusations, external comments of rejection and anything that might offend. We must choose to stand and keep moving forward with clarity of vision and purpose.

Vision must be in the forefront and the windshield kept clear at all times. Let me share how important vision is to you through a miraculous story of God's divine intervention over a windshield. You will be amazed at God's goodness and how He can accomplish whatever He desires. God wants us to have His perspective and point of view. He wants us to stay focused forward in faith.

Vision Matters: Saks Fifth Avenue— Windshield Story

You might be thinking. "Saks Fifth Avenue, what does this have to do with any windshield or vision?" What does this have to do with America? Stay with me and read on. You will find that your life matters to God in every detail.

My husband and I were scheduled for a business trip to New York a few years ago and a couple hours before I was driving on the interstate a rock flew off a truck and hit the windshield. You guessed it. The windshield cracked and it was damaged. I knew it would not be safe and I had to get it fixed. If I chose to ignore the problem, it would get bigger. I drove home and called the insurance company. I knew we had a zero deductible and full comprehensive. *We have that with God as well.*

The representative on the other end of the phone did not know what I knew. He kept telling me it was going to cost me $2,500 to replace the windshield. I explained our insurance policy and we had a zero deductible with full comprehensive. He wanted to argue the point like a broken record, so I chose to tell him that I was going to turn this all over to God and my husband. I had a plane to board shortly and was not going to miss the flight.

We have to learn to pick our battles in life. Some things are not worth wasting precious time. It is not wisdom to argue with someone who doesn't know what you know.

While the person on the other end of the line was shocked at my comment about God, I was polite and pleasant but ended the conversation as it was wasting my time and producing no results. I knew he had misinformation. My husband and I headed for the airport and boarded our flight. After arriving in New York, since Dan had a meeting, another friend and I chose to go to Saks Fifth Avenue to have lunch. I also had a dear friend that worked there as well that I wanted to see.

We had lunch and then visited the lady I knew who worked there. We met total strangers and I had a delightful conversation with one particular woman who asked me if I thought a garment would look nice on her. I proceeded to help her shop and we talked to each other like we had known each other for a long time.

My cell phone rang and it was the car dealership calling to report the same news about the windshield. I heard the same thing again. I told the service representative that I had turned it over to God and that if our President could get a bill passed, I surely could as well with the particular insurance company—which I named aloud.

The total stranger that I was helping to shop overheard and asked me if she heard me correctly. I won't name the company, but interestingly enough, this lady was the number one person over Human Resources at their corporate office and asked me to wait while she called the Vice President of claims. She handed me the phone and I shared the details with this man. He advised me not to worry and said he would handle it.

Twenty minutes passed and the phone rang. On the other end of the line was the VP of claims at corporate for this insurance company, advising me the bill would be totally covered. I called the dealership and shared the series of events. He was amazed at how I turned the windshield problem over to God, boarded a flight to New York, and how God had divinely connected me with leadership from corporate for the insurance company while having lunch and visiting a friend at Saks Fifth Avenue. It was totally a God set up and a show of Himself on our behalf. He never ceases to amaze me.

He cares about every detail. He cares about what matters to us. The very next day, a representative from this insurance company hand delivered a check to the dealership to pay the bill in full while we were still in New York and the car was still in our garage.

This is how God works. Jesus has already paid the full price for all mankind. Before you were ever born into this world, your debt of sin was paid in full through Jesus Christ. We must believe, receive, and confess Him as Lord to be a receiver of that gift! The whole world has been forgiven.

The enemy comes to steal, kill, and destroy. He wants us to think we still owe a debt that has already been paid. He wants us to get all worked up and lose focus. He wants us to miss our destiny and divinely orchestrated plans.

However, right in the midst of everyday life, God shows up and reveals Himself. It is important to Him that we see clearly—and stay focused forward in faith! If you don't get proper vision and start to see things clearly through God's eyes, you may very well miss your destiny.

We must stay focused on God and await His return. We must keep standing upon God's Word and moving forward with clarity of vision and purpose. We know He is returning but we are called to occupy till He comes. What does that mean? Do what you do and fish for souls. Souls are people that are in need of Jesus.

We must choose to occupy and be about the Father's business. That is simply doing business on purpose for God and advancing His kingdom here on earth. People are stressed, worn out, and weary with life. We have a lifeline of hope—His name is Jesus. We share Him by loving people and by choosing to share our faith and testimony, while other times we simply walk with them and take time to care by encouraging them and sharing our resources. In the midst of slowing down to show the love of God, we find fulfillment in knowing we are moving into God's next assignment for us. It is His anointing that empowers us to move forward and take back the ground the enemy has stolen. Even though we experience attack, we keep moving forward advancing the Kingdom of God. Always remember, Satan never attacks a retreating army. Keep moving forward.

Weariness And Pain

A hunger pain and weariness drove one man in the Bible to totally give up his birthright. In Genesis 25, the Bible tells us how Esau gave up his birthright because he refused to think past the hunger pains in his stomach. He had been out in the fields working and he was weary. I can just imagine that when he walked through the door of the house, his senses were very open to the smell of good food being prepared by his brother, Jacob. He asked Jacob for food and did a very dumb thing.

Jacob saw an opportunity and seized it. He apparently knew of his brother's shortsightedness for the immediate and took advantage of the moment. Jacob told Esau that he would give him red stew if he would sell his birthright. Esau was so weary that he said, "Look, I *am* about to die; so what *is* this birthright to me?" (Gen. 25:32, NKJV).

Perhaps Jacob did not want to delay gratification. He gave up his inheritance for a bowl of soup. The Bible commands us, "And let us not grow weary while doing good, for in due season we shall reap if we do not lose heart" (Gal. 6:9, NKJV). Don't allow your flesh to overcome the vision God has put in your heart. We must choose to fan the flame of eternal passion, ignore the enemy, ignore the critics, and ignore our own fleshly feelings.

Esau was more motivated by his flesh than by a vision of what God had for his life. He chose wrongly because he didn't know how to delay instant gratification. Samson is another man in the Bible who could not restrain his flesh and earthly passions or temporary desires. Both violated principles and tossed restriction to the side to fulfill a drive deep within. Their flesh drove them to give up God's best.

Self-discipline is not a term that most like to hear about. Neither is *submission* or *surrender*. Vision restrains us and provides boundaries that give protection. Anything that drives us can become an idol. The Spirit of God leads.

One of my favorite verses in the Bible is Habakkuk 2:2. We write the vision down and run with it. We write it down and make it plain and simple. Once I get a vision for a new book, I start it right then. I open a new document and begin. I start writing.

Everyone needs a vision for his or her life. God gives us vision in His Word. It is building His Kingdom—souls. We are called to build the church. It is God's divine plan to reach the lost. It is His plan to redeem mankind. If you are a believer in Christ, you are a member of the Body of Christ—His church. You are the hope of the world. Vision is highly important. Remember the windshield story—write down the vision God gives you, run with it, and do it with all your heart and move away from distractions.

Right in the midst of whatever God has called you to do with Him, always remember He is with you and will provide a home base. We gain wisdom and strategies and learn how to do life and work smarter. We surround ourselves with other people with different strengths and weaknesses in order to build each other up—it's called building a team. God will divinely position people around you and connect you with people of divine purpose. Look for them and expect them!

American Idols, Distractions, and Deception

Idolatry, distractions, and deception come in all shapes and sizes. Athens was full of idolatry and thousands of perverted idols lined the streets as Paul walked through the land. Paul was one man, a little man, but full of the power of the Holy Spirit. Studying the life of Paul gives me great hope and encouragement. If he could do what he did in the New Testament, we can make a difference today.

America has her own idols. It may be things and it may be people. Anything that takes the place of God can become an idol. In fact, *American Idol* is a show millions have watched. I have not watched the show but once or twice and I am not even sure that is the correct name, but as I was thinking about it, I thought about the idols in America. The Bible tells us: "Direct your hearts to the Lord and serve Him alone" (1 Sam. 7:3). God won't share His glory. He wants it all. *All* is one word with great impact. God demands all of our hearts.

You might be asking, "What is an American idol?" An idol is any unauthorized source—person, place, thought, or even thing—that you and I go to in order to meet a specific need. It is anything that takes the place of God in your life. For example, if you try to give your adult children everything they would like to have before they have worked to earn the money to buy it and pay the price, then you have just usurped God's authority in their life and tried to play God in their finances.

If we truly want to live in God's presence, operate in His power, and hear His voice, then we must turn to God with our whole hearts.

The Midnight Hour

Idols come in all shapes and sizes. For example, I had a young lady text me and notify me she had gained weight over the last few weeks and wanted to lose weight. She told me she was drinking red wine and champagne. I sent a text back to her advising if she would replace the alcoholic beverages with water, she would drop a few pounds rather quickly. She responded: "I like them so much because they are so tasty." Yes, something may taste good but not be good for our health. She liked the taste. My response was to simply stop complaining if she didn't want to make a change. Many like the taste of something that is not good for them. We just reflected on what happen to Esau due to taste and something he desperately wanted and lost his birthright.

Satan tries to lure us by twisting facts and making us think something is good for us when it turns into sin. Food is needed to live, but you don't live to eat. Sleep is necessary for rest and recovery, but too much sleep is not good. Sex within marriage is good, but lust and immorality are both sin.

Satan schemes his way into minds through trying to make a person think a God-given desire can be replaced with sin. It is deception. He plots to use whatever necessary to deceive and distract us from our purpose in God. We must learn to look to God's Word and His principles as our guide, first and foremost, and then we won't have as many problems. God's Word works. God's Word and our concocted ideas mixed within do not work.

Many years ago, I gave several gifts to an organization to be given away as door prizes for a charity event. While at the event, I noticed the total amount was not given away and inquired about it. The person I asked told me they decided the leadership needed the books and instead gave the remainder to staff. I couldn't believe what I was hearing. In my thinking, when you give something for a specific purpose, that is what it is for, right? If the organization really liked the book, they could have bought more and given them to their leadership themselves. This is how sin crouches at the door.

When anyone thinks they can justify sin, a door has been opened to Satan. People aren't born as murderers and thieves. One lie turns into another lie, and they just keep getting bigger. One form of justification leads to more. This is how sin begins in the heart of any person. No one can afford to go against the Word of God. Look what happened to Judas. We are either for God or against Him. It is all a matter of the heart!

God wants us to become whole and live holy. He doesn't want us to live a lie and have Satan enter our hearts like happened to Judas. Satan wants us all to focus on self.

We must choose to turn our focus to God. We must choose to stand up and take our *shield of faith* to quench every fiery dart of Satan. He is a real enemy and he comes to devour our influence—like a roaring lion. We must learn to be strong in the Word of God and in His might by putting on the armor of Christ Himself. (See Ephesians 6.) (Explanation: when we read and pray the Word of God, it becomes a part of our heart. When a fiery dart comes and attempts to pierce our heart, we are so full of God's Word that our hearts are moist and the fire is unable to penetrate.)

Nearly seventeen years ago while on a drive to speak at a church in Gastonia, North Carolina, I remember telling a friend that the enemy tries to keep us busy—being under Satan's yoke. He comes to steal, kill, and destroy. He tries to keep us busy so we don't hear God. He tempts all to overspend and work long hours so we have no time for family. His plan of demise is to over-stimulate the minds of all through television, computers, and all other forms of technology to the point of exhaustion where we don't know how to rest. (For further research if you don't believe me, study how brains are being rewired—called neuroplasticity. We must choose to renew our minds in the Word of God and learn to rest.) Rather than being busy, we must learn to be productive. We can choose to turn our country back to God, one person at a time, to every family, and every church across this nation. Will you turn back to God in prayer for America?

Ignite America

Are you fueling or fanning flames? As Christians, we need to find out what is in our own hearts. Are we going to sit back and do nothing while the world around us falls apart? Or are we going to get into the battle and fight the good fight of faith? (See 1 Timothy 6:12.) Can God count on you to do something to turn America back to God?

Wall Street may crumble, leaders may fail, but God will never fail us. The enemy is trying to destroy the spiritual foundation of America. God is waiting on us to turn back to Him. We are in need of a *great transformation*—from the crash of 2008 all the way back to 2001 and the events that occurred on 9/11—these tragedies happened and are still happening today. Will we turn? Will you do your part? People matter to God! Do they matter to you?

If someone knew the entire market was going to crash, would you want that person to tell you? If you knew your only son or daughter was going to spend eternity in hell, wouldn't you want someone to tell them of a better plan? If your grandchild walked into a street with a speeding car approaching, would you yell and run after that grandchild? Of course you would, right? If you didn't warn your grandchild, everything in life would change.

It seems everything in life has changed—all of a sudden. But in reality, it has been happening over time, little by little. Suddenly, everything seems to look and feel different. Lifestyles have changed and families are in chaos. While many think their well-planned lives are in order, their stock portfolios secure, their stash of wealth and real estate are enough, I've got news—we are headed toward the return of Jesus Christ and none of that will matter then to any of us.

I have been to many funerals and have never seen a U-haul carrying stuff behind the hearse. The only thing we will take to heaven with us will be souls we have led to Christ. God is sounding the alarm for us to wake up out of the slumber and live for Him. We are to be a light on a hill, a searchlight that is always on the lookout for people in need of God. People matter greatly to God therefore they must to us as well.

Technology Changes Everything

Speaking of things, technology is rapidly changing the globe. It is a great tool to share the Good News of Jesus Christ, however, you walk in a bank and tellers are missing and losing their jobs. Friends call me to share that a computer has taken their position. Jobs have been moved to foreign nations due to technology.

Technology changes everything and keeps changing itself. We have to stay up with what is going on in life. Many jobs have been created, and businesses operate and thrive by technology. God gave people creative ideas to actually build technology. It is a great tool to be used for good. But technology also changes the way we spend time eating meals together. Or rather, are we even spending time together anymore at all? Recently when our grandkids were over and we were having lunch, I asked them to leave their phones and all technology in the living room. I told them we were going to have lunch and talk. We enjoyed lunch and had fun talking and listening to each other. When I was growing up, we actually talked to each other at the table and listened to what each other had to say. For the most part, this has been lost in America.

Technology is a great tool for staying connected with those who live at a distance. But nevertheless, what on earth has happened to family time in America? Life has changed. We must learn how to use tools properly and learn to advance God's kingdom here and now in the earth. While technology changes daily and at a high rate of speed, God never changes. He is the Great I AM. God. Yahweh. Thank God.

The world is changing before our very eyes with increased volatility and uncertainty. It is all over the media and we can see the warnings and signs of the times unfolding before us that Jesus warned us about long ago. America is in great need of turning back to God. We are in need of the Messiah who has already come—and is coming back again!

Warnings and Confirmations

My husband was watching an old movie one evening and I couldn't help but notice what I was hearing. I was editing this book and chose to insert this for all readers. God gives us warnings and confirmations in the natural to show us what is actually happening in the spiritual realm around us. He is sounding the alarms for all to hear.

I believe this particular movie was made in 1998 and two meteorites were headed toward planet earth. Morgan Freeman was the actor portraying the President of the United States. A blonde lady was a news reporter and was giving the news as she was informed.

What really caught my attention was the fact that the spaceship that was launched to destroy the meteorites that were about to destroy the world was named "The Messiah." Did that get your attention as well? *The Messiah—Jesus Christ chose to die for all mankind!*

I watched briefly and noticed that the Messiah and the people on board had to die to divert the final destruction from the largest meteorite. One of the astronauts said he was as close to home as he would get—he was in the heavens. *I heard that, too!* Next, the news reporter chose to help others make it to some place that had been created that was named "Noah's Ark" to save one million people. This was all in this movie. *God is sending clues, loud and clear, to confirm that we are living in the last hour!*

At the end of the movie, the smaller meteorite created a tidal wave that destroyed New York, part of Washington, surrounding cities, and all within. Interestingly enough, a tidal wave did take out twenty-five-plus homes on the coast of Boston a few days after I saw this movie. God can use a movie to move us to prayer as well as warn us of things that are coming. This was portrayed in the movie similar to the flood and Noah's Ark that saved those within. In the movie, the government had built an underground shelter and it was named "Noah's Ark" to save those that had been chosen.

The Messiah did destroy the larger meteorite, but all died on board. The news reporter chose to help others and went to stand with her father on the beach, embracing him as the tidal wave rushed over them.

The only way America will be ignited for God is not *if*, but *when* she turns back to God! We must choose to embrace God and His ways. We must choose to honor His Word above all else. We must stay focused on God's kingdom, reaching souls and allowing the water of His Word to wash over our souls for cleansing on a daily basis.

Every person matters to God. He desires that none should perish. He wants all to turn to Him and come to know Him. He has given us the gift of forgiveness and redemption for all mankind.

It is time we raise the banner of God's love. The Bible says, "He brought me to the banqueting house, and his banner over me was love" (Song of Sol. 2:4, ESV).

What Flag or Banner are You Raising?

He brought me to the banqueting house, and His banner over me was love.
—Song of Solomon 2:4, ESV

No matter where you may live, there is a flag that represents that nation. We raise some type of flag or banner ourselves, whether we realize it or not, by the way we live and respond to people and situations. God used a donkey to get one man's attention in the Bible. He used people with severely messed up lives! He had a group of twelve disciples that fell asleep on the job at the most critical hour and He can use you and me today. He can also speak through a movie.

You probably have seen the movie *Braveheart* and most likely remember a scene with the flag, which brings me to this question: what flag have you chosen to raise and fly in America? If you are a person who doesn't watch movies—that's OK. Stay with me anyway. If you saw a group of nicely lined up snowmen with fishing rods facing the water from the banks, what would you think? I began to think about all the snow that has fallen across the nation and how snow forces us to stop and see what really matters in life. A member of our family sent me a picture of snowmen that were all dressed up and had banners attached to their fishing poles. Their banners were still flying in the midst of snow.

When I think of fishing, I think of going after souls. Souls are people, and people matter to God. Jesus chose His twelve disciples and told them He would teach them to be fishers of men. Your life matters to God. People matter to God. Do they matter to you?

People matter so much to God that He gave His only begotten Son Jesus Christ as a living sacrifice. We touched His heart to give His best. He gave to redeem all mankind. It is obvious to me that God cares about the people in the world.

By the same token, what touches our hearts has the ability to change us. Think about this for a moment. If it gets to the heart, it is something you become in life. You are moved to action because of passion. When America turns back to God and allows His love to overflow, she will once again become a nation unto God—fulfilling her call.

But over these past few decades, America has asked God to depart. God has not forgotten America—but she has forgotten Him. Where did this nation go wrong? Was it the one woman that we allowed to get prayer taken out of schools? Was it the compromise in the White House that has trickled all the way down to local government offices?

Whatever is in the head eventually shows up in the body—whatever you see in the body is somewhere in the head.

True leaders lead people with standards and moral integrity. True leaders lead people based on standards and are not moved by money, manipulation and messages. Politicians are elected and can sometimes be persuaded by money to go against their own word to the people. But we need leaders that will stand up and honor God's Word. We need to stand up and through a solemn assembly must precisely and respectfully call political leaders to God's principles for government. (See Romans 13:1–7.)

I have heard it said that everything rises and falls on leadership. The president is to lead the nation. A business owner leads his or her business. Husbands lead their wives. Mothers lead their children. Fathers lead by example. Pastors lead their churches. I have been thinking, rather than teaching on leadership, why don't we teach on how to follow the Holy Spirit and stay under His authority and His leading? A friend of mine and I were talking and she said that just maybe we should start having *follow-ship* conferences on how to follow after God with a whole heart. *Good word!*

A leader is only able to lead someone as far as they have gone. A teacher can only teach what he or she knows. We live with so much technology that we have no excuse to have any ignorance. We are following someone, whether we know it or not. We are either becoming one with God or one with the world.

Becoming One With God

In marriage, when you make the commitment to love your spouse, you truly engage on a path of becoming one. The two stand together through thick and thin and for richer or poorer, and in sickness and in health. Nothing can touch them when they stand together as one—always guarding their heart.

Every Christian must decide to no longer serve two masters and guard their heart. God makes it clear that we cannot have the world and have Him at the same time. (Read 1 John 2:15–17, NKJV.) We must decide to consult God in prayer on all matters of life (Luke 9:23) and we must choose to make Him Lord of all.

When a nation turns to God and relishes in His love, the love of God will prevail. Nothing is impossible for a nation whose god is the Lord. She may be nearly unstoppable and many have said, "unsinkable."

Most people remember or have heard the story about the Titanic. The crew that was on "lookout" gave warnings that were totally ignored. The iceberg that was seen was a warning to turn back. The warnings were ignored until it was too late and today we know what happened. Movies have been made about the Titanic. You may or may not have seen any of them, so let me share briefly about the Titanic.

She hit an iceberg and sank with hundreds and hundreds of people meeting death in frigid water with no land in sight. The very luxury ship (cruise liner) that was unsinkable, according to man, sank at sea. There were not enough lifeboats on board to accompany emergencies because the ship was labeled "unsinkable." The iceberg was under the water and ripped a hole that brought on sudden disaster. By the time the actual iceberg was discovered it was too late, for the damage had already been done.

In life, it is the hidden issues that we refuse to deal with that either make us or break us. I believe it is better to be 5 percent seen and the rest hidden in God—anchored in Him—and living out of a pure heart that desires to please Him above all else.

Is your heart becoming infected by the world and wrong belief systems, or are you impacting the world for God?

Matters of the Heart

The heart is necessary to life. Our heart matters to God as well. Motives of the heart show up in our actions.
If you have moved from a mandate from God where He has revealed His divine assignment to driven ambition, there is a definite heart issue. If you have moved from knowing God and talking about Him with others, and are now consumed with work that you have forgotten God, there is a heart issue. If you have thrown people by the wayside and pushed people out and put others in to your own liking, or you have stolen finances from your employer, business, or family, there is a heart issue. If you have chosen to do whatever it takes to get to the top of your organization and done things that don't line up with God's Word, there is a heart issue. Judas had the same problem. Satan entered his heart and he was overtaken.

Sometimes people climb to the top of the ladder and suddenly realize the ladder is leaning on the wrong building—we must learn to lean on God.

Matters of the heart are important. You can't live without a heart. We all have to deal with life issues as well. When my husband's heart stopped beating at Mercy Hospital in 2012, had God not intervened, I would be a widow today. God brought him back to life. We need God to bring America back to life in Him as well. We are a nation in need of God.

If you are alive and breathing, you have most likely experienced hurt from a person or problem at some point in life. Even if it is something you didn't cause, but rather an injustice that you've experienced, you still have to move forward for protection.

There are certain things all people have to do in life to truly live out of their heart. Forgiven people forgive others. Forgiveness doesn't mean that others aren't held accountable by God; it simply means we move forward and trust God to bring justice in His perfect timing.

The Bible says, "Do not repay anyone evil for evil. Be careful to do what is right in the eyes of everybody. If it is possible, as far as it depends on you, live at peace with everyone" (Rom 12:17, NIV). An attorney told me something I will never forget. He said, "Revenge is best served on a cold platter." How true that is in life.

Choose to be released from the prison of bitterness today by choosing to forgive others, yourself, and perhaps even God, and move on. Make that decision today to be released in full potential to fan the flame in others for God. Eternity is all that really matters. We are being trained in this life to reign with God for all eternity. We are being trained to live in the agape love of God. Forgive and live!

The Bible says to live at peace "as far as it depends on you." What this means in real life application is this: it doesn't really matter what the other person does or says, whether they react or blow like a volcano, or even if the person is dead doesn't matter, either. Our God-given responsibility is to decide to forgive and move forward in life. *Forgiveness does not eliminate consequences. The Bible makes it evidently clear that God will repay those who do harm to His own.*

Stop and forgive. Don't keep stewing with rage over getting revenge. The Bible says, *"'I will take revenge; I will pay them back,' says the Lord"* (Rom. 12:19. NLV). Don't allow another day to pass you by with holding a grudge or bitterness in your heart. Choose to forgive. You have a race to run to the finish line.

Race to the Finish

We have a race in life to run. At the finish line, we will spend eternity in one of two places—heaven or hell. We must choose now while we are alive, and learn to run the race well by trusting God and removing all hindrances.

Even on a racetrack, the drivers must make a decision to move forward or get run over. If anger can move a person to jump out of their car on a track and lose all sense of reasoning, they will most likely die in the race. Drivers don't stroll around the track with other drivers flying by them when they are thinking correctly—they choose to get in the race. They make a choice to go for it. They circle to the finish, keeping their windshields clear with proper fuel to finish.

The driver also has a crew that he or she depends on for quick pit stops to replenish. Maintenance and replacement of tires is sometimes a necessity to be able to finish the race as well. Every driver has to make sure they can see what is out in front. They are moving at such a high rate of speed that if they don't, disaster will be the end result. Remember the windshield story I shared earlier. If God cares about a windshield, how much more does he care about your life? I committed the windshield problem to God, got on a flight to New York, went to have lunch, helped a total stranger shop for clothing afterwards, and she just happened to be an employee of our insurance company. That is totally just like God our Father. Praise Him!

Like the small windshield problem to the crisis we have in America, we can obviously see we need God's help. America has lost her sense of vision and purpose. People are desperate and living in crisis.

Only God can take a mess and turn it into a message. Only God can take a messed up life and turn it around for good and His glory. Only God can turn a test into a testimony when we choose to obey Him and trust Him. Only God can turn a trial into triumph. Only God can take a tragedy and turn it into an amazing testimony of His goodness. Only God can turn a victim into a victor. Only God can take a crisis and birth a deep heartfelt *cry* for revival in a nation. Thank God for His mercy and grace. We have victory in Christ at every turn when we choose to follow Him and obey His Word.

Bad things happen to good people. We have to choose to get back up, stay in the race of life, and move forward with God. Many people who have experienced horrific things go out and speak to others about the issues they once faced. God equips and empowers us to help others when we turn to Him.

Only God can take what we commit to Him and take care of it every single time. If He can do what He did with the situation with the windshield, he can surely take care of all. He cares about the details in life. This should be evident to you through the divine intervention over a windshield. God shows Himself strong over every problem that we turn over to Him. He is a very present help in time of trouble.

How much more does God care about souls, families that are torn apart, and this nation? We must choose to turn back to Him in hot pursuit.

Hot Pursuit

In our relationship with God, we can live in hot pursuit all the days of our lives, having clear vision and walking out our destiny. In order to do this, one must live in *humility*, *obedience*, and *trust* in God. Many people trust in self. Humility moves a person to instant obedience. Obedience reveals a heart that totally trusts God. That is how we live in *hot pursuit* of God instead of being lukewarm in life.

We can live out of God's heart and have keen vision, moving into our destiny in God. Every person needs to move from blurred vision to keen, accurate understanding of personal destiny in God through seeing what God sees. We also have to learn not to despair in the period of adjustment and waiting. This is accomplished as we seek God and meditate on His Word, both day and night. We must not lose hope in the waiting or be moved to despair.

Don't despair over mistakes you have made, or even at the hand of others. Don't despair over mistakes and misfortune. Move from despair to pursuit of God. Choose to live for God and get anything that is not like God out of your heart.

You can learn to bishop your own heart. You can talk to your heart and tell it that it will forgive all who have wronged you. Hatred is not residing there, and neither is any other wrong emotion. Keep moving forward in faith.

We live out of what we know in our hearts and can sense in our spirit—moving forward with God for His kingdom purposes. Even in the natural, when you purchase a new prescription for contacts or eyeglasses, it takes time for your eyes to adjust accordingly to the new lenses. Your view in life can be distorted because of what you've experienced in the past. You can be misguided and believe a lie. Let's take a look at the lie that was bought and believed by those on board a cruise ship.

The Titanic

The *Titanic* was said to be "unsinkable." This was man's opinion, and not a fact.
TITANIC FACTS*: At 11:40 p.m. on the night of 14 April 1912, en route to New York and on her maiden voyage, the RMS *Titanic* struck the iceberg that would ultimately lead to her sinking less than three hours later. At around 2:20 a.m. on the morning of 15 April, RMS *Titanic* disappeared beneath the surface of the Atlantic Ocean, a disaster that resulted in the loss of more than 1,500 lives, almost two-thirds of the people on board.

The *Titanic* was equipped to carry sixty-four lifeboats, but only carried twenty. The first boat out only had twenty-eight people in it with a capacity of sixty-five. She received six warnings about icebergs before the collision. She sank in 160 minutes (2 hours and 40 minutes). The temperature of the seawater was -2 centigrade. The total percentage of passengers and crew who survived was 31.6 with 53.4 being the percentage that *could* have survived given the number of spaces left on Titanic's lifeboats. Two dogs also survived.

*(Website: www.titanicfacts.net, visited 4/30/15.)

As I was reviewing facts about the Titanic, I found some to be quite interesting. The number of *Titanic* crewmembers who survived is 214. The percentage of the crewmembers that survived was twenty-four. The percentage of male crewmembers that survived was twenty-two. The percentage of female crewmembers that survived was eighty-seven. The percentage of navigation officers who survived was fifty (four out of eight). The percentage of engineering officers who survived was zero (all twenty-five perished, bravely working to keep the ship afloat for as long as possible). The percentage of lookouts that survived (those that were watching) was one hundred.

I find it interesting that all those that were look-out crewmembers (*those who were watching*) survived. They were saved. This continually confirms the importance of watching and paying attention.

There is a story in the Bible about the ten virgins and their oil lanterns. Five were wise and five were foolish. While the story in Matthew 25 is both an adventure and a romance, the arrival of the Bridegroom (Jesus Christ) is expected. The Spirit of God has been provided ahead of time ensuring eternal light and joy to the bridal party. At the midnight hour in the midst of deep darkness the saints will go out to meet the Bridegroom.

The five wise virgins seem to be the center of the story as they are prepared and also know a crisis is coming and a time of great darkness. They also know who they are in Christ and what they are called to do. They are prepared to be faithful witnesses even in the midst of great darkness. Their devotion is to God and their worship is in spirit and in truth.

While we reflect on scripture and the five wise virgins, we would do well to think about what happened with The *Titanic* and all on-board. The number of passengers on board the *Titanic* that survived was 492. While I enjoy studying God's Word and digging for nuggets of wisdom, reading statistics and gaining understanding, it is vital we don't miss the spiritual alarms that are going off all around us. The alarms are sounding.

Someone didn't heed the warnings on the Titanic. On September 11, 2001, tragedy struck in several places in America! In the race of life, much like driving a race car on a track, there are turns we must choose to make or die. The Bible tells us that when we turn to the Lord, He removes the veil that blinds us.

God sends snow to the earth to stop us and cause us to see the real need of the world—turning to Him. When we are shut in due to snow, we have only need of basic essentials in life. Not much else matters. With snow-covered grounds and parking lots in front of businesses covered with ice, some owners don't much care if the snow is cleared. The people that lease the spaces do care, however, because it is their livelihood. It's how they make money to feed their families and keep the doors of the business open.

If a building owner only cares about the rent from a tenant and doesn't care much about the people or their business owners, they probably won't care much about taking care of the parking lot or care about the outside walls either. What causes anyone to lose the art of caring about people in any nation, business, organization, or family?

I know there are many wonderful organizations that do care, but the world as a whole is rather selfish. How can we move to caring about each other? How can we be the change around us?

With the busy-ness in America from the daily demands, life in the corporate world to life in retail, from life in small business to life in ministry, there is a huge difference in what people are paid to do and what people are called to do. Corporate America should be learning from the church how to abide rather than striving to always achieve more. The church should be showing the world how to treat people. If the church of Jesus Christ were doing what she was called to do, the world would be running to the church and filling the altars in prayer.

Has the world infected the church? Or is the church affecting the world? Take time to reflect on your local church. Are the walls filled with impoverished places and nations you have touched? If not, what fills the walls? Is the history of the church with pastors and spouses, all arrayed in different outfits? Is it a combination? What do you see? It is good to see history and reminders of how a church has impacted the community and nations. It is a reminder to us to keep moving forward because souls matter to God. We become one with His heart when souls matter to us as individuals!

What has happened to the house of prayer that Jesus called His church? What has happened to the local body of Christ? What has happened to America? Will she learn to abide in Jesus and ignite America? Is she so caught up in business that she has forgotten God and people?

Have altars become a stage for performance? Does anyone really worship God anymore? What is happening across this land? Do we have conferences about prayer and never really pray as a church? What happened to prayer in the House of God? Whose house is it anyway? Has God changed? The answer to that last question is a resounding no.

People move away from their moral compass in God to manipulation, motive change, and being driven rather than being led by the Holy Spirit. Has the church moved from leaning on God and being led by the Spirit of the living God to performance and people pleasing?

I fully understand that a church needs to be run like a business to a certain degree. Anyone with common sense knows that. The electric bill must be paid or the lights will be turned off. If the Body of Christ does not pray, we have a power problem as well.

I remember standing in line at a store one day and thought I knew a man in front of me. I thought he was a pastor of a church in another area. He had his son with him as well. I spoke to him for just a few minutes and he insisted I go in front of him. He suddenly turned around and started walking back down the checkout line. I heard him tell his son he forgot to bring his wallet and had left it in his wife's purse. He was gone before I could even offer to pay for his small purchase.

The Holy Spirit spoke to me—that He didn't want me to pay for the small purchase of technology—some type of listening and connection device. He was showing me that the power of God has never been for sale. It can't be purchased, and only comes through divine connection with Him! The power of God comes alive when we stay connected with Him through intimacy.

It wasn't that God was saying this pastor did not have any power—it was simply God's way of confirming to me what He had for me to write in this book. It goes for us all. We all have to follow Jesus Christ, stay connected, live in His Word, and pray. We go out in the world and shine the light in the darkness. However, it is not for sale. It can't be purchased. Jesus has paid the price once and for all—we have to turn to Him in repentance and prayer as a nation in need of God! Like the pastor and son that turned around and headed for the wife, God the Father sent His Son and has empowered His church—the bride of Christ.

Leading, Being Led, and Abiding

Pastors, church planters, evangelists and any ministry organization has to lead their organization—everything from balancing budgets, building teams, leading outreach initiatives, and fostering vision. And let's not forget leveraging finances and strategizing growth systems through discipleship programs. But in the midst of it all, children of God are called to abide in Christ. As sons and daughters of God, no matter what type of ministry field you are in, we are still called to live in peace and pursue God's presence.

Moving from striving to our personal decision to abide in Christ is a distance of choice and determination. It involves surrender of self-will and reliance upon God—choosing to be led by the Holy Spirit. If all you've ever known is performance and self-reliance in the name of doing it *for* God, you may experience a screaming fit from your soul. We have to crucify our flesh on a daily basis and choose to obey God.

God desires that we do what He has ordained us to do *with Him* not for Him.

We all experience hidden times where God is at work in our soul and preparing us for what He has called us to do with Him. God trains us through hidden times, sometimes years where our gifts and talents go unnoticed, so that when He brings us on the scene everyone will know it is the Lord's doing Himself. His personal training cannot be passed by in life. What happened with the *Titanic* proves that what is seen may not always be the most significant. What is hidden has the power to destroy.

On the other hand, the time we spend hidden away with God brings about power and potential that is greater than any nuclear device. Our time in prayer with God and the hidden times of the soul give us purpose and bring us to the place that we acknowledge we are nothing without Christ.

I can assure you now that if we could have a conversation with the people that were on the Titanic, they would agree that the iceberg had the power to destroy a ship that was labeled by man as "unsinkable."

When you are feeling uncelebrated by people or hearing negative comments, choose to treasure the time hidden away with God where His work in your life brings about life and not destruction. The iceberg that was unseen destroyed the Titanic.

Sometimes, like in the life of David, it is the thing that is unseen or the person we are not willing to confront that causes destruction. We must always trust the leading of the Holy Spirit. He sees and knows all!

On the flip side of what happened to a ship that was supposed to be so great and labeled "unsinkable," we can choose to stay hidden in God so that when God does release us for the next season in life, His power and purpose is revealed. Contrary to the world's way of thinking, where everyone strives for performance and to be seen on the stage of life, God's ways are far greater. Staying hidden in God and having our own personal quiet time with Him gives us great power, personal passion, and undivided attention for hearing and understanding the purpose God created us for in the first place—to know Him and make Him known.

Others may not necessarily notice the riches in your life that are being mined in the tough seasons. This is where life is uncomfortable and God is at work. Choose to relish time hidden away with God and trust Him for His perfect timing. This happened in the life of Joseph as well.

I have a feeling the people on the *Titanic* remembered what was important, thought about life after death, and were in a state of panic when they knew the ship was sinking. All were together, rich and poor alike, those with great wealth and worldly riches, and those that were workers on the ship itself. The musicians chose to play their instruments and entered into a place of worship while people passed by that cold and dreary night after the news was out that the *Titanic* was going down.

It reminds me of Psalm 96—about singing to the Lord! *"Oh, sing to the Lord a new song! Sing to the Lord, all the earth. Sing to the Lord, bless His name; Proclaim the good news of His salvation from day to day. Declare His glory among the nations, His wonders among all peoples"* (Ps. 96:1–3, NKJV).

Say among the nations, "The Lord reigns; The world is also firmly established, It shall not be moved; He shall judge the peoples righteously." Let the heavens rejoice, and let the earth be glad; Let the sea roar, and all its fullness; Let the field be joyful, and all that is in it. Then all the trees of the woods will rejoice before the LORD; For He is coming, for He is coming to judge the earth. He shall judge the world with righteousness, And the peoples with His truth" (Ps. 96:10–13, NKJV).

He is coming back again. God wants His church to arise and shine, so that corporate America and the nations will see and know Him. What a tragedy it will be for many to have gained what they think is wealth yet miss eternal life in God. The people on the *Titanic* bought the lie that the luxury cruise ship was unsinkable. Satan wants you to think you have all the time left in the world. Life is but a vapor—you don't have a clue what tomorrow may hold.

As a matter of fact, right in the middle of editing this book, I received a phone call with the news that Mother's brother had a massive heart attack and died. We never know the time or hour. I had a three-day wait again on finishing this edit. God is waiting for us to return to Him for an edit as well.

That is why it is vital that you turn to God while you still have breath in your lungs! You may already be an on-fire Christian, or you may have heard about God and don't have a personal relationship with Him. You may be a pastor or a church planter, but you can be doing work *for* God and not be in relationship *with* God. In fact, I remember hearing the testimony from a pastor who shared he was actually a pastor of a church for seventeen years before he realized he wasn't even born again. He gave his life to God and has a thriving church today, outreaches, and a Christian university.

You may be a pastor of a huge church to a person who goes to church every Sunday. You may now have moved from being on-fire for God to cold and the frozen chosen. You may be on one side of the fence or the other. Perhaps, you are even angry with God because life did not go as planned.

You may have never stepped foot in a church or you may have been wounded in one. You may feel like you are a mess, or you might be the one that can sing, "It is well with my soul." You may know how to depend on grace, while others only know how to define it. No matter the case, we have to learn to sow grace and realize the church is supposed to be a place of refuge where people feel welcome and can be rerouted back to God.

In professional racing, drivers have to make the turns or they will experience burn out or even death. Many commuters turned back on that early morning of September 11, 2001, due to coffee spills and sick children and missed a tragic death. My prayer is that no matter where you are on your journey in life, you will make the turn and live in hot pursuit of God.

The *Titanic* did not heed the warnings to turn back. The "unsinkable" did in fact sink at sea due to the iceberg. Will we as a nation, heed the warnings from God and turn back to Him? Will you do your part in praying for America to turn back to God? Will you turn to God in prayer on a daily basis for this nation?

In the midst of the present storms we are facing as a nation and individually, will you turn back to God in prayer and lead others to a place of abiding through example? Jesus is the anchor that holds through every storm!

Leading, Being Led, and Abiding

> Storms in Life will Come
> Jesus is our Anchor through Every Storm!

Pursuit or Competition

Would you say most people are in pursuit of God or moved by other things like competition, Hollywood, gain, or even their personal life plan? Let's take a look at competition and how it pits people against people. If you have ever played sports, you obviously know that competition requires the subjugation of some for the success of one. It happens in business, in government, and other facets of life. We must learn how to operate in a world of relentless change, ferocious competition, and unstoppable innovation by following the principles found in God's Word.

Companies compete ferociously to create the newest and greatest product, hoping to gain greater market shares than their competition. People may pretend to be your friend but only try to get close to gain secret marketing ideas and financial gain to promote their business and destroy yours. Sporting franchises rely on their team's success over the competition to grow the franchise. Politicians spend millions of dollars to learn what to say and how to say it at their campaigns to beat their opponents. Some politicians even strategically attain position to promote their own purposes and fill their own "back pockets." Colleges also view ratings and rankings as indicators of their success over the competition, and then use them as tools for bragging for self-promotion.

Do these sound like Kingdom principles? It doesn't sound like competition is a Kingdom value to me. Unless America turns back to God in this final hour, we are headed for disaster. God is sounding the alarm for the church to wake up, arise, and to get out and harvest the fields—people are lost and don't know their need can be met by God. People are living in a state of emergency and God is the answer.

We have all experienced emergency calls and connections. Right after the tragedies that occurred on 9/11 we saw a nation of people fill churches for about three weeks. Unfortunately, life went back to what was thought as normal. There is nothing normal about America my friends. America as a nation is just as bad as Sodom and Gomorrah. A nation that was founded on God and under God has turned her back on Him.

We must move from pursuit and competition to the filling the altars again in prayer and turn to God. We must lift our eyes to see God's perspective.

Jesus said, "Behold, I say to you, lift up your eyes and look at the fields, for they are already white for harvest!" (John 4:35) –Jesus walked in such anointing carrying the Spirit without measure that he instantly defied natural principles that reveal spiritual truths for us today. When we move away from pursuit and competition to the things of God, lift up our eyes and see the harvest of people, we will become empowered and directed by the Holy Spirit to do more in less time while following after God.

With revelation from God, every day is harvest day. We are empowered to pray for people, no matter what they are facing, and expect them to receive breakthrough, healing, and be delivered from the powers of the enemy. When you choose to put revelation from God into practice, what used to be impossible will be ordinary as you step into your God-given authority. You will be moved from worldly pursuits and competition to a life of expanding faith and miracles, instead of a mere observer. It is a divine gift to fully rely on God and operate in Kingdom power.

The Gift of Fully Relying on God: Christmas Beau

We must choose to become one with God through spending time with Him and learning to trust Him. God teaches us in small ways to learn how to rely on Him. He trains us in the natural through details in life. He can use anything and every one of us.

A dear friend of mine gave me a beautiful Pandora bracelet with a frog charm on it. As a matter of fact, she gave me one, my sister, and our mother as well. She told us the frog represented "fully relying on God" in life. I liked that. It had a little gold crown on its head. It was a reminder of where our faith must be at all times.

God connects us with people of His choosing. He connects us on purpose. He gives us blessings as sweet reminders of His goodness and great love. There are good people that love God here in America—and across the nations.

Let me share another sweet story. Jesus shared stories, told parables, and met people in their place of need. He met the woman at the well in John 4 and brought her to a place of encounter. She in turn went out immediately to share about this man named Jesus with her entire village.

Stories build our faith and are great reminders of God's goodness. Don't be afraid to share life with others. God put us here to encourage each other on in life and to have relationship. He positions people to walk with us—in the good and bad times.

I love God. I love people and I love animals. After the passing of all three of our cats of over twenty years, I told my husband I would

The Gift of Fully Relying on God: Christmas Beau

like a little white dog, perhaps a Bichon, Maltese, or a Westie. I will never forget what he told me. He told me I couldn't get a dog till after he died. I think he was kidding, but wait till you learn what happened.

Several years had passed since he told me that, and I remembered that he did actually die at Mercy Hospital in 2012 but God raised him back up. Perhaps, now the time was arriving for me to get the puppy. Does God ever have a sense of humor?

Anyway, a few weeks after I received the gift of the Pandora bracelet, I chose to buy a small heart charm that had paws on one side and "MY SWEET PET" on the other as an act of faith for that new addition to our family. I figured if I don't have enough faith to believe God for a dog, I better not pray for any other people needing healing at all. Just because we have seen God do great miracles in the past doesn't mean there won't be more!

On Saturday, October 18, 2014, we were driving over to the Belmont Fall Festival to spend time with grandkids and to be there for them for their live podcast. On the drive over, we were talking and listening to the radio and all of a sudden, I said, "I'm going to have that little white dog and a new house, too." I didn't really know where it came from, but something rose up within me and I decreed and declared it by faith in God.

After the event was over and we were about ready to leave, the thought came to my mind, "I want to go over to the pet store, The Last Place On Earth." I told Dan, and he said, "What?" I told him that I wanted to go see the pets and I knew it was really probably the *last place on earth* he wanted to go to that day.

He explained the reason he didn't like to go to pet stores is because there are many animals in need of homes and they all look so sad. Well, anyway, off we went. We arrived and there were several little puppies as we journeyed through the front, passing the loud birds and aquariums. There was a little Shih Tzu puppy, a Westie, and a few other puppies in the pet store. I picked up the little westie and showed him to Dan. All of a sudden, I noticed a cute little white dog that looked like a lamb in a crate with a Chihuahua, so I asked the pet store clerk if I could see him.

I thought he looked sad as he waited there with his crate buddy. I asked Dan to hold him and I remember the clerk saying he couldn't believe this little Bichon Frise puppy had been there for nearly three weeks. He told Dan he had told another clerk that his family had not arrived yet and he was waiting for them. My husband said, "I think she has arrived."

Yes, you know the rest of the story. We went home with that little white puppy. Mother said he looked like an angel. We discussed names and how Angel is cute and a girl's name, but that angels are really always male. I called him Christmas and then Bow. I chose to name him "Christmas Beau" because he was a gift from God.

Now I have the puppy. Did you know God has a new place in heaven for us to live too? He has prepared a place for us after this life—it will be our new home in glory with Him! You might not have noticed my declaration about a new puppy and new home in the same sentence—but it is totally a God thing. He is training us here in this life to reign with Him in the next. He is training His Bride (the Church) for her exalted position of co-rulership with the Son over His vast, ever-expanding, eternal kingdom in the ages to come.

Turning back to God as a nation in prayer is part of our training. God is training us how to use the weapons of prayer and faith in triumphing over evil. Jesus prayed for us to have unity. There can be no unity without love. A love deficiency manifests itself in discord, division, and fragmentation.

Pray for America! Stand up again and believe God and His Word! Will you trust Him? God wants to use you as an individual and America in greater ways to advance His kingdom here in the earth while there is still time.

Begin to declare that America is "One Nation Under God" again. It is important what we say. Remember what I said about having a puppy and step out in sharing your faith. Love God, love people, and pass it on!

The Gift of Fully Relying on God: Christmas Beau

Ministry in Action

God can use anybody in ministry. We are all called as ministers, cleverly disguised in whatever sphere of influence we find ourselves. When we choose to fully rely on God, we move to a place of inward trust that is unshakable. God can use anything and anyone in His plan. Listen to this!

Did you know that God already used Beau in ministry? Because I listened to the Holy Spirit's leading when my son recommended a groomer in Belmont for my new puppy, and I obeyed, the Holy Spirit positioned me with a lady from King's Mountain who donated shoes to people in need through our non-profit ministry. I stay in awe of how God works in our lives on a daily basis.

I had to choose to turn out of my driveway and go the distance—drive to Belmont. God sent a woman all the way from King's Mountain to the same place. We have to learn to go up to the mountain of prayer with God—and meet Him on His terms. We are called by God to spend time in prayer, outlive our life here on earth, lead souls to Him and have joy in knowing Him until He returns. He is returning sooner than most may think.

God has a way of putting people together for divine purpose that we couldn't rig if we tried.

Another day while I was on the phone with my sister, I was talking about her relocation and gave her a scripture about moving. All of a sudden, Beau picks up his small bed with his mouth and moved it in front of the pantry door. He picked it up one more time and moved it to the back door. Beau was moved to action when he heard the Word of God.

The Word of God works when we choose to obey it. Beau didn't have to forgive anyone, or reason and doubt in his mind, he was just moved to action. If a new puppy can rise up and move, so can we as a nation. *We have no excuse!*

With a nation that rejects Christ, where we have our freedom of religion experiencing attack, to the point of disallowing anyone to express public faith, we are seeing Christians missing in action. The enemy is doing his best to stop ministry. Instead of being a person with a ministry in action, Satan wants us to be MIA—missing in action.

Beau was moved to action, what about you? Will you stand up and unite with other believers who know Jesus Christ is our only hope for America? Will you move into action?

Whole families and spouses have waited for years just to receive one letter that brings a glimmer of hope for the return of a loved one during war. Many families have been devastated due to a spouse missing in action, only later to learn they were killed in combat. I have good news! Jesus is alive and He has already won the victory for us. Our part is to stand up and believe. Jesus gave us a love letter—His Word—The Bible.

Like the thousands of people awaiting the return of a loved one, we are awaiting the return of Jesus Christ. We know He is coming back again. Some of you may be reading this book and living in fear, anger, rage, and great pain that causes you to blow up and lose your temper and want to control everything. You go thirty days and blow again—it is time to stop wounding your own family. It is time to stop attacking the Body of Christ. We are called to mature in Christ rather than live in drama and dysfunction.

We must choose to be about the Father's business—ministry in action—in whatever sphere of influence we find ourselves. Otherwise, we will be used by Satan to send people off missing in action—even our own families.

Whether we have two minutes left on God's clock or we have one hour, we must turn to God now with all our hearts. Whether we have one year left or less, we must do all God has put in our hearts to do with Him *now*. It is simple—He gives us vision and we write it down, listen to Him for instruction, obey and get out and do it. It is that simple.

No matter what type of business or position we hold in life, we are to advance God's kingdom in the midst of the marketplace. That is where we are to witness for God—right in the midst of wherever God has called us to be. Some are vascular surgeons, heart surgeons, business owners, employees, employers, college students, some are administrative assistants in prisons, to working in media and right in the midst of your own family—we are called to walk in God's agape love. In some seasons our ministry is primarily to our own family.

You may be a stay at home mom or the CEO of a major corporation, but neither is small in God's eyes. This is why the enemy tries to get us worked up, angry, bitter, and rather than using the opportunity to witness, we make more casualties. We are not only called to witness to others, but greater than that we are called to reveal the love of Christ in our home first—and then to the world.

God loves the world so much that He may give you a new business idea. He may put the dream in your heart to build hotels and resorts to impact people's lives through God's love exhibited within each place. He may give you a business that finds people jobs so you can reach masses of people across the globe. One of our partners and friends buys Christian books and gives them to clients. As a matter of fact, before I ever published my first book, I bought and gave out thousands of books by other authors to people everywhere I went—from people I knew to total strangers. There are many ways you can touch a person's life through the influence of Jesus Christ!

I know personally that we can never out give God. He blesses us in our obedience. God will use you in greater measure for deeper impact when you choose to step out in faith and trust Him. Whatever He puts in your heart to do, simply do it. "Whatever He says to you, do it" (John 2:5).

I pray God gives you new ideas to share the Good News of Jesus Christ. People are God's priceless treasure. Do whatever God has put in your heart to do with Him with all your might. The only thing that matters for all eternity will be our obedience to the Holy Spirit here on earth and doing our part to fulfill the Great Commission—advancing the Kingdom of God!

God's Priceless Treasure

(Note: this was also the title of my first book, *God's Priceless Treasure: How to Overcome Challenges, Be Transformed, and Know Your Purpose*. It is a book that will inspire you to believe there is hope for anyone when we choose to persevere through challenges and trust God.)

We are God's priceless treasure. Jesus came into this world to redeem all mankind. Every person is like a precious gem that needs lifting out of the dirt and washed by the blood of Jesus.

God is a good Father. I had a great father in the natural. My father passed away on January 30, 2010 at 5:17 P.M. with snow-covered grounds in a hospital in North Carolina. I remember distinctly learning the nurses were trying to give my father extra morphine, wanting to remove the bi-pap machine in order to send him on out into eternity and create another bed for the hospital. I chose to confront and asked for his oncologist to come in to speak with us.

I remember it like it was yesterday. I explained our belief in God and that is was His right, and only His right, to determine when Daddy was to go out into eternity to be with His Lord. My father did not want to smother to death and he had shared he felt like that was what was happening when they removed the bi-pap machine.

Instead of the hospital staff getting rid of my father, we chose to stand up and confront. He lived an additional seventeen days where we surrounded his bedside and had sweet fellowship with our father who loved us. God took him in His own timing.

One of the nurses came back over to me and asked me to pray for her. She said she didn't feel like what they were told to do was right. I prayed for her and I explained to her that was how the Spirit of God convicts.

I don't believe it is our right to determine when or how we die. Countless numbers of children are murdered on a daily basis through abortion. Similar to the spirit of death that came through when Herod decreed an order to kill all babies, we can see the rise of that same evil spirit across this land. People are fixated with television shows and movies that depict death and gore. Many think *monster dolls* and other toys are harmless, but they are not. They open the door to the enemy. Movies and shows that depict witchcraft and sorcery are just as evil—and have infiltrated the minds of millions of kids, not to mention adults. Many have become fixated on zombies, hunger games, eating people and all sorts of evil.

Tragedy has already struck America—long before attacks by terrorists and market crashes. People have willingly and unwillingly, some knowingly and some unknowingly, opened the door to the enemy. We are all in need of a Savior, long before tragedy strikes. The Bible tells us that once a person dies, he will face the judgment of God. We must choose before death how we will spend eternity. *It will be no one's fault but your own if you choose hell. Make sure of your choice right now, before it's too late.*

Hell was created for Satan—not people. It is your choice. Where will you spend eternity? Will you turn to God now, before it's too late? Just like my uncle who passed when his heart stopped beating, we will find ourselves either in the presence of the Lord Jesus Christ, or separated from Him for all eternity.

If we die before the rapture of the church, we will most likely be placed in a casket. The casket where we are placed at death is actually a hope chest—where we await the return of Christ Jesus. The dead in Christ shall rise and those who are alive and remain will meet Him in the air in the clouds.

Our only hope is to share the gospel—the good news of Jesus Christ, with boldness and confidence to shake the nation. We are to take the kingdom of darkness and snatch people out of darkness like saving them from a fire. Life is short. Eternity is forever. Before death or tragedy strikes, make the choice today. Life is all about choices. We choose life or death. When we choose God, we gain eternal life.

What about you my friend?

A Leap of Faith

(Note: this was also the title of my second book, *A Leap of Faith: 25 Days At the Mercy Seat*)

When we learn to trust God we are prepared when trouble comes or tragedy strikes. Tragedy can strike at any moment in time. Life does not always go as planned.

Do you know how to share the hope we have in God when tragedy strikes? Do you ever feel at a loss when someone is walking through a major crisis? God wants you to be equipped and encouraged to help others who are walking through tough times.

With the growing debt in America and the moral decline, this nation is far from the standard that she was founded. We are still *one nation under God* but we don't much look like it. Our nation will not look like a nation under God again until our leaders turn to Jesus Christ in prayer. We must repent and turn back to God as a nation to have hope for America. Without God, our lives and the lives of our loved ones are in jeopardy.

Knowing the future of our grandchildren is in jeopardy with the reckless spending, godless government, and the attempts to shut anyone down who speaks the name of Jesus –as well as attempting to change the laws of God, what on earth has gone wrong?

Do you believe in God? Do you believe He is willing and able to fulfill His promises to you? Do you believe He can turn the heart of a king? He says so in His Word. (See Proverbs 21:1.)

Do you believe He really wants to reward those who seek Him? I submit to you that our focus has been misplaced. Our gaze must be

A Leap of Faith

upon *Him,* the one who holds the key to the manifestation of all our God-given dreams and desires.

When a nation turns to God, it is blessed. Wherever Christianity flourishes, there will be resurrection power available and vibrant life, not death. We personally experienced this at Mercy Hospital, when God raised Dan back up when his heart stopped beating. He went through two open-heart surgeries, two strokes, and spent 25 days in Mercy. We must choose to allow the Great Heart Surgeon—Jesus Christ, to do what only He can do in our hearts. For it is Jesus Christ who opens our eyes and hearts to see the lost and have compassion. We are moved from selfishness to sacrificial living and giving.

Just like the Pharisees and Herodians sought Jesus to destroy him in Mark 3, right after he healed the man with the withered hand, the same happens in life to us after a huge miracle. The enemy tried to stop Jesus because of His following. The same is happening with Satan today. He wants all he can get to go to hell with him. He knows his future and that time is short. If you don't believe me, read it for yourself in Mark chapter 3. Jesus withdrew himself to the sea with His disciples and multitudes followed Him. I hate the devil but I love Jesus. God desires that none should perish, but those that don't turn to Him and choose Him will in fact live separated from God for all eternity.

None of us are perfect.

We have all fallen short and are nothing without God. Jesus is the only perfect man that ever lived on earth. He left heaven and came to earth to redeem all mankind. God is sounding the alarm for us to turn back to Him. He desires that we follow Jesus like the multitudes in Mark chapter 3. As believers, we are chosen witnesses for Christ Jesus. We are to speak the truth in love.

Sometimes the only word that fits a job description is speaker, advocate, minister, etc. I don't really like to use the term speaker because a speaker is really something that magnifies noise. We are called to be Christ followers and advocates for people in need of God. Jesus gave His life that we might live. We must share the good news of the Gospel. That is the Great Commission.

When we learn what being a Christ follower really means, we will see a nation that turns back to God, flourishes, gives sacrificially and lives that way on a daily basis. It is a personal choice. We must take time to stop and help others who are stuck in the mire of this world. We must choose to shine the light of Jesus to a lost and hurting world around us.

People are genuinely hurting and suffering. Study and learn what the Bible says about suffering. The effects of trauma and the process of grief can be debilitating when a person doesn't know how to move through to healing. Fear, failure, rejection, discouragement and even compromise can hinder spiritual progress and fulfillment. God is looking for those who will hear Him, believe Him, and move forward to speak purpose and destiny into others.

There are basic principles I have learned that I want to share with you:

Listen to God's Promises

The first thing Abram did was listen to the promises of God. God promised to make Abram into a great nation, to bless him, and that he would make him "a blessing." Those are huge promises. Abram did not move to reasoning or questioning God through doubt. He believed God and did not worry or fret.

Abram accepted the promise as true and expected it to come to fruition—just as God had said. The first step to receiving God's blessing is accepting His promises as true. You don't have to make sense of it or try and figure it all out. It doesn't even matter if you think you "deserve" it or "don't deserve" it. God is able and willing to do far beyond whatever we can think, ask or imagine.

Respond In Faith—Simply Believe God

Abram responded to God's promise by leaving his father and family as the Lord directed him, and in the exact direction. Genesis 13 tells us that God blessed his family as they went, but particularly notice that Abram doesn't question God's direction at all. He simply

A Leap of Faith

obeys through responding in faith. He doesn't try to figure out all the intimate details.

Abram simply trusted God and that is what we are called to do as well. Don't allow fear to get in the way or even wonder about what others might think. Don't fear what you might encounter along the way—just do whatever He says to you. "Whatever He says to you, do it" (John 2:5). God calls us to move forward trusting Him in every step.

Trust God

A heart that trusts God moves to action. If I had not learned to trust God because of *His training* in my life, I would be a widow today. It's not enough to hear God's promises, or even to act on them. We must have *trust* in God and believe His promises. We have to trust Him from the heart. In John, the Bible tells us the Holy Spirit is the Spirit of Truth—this gives us great insight and wisdom to trust in God. (Take time to read John 14, 15, and 16).

You will notice in Genesis 14 that Abram's trust in God did not falter, even when things did not *seem* to go as planned. You will see Abram even turning down what would seem to be a gigantic blessing from the King of Sodom. Abram knew in his heart that he didn't need the blessing from Sodom. God was for him.

Abram was expecting a blessing from God. How many of us are willing to turn down what seems huge, gigantic, or an enormous blessing in exchange for the heavenly blessing we know is coming from God? Take a minute to ponder if your trust is truly in God's promises, or is it in the financial or material "blessings" that you are aiming for in this life? God loves to bless His children—but He wants us to seek His face and not His hand.

Give All Praise and Thanksgiving to God

At the end of the day, do you take credit for how well you've spent your money, how well you've managed your assets, or how well you think your family or business has turned out in life? Do you take credit for any of this? Do you turn to God and give Him all the praise?

Scripture says: "Abraham believed the Lord and he credited to him as righteousness" (Gen. 15:6). We find that Abram didn't need to take credit for the blessings he had received from God. He knew the true source of all of life. He was totally committed to God. Are you?

HEART CHECK

Is your faith in God contingent upon what you see, hear, or feel?

Where do you really place *your* trust?

Are you reading God's Word and following His instructions?

What evidence do you need to believe what God says to you?

What is the level of your intimacy with God? Do you truly *know Him,* or do you simply *know about Him?*

Are you abiding in Him so that you hear the voice of God's Spirit? How do you know?

Do you rest in God during times of waiting?

God's Emergency Room

Have you ever experienced times of waiting in any emergency room or E.R. Department? Unless it is your heart in most cases, you have to wait. The heart has to work properly in order for us to have life. On a spiritual note, our hearts have to be right as well.

Let me ask you a few questions. What is your first thought when a family you know personally faces tragedy, experiences loss of business, or has a drastic loss of income due to unforeseen circumstances? Does your heart respond with the love of God or do comments spill out of your mouth that are not godly? I've heard people say things that have taken me by surprise at times and wonder what on earth is wrong with their heart.

We have all said things that don't sound quite right at times. Words are spoken and people misinterpret. Even texts can be misinterpreted. God is at work on all of us and nobody has arrived to perfection. As a matter of fact, just when we think we have achieved or mastered one area, it may fly apart or unravel at the seams—thus finding our total need of God.

What causes any person to say something that is hurtful about someone else facing personal loss or tragedy? It can happen to anyone. I will never forget a young lady the Lord had me ministering to many years ago. She rededicated her life on a Christmas Eve. I shared the great news and invited her to come to our home church at that time. She came for a few Sundays and I encouraged her to attend a church a little closer to her home so she wouldn't have to drive so far.

A few weeks later someone handed me a magazine saying, "Here is a picture of your new convert." It was a picture of this lady with a champagne glass in her hand. She was posing for a picture for an award ceremony in New York.

I remember thinking to myself, "What on earth is wrong with this woman's heart? Why would she go to the trouble to show me a picture of a new believer?"

What I learned is this; people get saved and then God brings about cleansing. You can't clean a fish till you first catch it. Sounds correct to me, how about you? However, as believers in Christ, any person can get cold hearted and lose their heart for souls. We are called to be about the Father God's business—fishing for souls. This is an area we must each tend to on a daily basis. We want pure hearts that want to please the Father God—and help people, not hurt them. *None of us can boast about anything but Jesus Christ. We are nothing without Him. He came for the broken—that is all of us.*

God desires to use each of us in various ways to encourage one another. This means we must be alert to the people the Lord brings across our path. We must choose to make ourselves available, even when we feel we have nothing to offer or when it is not convenient. One of the prime examples of an encourager in Scripture is Barnabus. His name means "son of encouragement," and that is exactly what he was. Will you choose to be an encourager—to the ones who may have grown cold or wounded *and* the ones on a new journey of faith? *We all need encouragement.*

We must choose to lead people to Jesus through love and not condemnation. As believers, we must not get on one "band wagon" or another, blasting people out who are practicing a sinful lifestyle, or what may *appear* to be sin, to telling people about someone else's past life to bring shame, or slashing people up with our tongues. *All* is sin to God. God is calling us to be instruments of healing to *all*. *We must choose to be sensitive to people and ask God to give us pure hearts that are tender toward others who are hurting or who may be walking in a place we have not traveled. God's emergency room is just that—He desires to be God over every situation and in every heart—to those who will receive Him.*

Lowering Your Nets

The only way you catch fish is to lower your nets. It's time for America to go back to fishing. Fishing! "What does that mean?" you might be asking. Fishing is about souls.

Jesus thought it was important enough that he called four fishermen to be disciples as we read in the gospels. The Bible says, *"And Jesus, walking by the Sea of Galilee, saw two brothers, Simon called Peter, and Andrew his brother, casting a net into the sea, for they were fishermen. Then He said to them, "Follow Me, and, I will make you fishers of men." They immediately left their nets and followed Him. Going on from there, He saw two other brothers, James, the son of Zebedee, and John his brother, in the boat with Zebedee their father, mending their nets. He called them, and immediately they left the boat and their father, and followed Him"* (Matt. 4:18–22, NKJV).

Two were casting and two were mending. We have to catch a fish before we can clean it. By faith we understand the Word of God. We are called to bring in the lost and help them walk to the other side of healing. We are *all* in need of repair, preparation, and restoration. God wants us to search for the lost and hurting. It is He who brings about the mending and setting in order. It is the process of our journey in Christ Jesus.

All things are passing away and time is short. It is time to lower our nets and go for the masses. It is time to expect a great harvest of souls because that is why Jesus came in the first place.

"The end of all things is at hand" (1 Pet. 4:7). This world is not our home for we are about to depart. Prepare now for moving. I love that thought, don't you? It is fun to move to a new place. It's

fun to move into a new home, beautifully decorated and fresh with new fixtures. It's fun to travel to new places. It's fun to travel with friends too—as long as they don't gripe and complain over everything. Thank God we have wonderful friends. We must choose to have no room for complaining.

No Room in the Inn

There should be no room to complain about anything. The King of kings and Lord of lords was born in a manger—talk about humble beginnings. There was no room in the inn.

The End is in sight and it all began in a lowly manger. There was no room in the Inn for Jesus. It all began in the Middle East and it will all end in the Middle East. The whole world is watching what is happening there right now.

While there is still time available for you, right now, there is room at the cross, if you will turn to Him now. If you are reading this and are not assured of where you will spend eternity, turn to God in prayer, repent of your sins, and receive Jesus as Lord and Savior.

No matter where we are on God's clock, at the last hour or even a two-minute warning, if you are breathing there is still time. Choose to move forward in faith in God and trust Him for the outcome. Jesus has made room for you. He has equipped you and empowered you with gifts and talents. Your gift will make room for you. The gift of Jesus drew shepherds and three wise men from the Far East.

If you are still breathing, there is room for you at the cross of Jesus Christ. Wise men came in search of him at His birth. Wise men and women receive Him today on earth. Don't wait another minute to make the choice for Jesus. Open up your heart to receive Him now if you have not done so already. Take time to spend in His Word and read the Bible. Sit and wait in His presence and listen to His still small voice. It will prepare you for things to come in your daily walk.

A Deeper Walk With God

We learn how to walk in a deeper place of trust in God when we walk through trials that come in life. We learn how to respond to people and listen to the still small voice of the Holy Spirit when the lab technician is moving too slow with drawing our blood. We choose to be patient and learn the person is new on the job. We suddenly realize that we are responding differently than we did several months ago—before we accepted Jesus and started our walk with Him. We begin to see growth in ourselves.

We come to a deeper place in God after the long walk down the hospital hall since the funeral home has been called in to pick up Mom or Dad who just passed away, and the nurses who asked you to leave the room—that is a place of pain my friend! It may be the call with the news your son has been killed in battle, or your spouse was just killed in a fatal car wreck. It may be a letter from a doctor's office advising you to come back in for additional treatments—the cancer has returned. It may be a notice of a lost job because the company is cutting back. Whatever the case, we all find we experience times of pain and waiting.

Your time may be in an operating room waiting room where you sit and wait till the surgeon walks out and you can tell by the look in his or her eye something went wrong. The phone call that came with the emergency room attendant on the line, to the coworker telling you the owner asked for your keys—you just lost your job after thirty years of loyalty. All of these are stressful moments that come to us all. We live in a fallen world where bad things happen.

Sometimes, we think the loss of a job is a tragedy when in reality, it may be God's way of pushing us out to do that *thing* He has put in our hearts to do with Him from long ago. It may be God's way of protecting us from something far greater. I can imagine the people who had sick kids that stayed out of work on September 11, 2001 and missed the attacks on the Twin Towers are still thankful, even today. Many others in Washington were injured and killed. Those who chose to stand up on the plane to confront the hijackers lost their lives as well.

It is the times of trial and when we feel like there is nowhere to turn, that sometimes we turn to God in that very crisis. God does not cause the problems, but what the enemy means for harm, God turns for our good and His glory. Our part is to seek Him and turn to Him with our whole heart. It is not in testing other religions or getting caught up in religious debates that we come to know Jesus. It is in the seeking where we find Him and have a deeper understanding of His amazing love. This is where you and I come to learn He is the very air we breathe and our reason for living.

We are creatures of habit and sometimes we tend to put comfort over seeking God. Jesus says, *"Come unto me, all ye that labor and are heavy laden, and I will give you rest. Take my yoke upon you and learn of me..for my yoke is easy, and my burden is light"* (Matt. 11:28–30, KJV).

There are times in life when you don't know what needing Jesus is all about until you have no other choice. America needs God. The only way to turn America is through prayer. *God save America and turn her back to You Lord.*

One of the reasons why America is like Sodom and Gomorrah today is due to the total lack of prayer and no recognition of God. One woman was used by the adversary to remove prayer from schools and now we have a nation who changes laws to suit worldly ways of living that clearly go against God's Word and the very foundation of America—one nation under God! We must get back to praying.

Prayer changes everything—mostly you. Prayer changes outcomes *when* we choose to pray. Leaders prayed and masses filled churches for about three weeks after 9/11 and then it was life as normal again. However, was it really normal? No!

We can change the world on our knees. Will anyone join me? Jesus prayed all night in the Garden of Gethsemane. His disciples fell asleep. The modern day church is mostly asleep. We have classes *on* prayer but rarely are prayer meetings actually held anymore, and when they are very few people show up to pray.

We have become a nation void of prayer. Many churches have become like cruise ships and stages for performances rather than a "house of prayer." Jesus turned over tables for that very same reason found in the Word of God. While there is nothing wrong with having performances and events that draw people to Jesus, we must not be a church void of prayer and the love of God that brings repentance and revival.

We can have revival if we will choose to start prayer in our homes, one person at a time, and one family at a time. The Lord gave me a vision of North Carolina with lights in homes coming on, one by one. Then it spread across the nation. Will you join me in prayer? Will you be one that chooses to inspire others to turn to prayer for the nation? You can start a family time of devotion and turn back to God together. A great tool is *Sparkling Gems*, by Rick Renner.

Renewing the mind in the Word of God on a daily basis and praying will bring realization that God's mercies are new *for you* each morning. You will go into a deeper place with God and grasp the truth that you are free and forgiven, with no more designer baggage to haul around. Instead of living with regret, you will live as a catalyst for change to a world in need of Jesus.

Be A Catalyst For Change

Are you afraid to confront the enemy or do you embrace the enemy and choose to allow America's demise? Are you the one who procrastinates and waits till it is too late to turn? Not making a decision and being passive is actually making a decision. Sitting back and doing nothing is living in denial, indecision, and hopelessness.

I was having a conversation with a person just the other day and encouraged them to talk to someone specifically about an issue. This person said, "You always want to get in a hurry and move too quickly." I looked up and saw a billboard and it said: *the time to talk is before it's too late!* Can I get a witness? God makes Himself evidently clear. Every person has to admit there is a problem before it can be fixed. Someone has to stand up. Deborah chose to stand up and go out to battle with Barak in the Book of Judges. Esther chose to come before the King. Will you choose to stand up for America?

Be a catalyst for change in America: Ignite means "to spark, to ignite, energize, mobilize; something that accelerates a reaction. Pray and ask God to ignite your heart again for Him and for this nation. Stand up and start praying for the lost in your family, your neighbors, communities, cities, and this nation!

> *We are hard pressed on every side, but not crushed; perplexed, but not in despair.*
> —2 Corinthians 4:8, NIV

Where Do You Turn?

I am asking the question, "Will America turn back to God?" On another note, what do we do when life turns against us? I hear people daily asking similar questions. Why is there so much evil in the world? Why is the world in chaos and confusion? If God is really who He says He is, why would He allow devastation?

Nobody will ever forget September 11, 2001. I remember the news and the pictures of the hijacked airlines flying into the twin towers of America's tallest building, the World Trade Center in New York City, and a third crashed into the Pentagon in Washington, DC. Thousands lost their lives as merciless terrorists chose to bring about destruction in America. Hundreds of heroic firefighters, police officers, and emergency personnel lost their lives trying to pull people out of the masses of destruction.

The heroic people who chose to take a stand on a fourth hijacked plane which was most likely headed for the United States Capitol or the White House, sacrificed their own lives to keep it from reaching its intended target for destruction.

I remember the phone call from my stepdaughter asking me to pray as she and her husband were stranded in another state and couldn't get a flight or a rental car due to all the chaos. I saw the breaking news just before she called.

I learned we have a neighbor whose husband ran across the Hudson River to a financial institution to save this land from total financial destruction just after the attacks. He was also included in the group of people who were covered with white powder that later brought about cancer in his life. The police dogs that searched for people through the debris also lost their lives to cancer as a result of that same white powder.

Interesting enough, I remember the jet that landed on the Hudson and lives were saved by a heroic act of the pilot and crew. The Holy Spirit prompted me to look up what the Hudson meant and what I learned was quite interesting. It means a *place of landing*.

This tells me it is important what something or someone is named. The Bible lays this out for us as well. What will it take to turn America back to God? What do we learn from the mystery of suffering in this land? Will we stand with Israel? Will we stand with Jerusalem? If you take a closer look at Jerusalem, look at what we see: JER USA LEM. Will we stand as the United States of America with Jerusalem?

It all started in the Middle East and it will end in the Middle East! The whole world has her eye on the Middle East right now. Pray for America to turn back to God.

The Bible says, *"Turn Thou to me and have mercy on me, as is Thy way with those who love Thy name"* (Ps. 119:132, KJV).

Evil and Suffering

Evil and suffering are very real. It would do us well to learn that evil and suffering does happen in the lives of good people. For example, take a look at the life of Joseph in the Bible. Evil and suffering can be seen on media and in our own personal lives. No one is immune to suffering. Tragedy can touch anyone.

The Bible says, "What does a man get for all the toil and anxious striving with which he labors under the sun? All his days work is pain and grief; even at night his mind does not rest" (Eccl. 2:22–23). We live in a fallen world and bad things happen to good people.

God is more real than all the pain and suffering. I have often heard the phrase *time heals all wounds*. I don't really believe that. I do believe that the choices we make when we suffer, deal with disease, encounter evil and wrongdoing is what makes a difference in our healing. When we turn to God and repent, He will heal our land.

Healing comes when we choose to turn to God and apply His principles to our lives. God is just as real as the pain, tears, and heartbreak we experience. He is more real than anything in life. He wants to make Himself known to each of us and He goes to extreme measures to do so.

He loves us so much that He chose to send His only begotten Son Jesus Christ to die on the cross for our sins. He is not in the tomb because Jesus arose three days later and is seated at the right hand of the Father in heaven right now. He is interceding for us that our faith will not fail. I believe He is holding time back so more can come to know Him and receive His saving grace.

Evil and Suffering

Jesus knows exactly what we suffer in this life. In the midst of life tragedies and heartbreak, He wants us to be assured of His divine presence and great love. He knows what we are walking through because He allowed His beloved Son to suffer the pangs of death and hell. God understands our suffering and the days we even wonder what on earth is going on around us. Why the attacks and difficulties?

Can we honestly believe that God is loving and merciful in the midst of pain and suffering and even tragedy? Right in the midst of the greatest tragedy or life experience, God wants us to remember Jesus Christ died and rose again for us. Even when we don't understand, God wants to assure of His great love. This is one of the reasons He goes to extreme measures to make Himself known to us in daily life. We see His hand in the smallest details and realize His great love for us as individuals. God loves us so much that He sent His Only Begotten Son to die for us on the cross at Calvary.

The greatest suffering ever known in human history was Jesus Christ's suffering on that cross where He gave His life that we might have eternal life.

Jesus prayed, "My Father, if it is possible, may this cup be taken from me" (Matthew 26:39). The "cup" Jesus was referring to symbolized the suffering He was about to endure in life. Think for a minute with me about what Jesus was referring to as He prayed this prayer only hours before He was arrested. That cup contained every murder, every evil and theft, every adultery, every injustice, every evil thought, deed, and every evil word—all the sins of the entire human race.

Jesus Christ, the sinless Son of God had all our sin transferred to Him in order for God's full judgment to come upon Jesus instead of us. Jesus took upon Himself the very death and hell you and I deserve in life. God demonstrated how much He loves us.

It's natural for anyone to ask, "Why is this happening?" More importantly, what God wants us to learn through it is the best question for us to ask the Lord. Did you know that how you respond to life tragedies is on display for others to see? People watch how you respond or react in life.

When we fail to recognize and remember the love of God, we almost always end up taking a wrong turn in life. People react in rage, bitterness, anger, hate, jealousy, envy, or even despair. People lie, steal, and cheat to get what someone else has in life. People murder and falsely accuse others to save self. Look at the life of Judas—how he betrayed Jesus.

When anyone reacts there is always a price to pay. Ungodly responses open the door to destruction and can make the situation worse. We poison our own souls and destroy other relationships and our relationship with God.

No one likes to be around a person who is filled with bitterness and revenge. Let me briefly share about Luke 17:6 and the power of forgiveness as well as what happens when we don't choose to forgive.

THE POWER OF FORGIVENESS

Jesus spoke of the sycamine tree in Luke 17:1–6 (KJV). In many other translations, the word *sycamine* is replaced with mulberry. The word *sycamine* that Jesus chose to use has great importance for us today as believers.

We must choose to pursue forgiveness on a daily basis. Our hearts can become stony with offenses if we allow them to stay and get lodged in our hearts. Then we are not able to clearly hear the Lord. We need His direction. Would it not be a shame if the Lord were trying to get your attention to pray for someone you love, a grandchild, son or daughter, who was in severe danger—and you couldn't hear God because you were angry and carrying hurt in your heart that blocked your ability to hear God's voice?

I learned some interesting facts about the sycamine tree from listening to Rick Renner's teachings:

It had the deepest root structure of all trees in the Middle East. This explains to me that when we stay angry, we can develop a root of bitterness. The sycamine also grew best where there was little or no rain. (A root of bitterness will grow where no fresh rain of the Holy Spirit of God and the Word of God is applied). The wood of the sycamine tree was also the preferred wood for building caskets that reveals a root of bitterness will eventually kill you. The fruit of the sycamine tree gets increasingly bitter the more you chew it. When we choose to rehearse wounds and hurts, we become bitter.[1]

We are to be carriers of the Word of God—the Blessed Hope—to a lost and hurting world. We are not to be filled with bitterness. We are called to be a light in the darkness.

Lastly, the tree was not naturally pollinated. When a wasp would stick its stinger into the fruit of the tree it was pollinated through the sting. (A root of bitterness starts with a sting or a fiery dart the enemy sends through somebody intentionally or unintentionally and it becomes a part of the heart through the hurt or sting).

If the tree is thrown into the sea, it will die and never grow again. The sea of God's Word—both salt and light—enables us to have the power to continually walk in the fruit of the Spirit rather than living each day in the flesh. Tests of whether you are living in the flesh or in the Spirit are revealed by what you do when faced with opposition. Are you doing what God's Word says *or* are you controlled by your emotions, what you see, hear, and feel? Choose to forgive each day. Don't allow the enemy to ruin another day by his evil schemes.

Our Response

The Bible also says, "All his days he eats in darkness, with great frustration, affliction and anger" (Eccl. 5:17). Doesn't sound good to me, does it you?

When we respond to adversity in a godly fashion our inner man is renewed and we become more like Christ. The more ease, comfort, and pleasure we experience in this life can cause any person to forget that all blessing comes from God. A false sense of security that does not come from God can rise up in a person when he or she gets too comfortable with anything. God is the one who blesses us and we must never forget that all wealth comes from God. It is He who gives us the ability and not we ourselves.

When a nation forgets God and turns away from Him, the blessings are removed. Tragedy and attack does not mean that a person is living in sin. As a matter of fact, if you will take time to read the New Testament and pay attention to the hardships and tragedies the people faced, you will have a change of heart in life. People that are obeying God experience attack. What we must remember is that we may be walking through attack but God is with us. We are not *under* attack.

God allows things to happen sometimes not to punish or correct us, but to provide for us in an unusual manner. Have you ever been in a birthing room and heard the cries of a woman in labor pains? Sometimes when God is doing something new, He will allow labor pains to occur in the life of a person, a family, a relationship, an organization, and even a nation—not to punish or correct, but to provide for them. He sometimes allows us to go through a season of turbulent times in order to reveal His better plan that perhaps we have not noticed or chosen.

He sometimes allows us to go through attack to get us in rightful position for what He is trying to bring forth in our lives. How do we get in rightful position where God is in charge? We choose to love Jesus Christ with all of our hearts and His ways over our own.

Knowing the Enemy

Knowing the enemy and learning to prepare for adversity is key in life. The time to prepare for life disappointments and hurts is in advance. Don't wait till tragedy strikes to turn to God. God desires that we build a spiritual foundation that won't crumble under the weight of life circumstances. I believe we have been given mercy as far as time is concerned, so that we will turn back to God as a nation. Now is the time to choose to turn to God and follow hard after Him. The Bible says, "Remember your Creator in the days of your youth, *before* the days of trouble come" (Eccl. 12:1, NIV, emphasis added).

I am thankful I was raised in a Christian home to know God. When we are trained as a child to turn to God for strength, we are being trained to have faith in God. When someone is weak in their faith, he or she simply does not have the spiritual fortitude or resources to weather the storms in life that come to all.

Much like the foolish man we read about in the Bible who built his house on sand, we are foolish if we do the same. Jesus told the story to warn us that we will be defenseless when life's storms arise if we do not build our hope in Him. Jesus said, "Everyone who hears these words of mine and puts them into practice is like a wise man who built his house on the rock. The rain came down, the streams rose, and the winds blew and beat against that house; yet it did not fall, because it had it foundation on the rock" (Matt. 7:24–25, NIV).

Is your life built upon the rock of Jesus Christ? Do you even know about Jesus and His Words? Life is a journey and a house's foundation isn't built in one day. Our spiritual foundation and life is a journey or process. No one has arrived. We all have more to learn.

If you are still living and breathing, there is something you don't know in every situation.

Make it your goal in life today—to build a strong foundation, one constructed from prayer and the truths found in God's Word.

Life Disappointments

If you have any age on you, I can assure you that you have experienced disappointment in something or someone. It is common to all. It may be a minor issue in scheduling a flight for vacation, to a room change on your cruise, to a sudden storm that arises when you are out at sea in Greece. It may be an attack in the airport in Rome that you just missed as you left and headed for another city. It may be a ruined wedding day when suddenly the skies darken and you have to run inside to an indoor wedding unplanned.

Life disappointments come in all shapes and sizes. It may be a failed test, a business that fails to a business partner or family member who turns out to be like Judas—a betrayer, to a marriage that turns to abuse. It may be you found yourself at the end of a gun and had to choose life or death. We all have choices and we all face disappointment and adversity.

Unless we learn how to handle life disappointments, we will *feel* like we are on a roller coaster. Many end up blaming God and actually turn to hating God. The Bible encourages us not to forget God's promise that "those who hope in me will not be disappointed" (Isa. 49:23). Unless we had kept our hope in God at Mercy Hospital in 2012, we would have been devastated. If I had not learned to listen, hear and obey God, I would be a widow today.

Disappointment, failure, tragedy, heartbreak and heartache come to all at some time in life. Failure tries to take us out emotionally through anxiety, stress, worry, and even despair.

Why on earth would any person, any city, any state, or any nation turn against God? What causes a person to blame God and others?

Valuable Insight

We can find valuable wisdom and insight in Scripture. Let's look at what David did in a situation found in 1 Samuel 21:1—22:23. David was being pursued by Saul, and sought rest at the town of Nob. Ahimelech the priest cared for David and his men. When Saul discovered that David and his men had been at Nob, he condemned the priests who gave aid to David. Fearful of conspiracy against himself, Saul ordered eighty-five priests killed and the town of Nob destroyed. Only one son of Ahimelech escaped to join David.

David's faith had slipped as he ran from Saul. His desperation became evident when he met the priest Ahimelech and lied to him. Desperate David resorted to mistruth. This is the same David that remained strong and defeated Goliath through the power of God, he kept his cool when Saul lost his. This is same David who killed a lion and a bear. What happened to David?

Sometimes desperation or fear causes us to act rashly and to displease God. Sometimes the world tells us to do certain things, to focus on ourselves, to justify whatever we choose to do. God says to stay focused on Him, keep priorities right and follow Him always. Who are you listening to?

Instead of living in truth, David chose to live temporarily in denial and disbelief. America can live temporarily in denial and sit back and watch the nation's demise. What will you do?

Encouraging Yourself in the Lord

I would like to share great and valuable insight found in 1 Samuel 30 now for wisdom. We are called by God to forgive, walk in love, confront in love, and encourage ourselves in Him.

Forgiveness is choosing to see your offender through God's eyes. It's having God's perspective. We are designed to have relationship with God and people. We are to extend grace to others. We are to have fellowship with one another. We all come to a place of common ground—the all-sufficient sacrifice of Jesus Christ.

Will you choose to encourage yourself and inquire of God? Will you choose to pray with me for America to turn back to God? Jesus' final prayer is for unity and was like a military campaign designed to capture this rebellious planet for God. We must always remember that anyone can become rebellious toward God when the heart doesn't want to hear, change course, and deal with issues.

Jesus states the great objective that was precisely God's plan of redemption lived out through his life here on earth. (See John 17:20–26, KJV.) He outlines what God intends to accomplish in the latter part of verse 21: "…so that the world may believe that thou hast sent me," and in the latter part of verse, "…so that the world may know that thou hast sent me."

God's redemption plan is for the whole world. It is all about knowing God and making Him known to the world around us. "God so loved the world that He gave His only begotten Son, that whosoever believes in Him should not perish but have eternal life" (John 3:16. KJV). We sometimes forget we are part of the same world. The church is not here to save the world, but we are here to share our faith and testimony so others may be convinced that Jesus Christ is the authentic voice of God and that He is the authentic utterance of God's plan and purpose in human affairs. Also, that Jesus is the key to world history and reality; and that He is the revelation of God and the only way from man to God is through Jesus Christ the Son. Our job is to live a life of evangelism so others can become aware of Jesus and they can either accept or reject Him.

Will you choose to encourage yourself in the Lord so you can extend grace to a lost and hurting world—starting here in America? Will you choose to extend grace in your own home? Will you choose to extend grace in your business or workplace and in the marketplace?

Let's review the wisdom found together in God's Word. David and his men came to Ziklag and found it burned with fire, and their entire families had been taken captive. David and the people who were with him lifted up their voices and wept, until they had no more power to weep and were weary. David was greatly distressed because the people that were with him wanted to stone him—blaming him for all that had happened.

But David strengthened himself in the Lord. Then he called for Abiathar the priest, Ahimelech's son, and asked him to bring the ephod to him. Next, David inquired of the Lord, saying, "Shall I pursue this troop? Shall I overtake them?" And He answered him, "Pursue, for you shall surely overtake them and without fail recover *all*" (1 Sam. 30:8).

David and all that were with him were worn out and in deep despair. They had wept bitterly over the crisis. The people that were with David wanted to blame him. But David chose to encourage himself in the Lord. He worshipped God as revealed by the request for the ephod. He inquired of God in prayer. God answered David specifically and gave him instruction. God told David to pursue the enemy, and without fail, he would recover all.

I don't know about you, but I understand the meaning of all. That is a good word. In times of trouble, David turned to God for wisdom and help, while Saul consistently turned away from God, even at his death.

The church is supposed to be a house of prayer and a place of refuge—a place for us as soldiers of Christ Jesus to recover our strength.

We are to turn to God in everything. We ask God to help us learn to thrive again, to laugh, to forgive, and trust God fully in every situation. We all need encouragement. Leaders need encouragement. Families need encouragement. Look for people to encourage.

The little thoughts that come to mind to send someone a note or text of encouragement are coming from the Holy Spirit. The thought of a particular person that comes to mind—just may be a clue to pray for them. Don't ignore the promptings of the Holy Spirit.

We need hearts after God like David—pure hearts that desire to please God above all else. We want to become more like Christ and outlive our lives here on earth—advancing the Kingdom of God in this last hour. God is sounding the alarms and we can see what lies ahead if we don't make a turn back to God as a nation.

Will we wake up out of sleep and move forward with God? Will America turn back to God? Will you stop turning on the snooze button and get up and do all God has put in your heart to do with Him? *The time is now.*

Choose to encourage yourself in the Lord, worship Him above all else, inquire of God and He will give you divine instructions.

The Alarm Went Off, But No One Was Listening

Was it too late? Is it too late? The alarm went off but people stayed asleep. Have you ever slept through an alarm clock and missed an appointment? You rushed through the morning and forgot your briefcase, but flew out the door only to have a wreck and destroy your car on the way to work. Life that morning did not start out well.

On September 11, 2001 this happened on a much larger scale as people were killed in mass numbers. People were killed, some injured, and only the ones who chose to stand up saved another attempt for an attack, but they too were killed in the crash that took place. Many missed the terrorist attacks due to coffee spills, sick children and too many stoplights.

What happened next is very important to remember. People prayed to God on national television and churches were filled for about three weeks. After life seemingly turned back to normal, people forgot about God again. You know, I was thinking today, "What is normal?" The only thing in life that is still normal is the "normal" button on your washer and dryer. Life is not normal, in case you haven't been paying attention to the spiritual alarms that are going off all around us.

One woman stood up and got prayer taken out of the school system. One woman wrote a book called *Fifty Shades of Grey* that caught America's attention through the media. What is happening in the Middle East has caught the world's attention. Many other events have caught the world's attention, but what about Jesus who walked this earth and brought redemption to all of mankind—He is the Son of God—the Light of the World. Has He caught your attention?

I love the sunlight. I don't really even like to sit in restaurants where the light is too dim. It is hard to see the menu and what about the noise? It is difficult to enjoy a meal and actually have a conversation when any place is too busy and loud.

Why do people like to live in darkness? The light exposes the darkness so we can see and live in freedom when we know the truth. When truth comes out—light dispels the darkness. People sometimes don't know they are in the darkness because they have become blind through sin.

The light can go off in your dryer and you won't be able to see much inside. It's time to turn the light back on and replace it with a new bulb if it has burned out. It's time to turn the light back on in America. Jesus is the light of the world. His light reveals all. It's time to have our hearts ignited with passion for the lost at any cost. We are at the midnight hour.

The alarm has been sounding for some time now and people have fallen asleep and some are lethargic and don't even care. Some are in denial while some don't feel there is any hope. What can one person do?

Hearing has been dulled due to deception. What a person hears has the power to change their perception—both in the good and bad. Comfort also has a way of doing that. Could it be life has become so comfortable that it doesn't really matter what happens to the neighbors? Could it be that your love has grown cold and you are bitter over what went wrong twenty plus years ago? Maybe, it was just seven years ago or even last week, but you are still so focused on self that you can't see the big picture in front of you. Maybe you just don't know what to do, so you do nothing.

The Bible says, *"The mountains and hills may crumble, but my love for you will never end"* (Isa. 54:10, GNT).

God's love will never end—He is waiting for us as a nation to turn back to Him. The time is now!

"Tell Them I Love Them"

When a person doesn't feel loved by God, he or she won't be able to offer love to anyone else. When we experience the love of God personally, everything changes. Because of the nature of mankind, we must remind ourselves daily of what God thinks about us—He sent His Son that we might be saved. He has a great plan and purpose for our lives. (See Jeremiah 29:11.)

Every person matters to God. It is not what the world says or your peers. The perfect love of God removes fear.

God fully accepts us and loves us greatly. People spend far too much time and energy trying to earn acceptance from parents, peers, persons of influence, and even those they envy—as well as total strangers. God settled the issue of acceptance once and for all: *"Jesus...made us acceptable to God"* (Titus 3:7, CEV). The finished work of Jesus Christ on the cross of Calvary made us completely acceptable to God.

God's love for us is based on who He is and not what we do. We must learn to live out of our identity *in Christ* and know *whose* we are. Many live *in crisis* and don't know they can live *in Christ*.

We are deeply loved by God unconditionally and all we have to do is turn to God in repentance and receive the gift of forgiveness—salvation for all mankind. The whole world has been forgiven, but *only* those who call on the name of Jesus and receive the gift through repentance will be saved. There is no other way to the Father God but through Jesus Christ—His Son!

God sees us as extremely valuable and precious. He was willing to send His own Son to pay for our lives. He owns the whole world—He created all. If you have not personally accepted the gift of forgiveness that has been paid for once and for all by Jesus, why not turn to Him today? You *"have been bought and paid for by Christ"* (1 Cor. 7:23, TLB).

When a person experiences the love of Jesus Christ and receives Him as Lord and Savior, everything changes. The Holy Spirit of God equips every believer to show that same love to others as we follow Jesus Christ on our daily walk. We walk through the Word of God by reading and praying the Bible. We choose to forgive and don't hold grudges. We confront in love and help lift others up. When you realize how valuable you are, that you are accepted, loved, forgiven, and the Creator of the universe sent His only Son to die that you might have life, you are empowered to release love and build meaningful relationships.

There are millions that do not know the love of God. When a nation does not know God, life does not go well. Is God sending us great warnings? The Bible is being revealed before our eyes. What on earth is going on across the globe?

We are seeing a spiritual problem that is manifesting in personal and national problems. The world is in crisis with beheadings, houses burnt to the ground in many states, and storms raging. Earthquakes are happening in many places. We see the natural manifestations of Scripture happening across the globe. ***For example, the Blood Moon is a signal from heaven to us—the Moon represents the Church and the blood represents persecution. Christians are being persecuted and beheaded for their belief in God.***

We've witnessed the New Age explosion, the growth in occult activity, the headlong decline in public and private morality, the horrors of worldwide terrorism and the wide establishment of multi-faith beliefs that are all presently factors all contributing to changing society. All of this has served to alert the Body of Christ to the blatant fact that we live in a very different world than the people of my generation.

We are at a point of desperation and must have a supernatural sweeping wave of God's power and presence across our nation. Lord God, bring a Great Awakening to the United States of America. Turn the hearts of leaders to Jesus and back to the foundation upon which we were built. Before we lose all hope, let us remember our heritage.

The only hope is—the blessed hope, Jesus Christ. Has the church become too much like the world through compromise? As believers, we must check ourselves.

Cruise Ships

Compromise is when we come between God and His Promises. The church of Jesus Christ needs to lower her nets for a catch—the end time harvest of souls. Where is she? Is she sick at sea cruising in the name of God? I believe that we have been seeing a natural manifestation of the present day church with the cruise ships sick at sea and captains leaving their positions in God. Many don't even realize they have already lost their position due to their ambition of massing wealth and real estate, rather than going after the masses! There is a huge difference between ambition and our divine assignment.

Let's take a look at Luke chapter 5. Notice they had to be close to shore to lower their nets. In verse eleven, we see they brought their boats to shore, left everything and followed Him. Instead of the world following the church today, it appears the church is following hard after the world. Many sit on pews receiving the Word of God that is watered down and shallow, void of the real truth while many churches are alive and on-fire for God. The Word of God is personal. Jesus wants us to make it personal for others. I love the Church. God wants every church and every person to be ignited with a passion for the lost.

God desires that we build relationship with other believers and spread the Gospel to the world in need of Him. Relationship is not about being kind to get something or manipulating people to get them to pay for everything, or to get them to do everything for free; real kindness is having a pure heart that genuinely cares about others—loving people expecting nothing in return. And when we can help others out of own resources, we do so. (See Acts 2:44.) We are called to live a life that gives sacrificially.

We must have gratefulness over entitlement and realize we are here on earth "for such a time as this" to be the hands and feet of Jesus in the earth. We are personally responsible for evangelizing the entire planet earth before the return of Christ.

God loves family and unity. We must pray for our personal families and for healing for the family unit across America. I receive many calls from parents who are suffering from ungrateful adult children. Parents are hurting due to adult children not showing kindness and genuine love but rather only calling when they want money or need something. That is not relationship.

When parents give adult children things before they can afford them on their own, they are enabling them to live a lifestyle they are unable to afford in life. There is nothing wrong with helping children start out but we are not called to maintain them. We are called to entrust them to God and not play God in their finances, or any other area.

Work is required to make money—then you use your money to work for you in order to do more things *with God*.

In 1 Timothy 6:10 we learn that the love of money is the root of all kinds of evil. The love of money is greed—and there is a hidden spirit of mammon behind it. We must understand God is the owner of all and we are managers of His resources. This knowledge moves us from a place of entitlement to gratefulness. God is pleased with His children when we exhibit a heart of obedience and an attitude of gratitude.

Get Your Ticket Now

If you are hosting an event and have limited seating, you can't keep adding tables in a room with limited seating. Not only do you break the rules of fire code, you also create an atmosphere of stress—trying to accommodate those who wait till the last minute.

When there are no more reservations—that is what it means. The doors are closed. The ship is full. The resort or hotel is booked. The hour has come and Christ has returned. You have been left behind. Don't take whatever the *mark of the beast* is—don't deny Christ! Make sure of your salvation now!

If you are hosting a comedy event for 200 people and sell more than two hundred tickets, those who paid up front won't be happy with seating. You don't keep selling tickets, fully knowing you have no space for them just to get the money.

We have to learn to make sure of our ticket to heaven through receiving the forgiveness that Jesus already paid for in full on the cross. After you die, it is too late. Make sure of your reservations now.

Thank God there is always room for one more at the foot of the cross. Thank God the price has been paid in full for redemption and anyone can call on the name of Jesus and experience eternal life in Christ. I believe that we could be the generation that sees the return of Jesus Christ. The world will experience utter chaos and collapse of unprecedented measure across the globe when every authentic believer in Christ Jesus is taken to Heaven to be with Him. Make sure of your salvation today—before it's too late!

Teach Us To Number Our Days

When we turn the calendar page over to a new year, we come face to face with the fact that our days are numbered. The Bible makes that abundantly clear. Life is but a vapor. When God raised my husband back up in life as his heart stopped beating at Mercy Hospital in 2012, it was a fresh reminder to teach us to number our days. It was like new fallen snow falling on the ground. Like a snow covered ground gives a new perspective of life, watching God at work does, too.

The Bible says: *"Teach us to number our days, that we may gain a heart of wisdom"* (Ps. 90:12, NKJV).

Life has a way of giving warnings. God desires that each of us choose to make better use of the time left. Time is a gift from God here on earth. Time has little meaning in heaven. This precise moment you are actually reading this book is a gift from God. There is no better time than right now to renew the mind and learn there is more to come in Christ Jesus. Once you've experienced a touch from God, nothing else matters much anymore.

The last hour is here and Jesus is coming for those who have received Him. Knowing Jesus is worth more than the entire world.

Lord, make me to know my end and what is the extent of my days; let me know how transient I am.
—Psalm 39:4, NASB

God is continually putting people together who have a heart for Him. He is moving us to the frontlines to walk out in the divided communities to encourage reconciliation and forgiveness. Life is short. There is no time like the present. He is teaching us all to number our days.

That longing that is deep within your heart is the Holy Spirit nudging you to move forward *with* Him. He connects us with other people of purpose and passion. The Bible says, *"All this is from God, who through Christ reconciled us to himself and gave us the ministry of reconciliation"* (2 Cor. 5:18, ESV).

Across America, tension, fear, and threats of terror are high, but it is not hopeless. We have hope in Jesus Christ—for He is the Blessed Hope! God loves all people and the transforming power of the Gospel of Jesus Christ brings repentance, healing, and forgiveness. Beyond that we find reconciliation and hearts healed with relationships restored in many cases.

You can make a difference. God works through people to change the world through the power of His Holy Spirit. People across America and the nations are in search for the truth to fill the void and emptiness in their hearts. It is God they need. America is in need of spiritual awakening again!

Lord, revive us again.

On The Job Training

Training on the job can be a little tough. You have to watch your leader and learn from him or her. Thank God the Holy Spirit is our teacher and He is training us when we pay attention to Him and obey. He is our comforter and a "very present help in time of trouble."

There is much unrest across America. People are living with stress and all kinds of pressure. We all need peace. You can try rearranging your library of books to look like you are at peace, but it doesn't really work that way. Everyone needs encouragement and we are *all* a work in progress. Being unwilling to recognize that we need encouragement at times simply means a pride issue. We all have new things to learn in life. We can all improve and learn to work smarter.

It can be easy to get caught up in a "microwave mentality" with wanting everything a certain way or done in a hurry. While multi-tasking is a great way to get things done on a corporate level for business or even ministry success, it has the potential to destroy relationships. If you begin to think you can multi-task during your prayer time, it's pretty much over. You will be circling like the Israelites before long.

We must be willing to ask for prayer and learn to endure during uncertain times. Jesus prayed for Himself. One of the hardest lessons to learn as a Christian is waiting and trusting God in uncertain times between a promise from God and its fulfillment.

The purpose of prayer is communion with God. Jesus prayed before making decisions (Luke 6:12–13), he prayed for wisdom and guidance (Matthew 14:23; John 6:15), for strength (Luke 18:1, 22:40–43), and for his disciples (Luke 22:31–32; John 17:9–22).

Let's not forget this point. Don't confuse principles with application when you are not actually putting it into practice yourself. It takes great humility and godliness to receive correction. We all need correction in life. No one is exempt.

You may be a captain of a ship at sea and need correcting. If unwilling to receive, well, you may end up like the Titanic. You may be an airline pilot and miss the warnings to change your altitude. You may be driving at a high rate of speed and unwilling to slow down, racing to make an appointment. The unknown car coming through an intersection may take you out.

I thank God that He loves us and sends people to help us get back on track. Everyone needs somebody sometimes! Don't ever forget it! We all need each other. No man is an island. I don't know about you—but I will take all the help I can get from God, however he wants to send it. He is our heavenly Father and He is the Creator of all. He knows everything and sees all.

We must learn to run everything by the Bible and find out what God says about any given situation. The Bible is God's training manual that gives us wisdom and provides protection when we choose His ways over our own.

I have often heard the canned phrase that goes something like this, "You can be so heavenly minded, that you are no earthly good." I don't believe that for one minute. I do believe anyone can be so legally (or religious) minded that they are blinded to spiritual things in God. The Bible gives us a clue to Jesus' attitude toward the religious leaders of His day, as they were bent toward the letter of the law but quite insensitive when it came to discerning spiritual matters. This gives us warning that anyone can become religious—and totally miss God. This is why we must continually guard our hearts and obey God.

> *It's useless to bring your offerings. I am disgusted with the smell of the incense you burn. I cannot stand your New Moon Festivals, your Sabbaths, and your religious gatherings; they are all corrupted by your sins.*
> *—Isaiah 1:13, GNB*

God proves He uses ordinary people (with pasts that have been healed) whose power and authority in Christ make them extraordinary warriors for God. The Spirit-filled life is a weapon of defense against the enemy and a live demonstration there is potential for every human being under God.

Don't ever give up on anyone. Keep praying. Don't give up on America. Stand up and make a difference.

You might be saying, "How can I make a difference?" You can connect with other concerned people for America. You can email and call your leaders in Washington. You can pray and fast for this nation. You might be the one who stops and talks to one person that changes an entire city. Jesus did it. Let's reflect on Jesus' conversation with the woman at the well.

In spite of her five husbands and living arrangements with one that was not her husband at the time, she must have totally understood something of what Jesus was talking about as she rejoiced and became an evangelist. She told the villagers, *"Come and see the man who told me everything I have ever done!"* (See John 4:29, GNB) *A great many of the villagers later gave testimony and said, "We believe now, not because of what you said, but because we ourselves have heard him, and we know that he really is the Savior of the world"* (John 4:42, GNB).

During the culture and time period, if a woman committed adultery, she was stoned to death. This reveals the woman at the well must have been barren and discarded. Women could be discarded who could not have children. Otherwise, she would have been stoned and not lived to share the story. This is a reflection of America and many other nations as well.

People in America must feel discarded and barren themselves with all the covering going on. Hollywood has millions, yet divorce and still have major issues. That gives the answer to the money issue. Money doesn't make people happy and fulfilled. Yes, it takes money to live and money is a tool.

The truth is, we have all been created with a void in our hearts that only God can fill. America needed God just after the alarm on 9/11/2001—for about three weeks. America needs God now like never before.

How many years ago was it that prayer was taken out of schools? Now, we have mass killings instead. We moved from spit wads of gum to murder. Instead of kids growing up and playing ball with dad in the yard, they sit for endless hours in front of TV and playing "killing some zombie" or game that is about destroying an enemy.

With the murder in Oklahoma of the Australian boy who was here living his dream, we can see teens are bored and must think killing is a game. There is absolutely no value of life. The spirit of death and murder has infiltrated the minds of youth. Perhaps, this young man from Australia came here to live out his dream—only to find his life cut short at the hands of teens.

Three teens told the police they were bored. People who are bored feel they have no purpose—and nothing to do. Murder? What has this nation come to?

The truth that Jesus proclaimed to the woman at the well was simple but incredibly profound—*"God is Spirit, and those who worship Him must worship in spirit and truth"* (John 4:24, NKJV). God's Word says we were made in His own image. Man must also have a spirit with which is it possible to both worship God, who is Spirit, and have a relationship with Him as well.

When people are valued, affirmed, and have purpose they don't get bored. They value life, have something to live for, and move forward. They make choices and make things happen.

You can make a difference in your community. Start a fellowship and invite young teens to play sports. Start a home Bible study. You can do something. Get up and get moving. God has put something in your heart to do with Him. It's not too late to make a difference. Even if you change the life of just one for all eternity, it is worth it. Souls matter to God. Get out and be the change in the world you wish to see. You can choose to make a difference by following after God and seeking out the lost.

With the news and media filled with crisis and hopelessness, we have hope in Jesus Christ. With the world collapsing around us as we have known it, we still have hope in Jesus—The Blessed Hope. Share your faith on the job and in the marketplace.

Collapse

Could it be the once great nation of America is headed for economic collapse due to 2015 being a Shemitah year, or will we turn back to God and be blessed? I heard on the news some time ago that hundred dollar bills were being re-inspected and would be destroyed because they were defective—30 million dollars in one hundred dollar bills. "You've got to be kidding, right?" Is that what you were just thinking in your mind?

If America does not turn back to God, we are in trouble. There are consequences to sin. Sowing and reaping is a biblical principle (Gal. 6:7), but don't confuse this with God's judgment because Jesus has already taken the judgment of this world in Himself. There will be judgment after the church is gone in the end of the ages.

As I picked up *The Mystery of the Shemitah* to read a bit last night, the chapter I turned to reminded me of the dream the Holy Spirit gave me concerning driving on Sunset Avenue I shared at the beginning of this book. Interestingly enough, on page 196, I read in the book where Jonathan Cahn shared how the British Empire had been called "the empire on which the sun never sets," but the sun did set. This collapse was connected to the First World War—and it happened in 1917, a Year of the Shemitah.

We are seeing signs and wonders as well as confirmations everywhere we turn. God is sending Jesus for the church, but we must work with the Holy Spirit to harvest the fields and occupy till He comes. We sow and plant, and He brings the harvest. Speaking of sowing and planting, my precious mother recently planted some flowers around the mailbox at our home and the very day she planted them in the ground, she received a phone call from someone who wanted to plant and harvest her fields at her home and take care of them for her. See how quickly we sometimes reap a harvest? When we plant in good ground, no matter how small we may think it is, God brings the harvest.

Many Christians are taking a stand for God in this nation, however we must choose to repent as a nation before it is too late. Like the flowers at the mailbox, we are called to be a sweet smelling fragrance sharing the Good News of Jesus Christ to all we meet in a world of chaos and sin.

The symptoms of godlessness that nations were judged by as recorded in the Bible are now prevalent in this country today. Everything from greed, abortion, making laws that go against God's Word, witchcraft, false idols, and sexual perversion all lead to the moral decline of a once great nation.

Because of the godlessness in America, unless there is repentance and change, we may experience economic collapse that could make the depression of 1929 and recession of 2008 appear small in comparison. In Revelation, chapter 18, we read "Babylon the great is fallen,"—Babylon represents the value system of the ungodly age and the kingdom of Antichrist. It is called Babylon because it is a system with ideas and philosophies that go all the way back to the Book of Genesis.

Nimrod who built the Tower of Babel was mankind's attempt at humanism, for a man to establish his independence apart from God. Nimrod's name means "rebel," and is a type and shadow of the coming Antichrist who will rule over the last Babylon. Babylon stands for a wicked and vile system—where people are stealing, gouging, and doing all sorts of evil. It starts little by little, such as deception in leadership, business, and in family values. In Revelation 18, you can read about the destruction of the commercial Babylon.

We must choose to stand up, be willing to confront, and turn back to God! I had to stand up yesterday and confront. A business attempted to overcharge me and I had to spend over an hour on the phone, speaking with three different people, before I could get it resolved. If a person thinks they can get away with small things, he or she will keep moving forward full speed ahead. It would be like a head of any organization using company money to pay for all his extended family's vacations—and thinking God doesn't notice. How stupid is that. I had a professor in college who said, "You can't fix stupid."

Is the system here in America broken or have people resorted to thinking sin is okay? God speaks of the system as a city. Take time to read Revelation 18 and see the depravity including the sin of godlessness. We must turn back to God and repent for the nation. The nation is moving full speed ahead like a convertible with its top down in a storm with no covering. We must choose to stop, repent, and come back under the authority of God's Word.

We know the end of the story as believers in Jesus Christ, no matter what or when, we will rule and reign with Jesus Christ as He is coming back again to set up His kingdom.

People collapse from other things that happen in life as well. We must be willing to stand up and love people in the midst of pain, wrong choices, heartache, and even when they are being falsely accused or have made quick decisions in fear or without properly thinking. In the midst of economic or emotional collapse, people matter greatly to God.

Is it a race to see who can destroy America? The enemy comes to steal, kill, and destroy. Jesus came that we might have life!

It takes just one miraculous moment to save a life. Jesus did that for the woman at the well in Samaria. He did that for us. He did that for a man named Saul of Tarsus—and changed his name to Paul.

It takes only a moment for a woman to change her mind at an abortion clinic. When a woman actually sees a picture of her baby on an ultrasound scan she comes face to face with her preborn child. It's extremely sad that women wake up with nightmares haunting them about their loss of a child. Women tell me they feel sad, sick to the pit of their stomach, and empty, wishing they could make that decision again. They are bent over in pain and many collapse with a broken heart due to personal decisions for abortion.

Abortion clinics are ending more than a million innocent babies each year and wounding women in the wake of calamity as well. Anyone can have a change of heart. When a woman changes her mind about abortion, she actually saves two lives—her own and the child.

Women are in need across this land of healing from the fallout of emotional devastation from having made one wrong decision—abortion. You can choose to be the one who stands up for life across this land. You can be used by God to stop abortion in one single moment.

You can choose to be used by God to stand up and save someone else from emotional collapse. You can walk with someone going through a season of crisis and bring hope. You can equip and empower others to get back up and stand on God's Word. You can help someone if you will listen to God and obey what He puts in your heart to do with Him. Be the change you want to see. This race in life matters!

Committing to the Race

Have you ever felt like your battery was low or that the flame on the torch of your life was growing dim? Have you ever felt overwhelmed from a task and just wanted to stop? God calls us to fan the flame and to spur each other on. We are to stay in the race and finish well. We have to work together and watch out for each other. As a matter of fact, if a racecar driver focuses too much on another competitor, he or she may wreck or even go in a wrong direction.

When life comes at you and catches you in a season of pain, it can seem like only a flicker is appearing on the torch. We are called to fan the flame in each other and ignite a revival in hearts across this nation. The mission field is home and abroad. Life is much like a race to the finish line to receive the prize; and as we run the race, we touch everyone around us.

Have you ever been to a race? If so, no doubt you have heard the famous words, "gentlemen, start your engines" to "drivers, start your engines"…and a flag starts the race and ends it as well. If the drivers simply sit in their racecars and never turn over the key to ignite the engine, they can be in the race but never move forward to actually commit to the race. You can sit in a racecar and perhaps even own it, but it does not necessarily make you an official racecar driver, does it? You can sit in a garage, but it doesn't make you a car either. In the same token, sitting in church does not necessarily mean you are a Christian.

To commit to racing you first have to qualify and show up on race day. The Bible reveals that no one comes to the Father except through Jesus. We must accept Him as Savior, believe and confess Him as

Lord to be born again. Then we are qualified through the blood of Jesus. We are in a race to the finish line where we want to hear the words "Well done, my good and faithful servant."

Many have tasted the good news of Christ or perhaps been in church and experienced the presence of the Lord, but are not regenerated or truly born again. A person can profess to be a Christian but not possess Christ. When you have truly been born again through the power of the Holy Spirit, you are changed. You experience a heart change. You no longer like the things of the old nature. The Holy Spirit convicts and warns the heart before taking a wrong path. You know that you know.

You will not want to displease God. You become a sheep in need of the Great Shepherd. Sheep don't like to be dirty. They want to be cleansed when they get dirty. On the other hand, a pig loves the mud and thinks it is normal.

Perhaps you have fallen back into some old lifestyle and need to turn back to God. It's not too late. You may have had an affair or blamed someone else for something you actually did. You can repent and return to God.

If you have not had a heart change, it's not too late if you are reading this book. You still have life and breath. The Holy Spirit can draw you to salvation through a worship service, a book, a television show or sitting by yourself on a park bench. Sin creates a barrier that blocks us from God. God sent His only Son to redeem us back to the Father.

The Holy Spirit will draw you and tug at the door of your heart. You may be sitting in a church service and feel an urgency to go to the altar for prayer. Don't ignore those warnings. Move forward! (Read Hebrews 10:24.)

Salvation

Where will you spend eternity? Have you made the choice? God has paid for the gift of salvation and you can receive the free gift today. People are lost and think what is right is wrong, and call wrong right. The Lord wants to help you put your past behind you. God wants to heal you individually and the nations. God will open your eyes to see hurting people in need of healing.

Salvation is a free gift but we must pray to receive it and accept Jesus through repentance. Salvation is being born of the Spirit of God. It is a daily walk of depending on God and choosing His will over our own. God's plan for our life is always the best. Every time we choose to do the right thing, even when we don't want to do so, a little part of our fleshly nature is crucified in the natural. Our spirit man becomes stronger and it is easier to choose God's way the next time.

One day our flesh will die, but our spirit will live forever. Accomplishments and accolades fade away, but spiritual fruit lasts forever. I must tell you that the only way to enter the Kingdom of God and have eternal life with lasting fruit is this: "Jesus replied, 'The Truth is, no one can enter the Kingdom of God without being born of water and the Spirit. Humans can reproduce human life, but the Holy Spirit gives new life from heaven. So don't be surprised at my statement that you must be born again'" (John 3:5, NLT). The Bible says, "Anyone who calls on the name of the Lord will be saved" (Acts 2:21, NLT).

Being born again is a phrase Jesus used to describe the remarkable experience that a relationship with God makes in a person's life. It is like starting your life all over again. Romans 10:9-10 says it plainly: "That if thou shalt confess with thy mouth the Lord Jesus, and shalt believe in thine heart that God hath raised him from the dead, thou shalt be saved. For with the heart man believeth unto righteousness; and with the mouth confession is made unto salvation" (KJV).

The process of believing from the heart and then professing a commitment to God is what enables the Holy Spirit to work a miracle of regeneration in your life—"the new birth."

Being born again is a matter of first believing in your heart that Jesus is the Son of God, that He died for you and then rose again from the dead. Second, it is professing Him as Lord. Professing simply means "commitment." Professing Jesus as Lord means committing your life to Him.

If you question your salvation or realize you have never truly been born again, Jesus invites you to accept Him as your Lord and Savior now. (Read Matthew 16:24.) Pray the following prayer:

Lord Jesus, I repent of my sin and confess that You are the Son of the living God, the Christ. I receive You as my Lord and Savior right now. Thank You for forgiving me and for the gift of Your Holy Spirit. Amen.

Remember when you first made Jesus the Lord of your life? There may have been no great fireworks, but you had a change of heart and a life change, right? For many people, the experience of salvation comes during a time of crisis or hardship, while enduring a messy divorce, the loss of a career, when going through financial crisis, bankruptcy, or perhaps during a time of confronting dependency. People come face to face with their own human abilities, and their personal need for God's assistance and intervention in times of crisis and challenging situations.

America must turn back to God and realize He is our only hope! The truth is that it takes God to overcome many of the extreme challenges and mountains we face during a lifetime, and sometimes it is at the point of crisis that brings us as individuals and a nation to recognize our need for the Lord.

While America is in trouble, there is still hope in the Blessed Hope—Jesus Christ!

Salvation

No matter if you have been a Christian for a long time or just now accepted Jesus as Lord, find a church to worship and connect with other believers. Also, be obedient in baptism. (See Acts 2:38.) You may have already done this and still have junk in your life, not knowing how to be free. Keep reading and learn the power of renewing your mind in the Word of God while finding true intimacy with our Lord!

Truth

After salvation, we need to be a disciple and continue to grow in the truth found in God's Word. The Bible reveals what Jesus told us. 'Jesus said, "If you hold in my teaching, you are really my disciples. Then you will know the truth, and the truth will set you free" (John 8:31–32, NIV).

Jesus never encouraged his disciples to place confidence in past faith or past experiences. Genuine disciples continue to obey the Words of Christ. There are many things that are true in human knowledge, yet there is only one truth that will set people free from sin and destruction.

In Hosea 4:6 God says, *"My people."* He is not referring to those in the world who are not born again or to those who are not serving Him, but He says, *"My people"* are destroyed because of one thing—and that is a lack of knowledge. This tells me a person can be born again and still remain in bondage. You may be in a storm of oppression or you may have a problem with raging anger, and live in a war zone in your own home. You may be in the midst of a battle for your life through no fault of your own.

I have good news for you. You can choose to live in victory and stand on the authority of God's Word that has already been given to you for *freedom and revival.* Acts 10:32 reveals God is not a respecter of persons. What He has done for one, He will do for you—and it is time to be set free!

"The word which God sent to the children of Israel, preaching peace through Jesus Christ; He is Lord

of all; that word you know, which was proclaimed throughout all Judea, and began from Galilee after the baptism which John preached: how God anointed Jesus of Nazareth with the Holy Spirit and with power, who went about doing good and healing all who were oppressed by the devil, for God was with Him."
—Acts 10:36–38

God desires that each of us step out and reach new people with the message of hope in Jesus. He wants us to stand up and pray for America. Preaching of the gospel will always draw new people, in spite of difficulties, opposition, and outright persecution.

As a Christian, you will experience persecution at some point. It may come through a family member, a son or daughter, or betrayal in some crazy manner. Peter said it this way. *"Don't give the opposition a second thought. Through thick and thin, keep your hearts at attention, in adoration before Christ, your Master. Be ready to speak up and tell anyone who asks why you're living the way you are, and always with the utmost courtesy"* (1 Pet. 3:14–15, MSG).

As we choose to meditate on the life of Christ, we find strength for our own. People may realize that you, like the disciples that followed Jesus, have been with Christ. The bottom line is you must spend time in God's Word—reading and praying it! This is how the mind is renewed and transformed in order to live each day!

Make no mistake about it—we are in a real battle here and now! We have a battle for the family unit, freedom of religion, for our nation, and the list goes on. The very minute we chose to receive Jesus and to side with Him, we engaged a real enemy who is bent on stopping the gospel message from coming forth through us.

Remember, because of Jesus Christ and the finished work on the cross, we are on the winning side. Persecution did not stop the apostles. Don't let it stop you either.

Because of Jesus Christ, we are the over comers in this battle. We have to stand up with faith in God and stand upon His Word. The shield of faith will quench the fiery darts of the enemy.

Anyone can get weary in battle. Physical and emotional attacks are very real. Financial attacks are very real. We have to choose to stand upon God's Word and not budge off of it. This is God's country! Don't ever forget it.

We must apply the Word of God to every situation. We do this by finding the promise in Scripture for the battle we are facing and praying it to God. It is the Word of God that we love and know and apply that brings change. Like the account in the Old Testament where a lamb was slain and the blood was poured into a basin—the blood had to be applied with hyssop to the doorposts of the home in order for the angel of death to pass over them.

Jesus Christ paid the price once and for all and He is the sacrificial Lamb of God. He is the Living Word of God. In order for us to over come and live in truth in this life, we must choose to apply the Word of God to our lives and homes as well.

Will you turn back to God for America?

God's Country

Have you ever been to the Olympics or viewed them on television? Whether you observed from the stands or from your sofa on the television, you saw the same games, just from a difference perspective. When you accept Jesus as Lord and are born again, you see life through God's perspective. You can view life through the lens of God's eye and His heart when you seek Him with your whole heart.

At the end of your life, you will receive rewards from God. He says He rewards those who diligently seek Him. He also rewards us daily with His benefits. In the natural realm, I might explain it this way. Most hotels have reward programs. You can stay in the resort and receive points for your stay as long as you are the one paying the bill at the time you check out. If someone else pays the bill, they get the rewards.

Your name has to be on the register and on payment for the bill. The paid in full bill has to have your name on it. Even though the owner of the hotel still owns the hotel, he or she will still give you the benefits by your participation of staying at their property.

Salvation is a free gift. There is a high cost of following hard after Jesus. It will cost you something. It will cost you everything. You are either totally in or not.

You aren't going to make it into heaven on someone else's salvation or relationship with God. You have to be the one personally committed to God. Your name has to be on the register—the Book of Life!

When we go out in the darkness and share the light with others, there will be some who won't listen. The Bible tells us what to do, *"And whoever will not receive you nor hear your words, when you depart from that house or city, shake off the dust from your feet"* (Matt. 10:14, NKJV).

Luke 9:5 also tells us to *"Shake the dust off our feet that hinders us from getting to where we need to be in God."*

Shaking

Have you ever been in a car that was going too fast and noticed it began to shake? Have you ever been behind a large transfer truck and felt the wind begin to pull you behind where you could feel your vehicle begin to shake a little? Have you ever been in a church service and felt the strong presence of God to the point you began to shake or your heart was pierced by the love of God in such a way that you knew He was and is real? I believe because God loves the world, He is going to *allow* a shaking.

God is going to start with the church first. While many have served the Lord in obscurity with a promise of fruit in heaven, we must realize there is a huge difference between the pastors who view their position as a job and the one who is serious about God and souls. There is also a huge difference between the missionary who does social work and the ones who are sold out to winning souls and obeying whatever the Lord asks of them. There is a vast difference between the teen that goes along with the crowd or even worldly Christian friends than the one who stands up for Christ at the risk of being alienated from friends. There is a vast difference in the business owner who gives to the Kingdom of God than the one who promotes destruction of mankind.

The world is in desperate need for those who will give all for the kingdom. We must be willing to take the initiative and stand up to stand apart for the kingdom. God promises to draw near to us when we draw near to Him. (See James 4:8.) The choice is ours.

God corrects those He loves, but many don't understand what that really means. Many perceive God as harsh and believe God corrects with crisis, disasters, sickness, disease, and premature deaths. Nothing could be farther from the truth. We live in a fallen world where bad things happen. We have all made wrong choices that bring about consequences.

It is critical that we understand God's methods and ways. If we don't, it will be hard to keep God as our first love. The Word of God teaches that God our Father corrects and relates to us by studying the human parental example found in Matthew 7:9-11 where Jesus is teaching His disciples, said "…if his son ask bread, will he give him a stone? Or if he ask a fish, will he give him a serpent? If ye then, being evil, know how to give good gifts unto your children, how much more shall your Father which is in heaven give good things to them that ask him?" (KJV).

Just as a parent tries to protect a child from harm, so does our Father God. Have you ever touched a hot stove? If you have, you know what happened. We teach our kids not to touch a hot stove because we love them and don't want them to get hurt. If they touch it, we discipline them to teach them a lesson to protect them from harm in the future.

The Bible says: "As many as I love, I rebuke and chasten: be zealous therefore, and repent," (Revelation 3:19 KJV). God corrects with His Word—not with natural catastrophes. The choices we make bring about consequences—both good and bad. America is headed for disastrous consequences of rejecting God if she does not repent and turn back to Him.

Repentance is not just an altar call where people come forward and weep at the altar to get things right with God. While that is sometimes an outward expression of inward repentance, it is not what repentance means. Repent means to go back to God's perspective on reality. Without repentance, we live in a carnal state of thinking. Repentance made practical is basically this: we gain God's perspective and live it as if we truly believe it!

God is not going to bypass the church and start with the world. He starts with His own. Will you submit and surrender to God's loving correction? Will you turn back to God in any area He illuminates or will you live in rebellion? I believe God is shaking anything that is not like Jesus out of our lives. He wants us to have pure hearts that live in childlike faith at all times—both good and bad.

Don't allow uncertain times to change your view of God. The Bible says, "And my God shall supply all your need according to His riches in glory by Christ Jesus" (Phil. 4:19). Uncertainty causes many to misunderstand who God is and they begin to believe the lies of the enemy. Let's get one thing straight: God is good all the time! The suffering we will experience in this life means living between conflicting realities—living through storms that come but praising and trusting God through them all!

Jesus desires that we view life with His perspective because His Kingdom is at hand. Jesus said, "unless one is born again, he cannot see the kingdom of God" (John 3:3). He was saying that when our minds are renewed, we will see the Kingdom as He did while here on earth. What a way to live! May He wake us up as a nation to destroy the works of the devil, demonstrate His love and power, and prove the Will of God here on earth! This is our privilege to partner with Him in the Great Commission!

Our Divine Roadmap

Second Chronicles 7:14 stands at the roadmap for revival. The church must turn back to God instead of blaming the world or society for our ineffectiveness as a church. Perhaps we need to take a good look to see if it is partly lack of prayer in the church, competition, or about something other than advancing the Kingdom of God.

For example, when you view someone living in sin, are you critical and judgmental or do you walk in love and stand in the gap through prayer? Do you allow others to use their words to defile your ears about anyone? Do you compromise in any area for your own position and worth? Do you use the world's system to manipulate the organization to obtain things you covet in the world through the church or through a business? Any level of compromise reveals a heart with places not fully surrendered to God.

This is why a shaking must come. Some Christians oppose revival coming before the end of the age and use the Scriptures that seem to reveal the church will be in a state of almost complete spiritual bankruptcy—materialistic, carnal, lukewarm—and "lovers of pleasures more than lovers of God." Scripture seems to paint a picture of the church being apostate and much like the church of Laodicea.

Throughout history, God has made it clear there will be a "remnant" of believers who have willingly gone through the necessary preparation whom will have part in the coming revival. Those who fail to surrender and submit to this preparation process, preferring to remain in their present day state of the Laodicea church, will have no part in the coming move of God. The Bible states that the lukewarm are to be "spewed" out of the mouth of God. (See Revelation 3:16.)

Did you know the Bible makes it perfectly clear that God is not pleased and will not live with a "blessings" obsessed, Laodicea type church in this present age? With the increasing darkness that has come upon the earth, His eye is searching to and fro for those that love Him and will be about His purposes in the earth today. He cleanses, refines, prepares, and will anoint such a people to bring light in all the earth. I believe this is why there is a "shaking" like we've never seen or experienced before with repentance that is first coming to His church.

God will not bypass His church and shake the world. He starts with His own. He desires that we all come to Him and be cleansed, mature, and have hearts of compassion that are moved to obedience immediately! He doesn't want us to sit back in silence and watch people become casualties of the war that is raging across the land.

> *"If my people who are called by My name will humble themselves, and pray and seek My face, and turn from their wicked ways, then I will hear from heaven, and will forgive their sin and heal their land"*
> (2 Chronicles 7:14 NKJV).

Silence

Have you ever had a bad day? Have you ever woken up and wondered why God answered everyone else's prayers and not yours? Have you ever wondered why the Internet goes out at your home when you are just about to email a very important document? Sometimes these are what I call divine delays in life. Waiting is not always fun and we don't understand why.

It is kind of interesting that right in the middle of a turnaround with editing even of this book, our Internet router went out. The lady on the phone with AT&T advised they could ship a router out immediately—either a Pace or MegaNet—and I thought this is great timing. One of the chapters within this book is about lowering our nets and going for the masses—not fish, but souls. We also have to stay in pace with God, in His timing and not our own.

Are you starting to see how God gets our attention and speaks through natural things in this life? My husband then called and asked me if I had taken time yet to call the American Automobile Association (AAA) and have a service person come out to jumpstart the battery in one of our vehicles. I had been sick with an upper respiratory infection and that car sat in the garage for a few days. It needed a jumpstart, much like we do sometimes in life.

When the service representative called to advise a technician would be coming out, I couldn't help but notice I already had this number keyed in my phone. As I looked back at the contact information I noticed we met this man on 3/31/12 when the same vehicle needed recharging. I was working on my second book at that time—*A Leap of Faith*.

Even though the car battery needed a charge, I chose to turn it around and gave the man a book to bless him. We can choose to view life as divine appointments in the times of silence, interruptions, and waiting or we can become frustrated and fearful.

God goes to extreme measures to get the Good News of the Gospel out to all mankind. He will interrupt the events of any given day for just one person. I believe there is something in my book that will bring encouragement to this man that came out to jumpstart the battery.

Silence, interruptions and times of waiting are all part of God's divine plan. It is sometimes hard to honor God's Word when it seems everything is silent from God. It is sometimes hard to wait in silence when you wonder what on earth is going on with that really big issue or while you are waiting on the doctor's report. What on earth is God doing in the silence? What do we do when it seems everything is silent and no one is responding to anything?

Sometimes in the business of life, the greatest thing we will learn is agape love. We learn this in times of waiting. We must first learn to never confuse what seems to be God's silence with His absence. When God is silent He is never still. He is at work behind the scenes working all things out for our good and His glory (Romans 8:28). Let's take a look at what the Bible teaches us to do in the silence.

Between the Old Testament and New Testament was four hundred years of silence. Can you imagine? No word, no voice, and no prophet sent by God. First, we need to understand why God was silent for four hundred years. What He was doing then can help us today.

Why study the four hundred years between Malachi and Matthew? Why talk about books that are not part of the Bible? Why talk about some books called the Apocrypha? Why talk about a family named Maccabees? Pay attention to the following historical information and note the types and shadows of history repeating itself.

*www.logos.com/400 Years of Silence

When the Book of Malachi closes you have a nation that is in love with idolatry, they want to worship the idols and gods of the heathen. They want to be like the world and live by man's law and not by God's.

The Midnight Hour

But when you start the Book of Matthew you find a nation of people who are worshiping one God and they are out to destroy every hint of idolatry.

When the Book of Malachi ends you have the Jews seeking to be part of the pagan culture. When you get to Matthew the Jews have rioted because of Herod building buildings for the pagan culture and putting statues and images on them.

When you leave Malachi there is very little or no interest in the Messiah, but when you come to Matthew they are looking for the Messiah. There have been a number of people who claimed to be the Messiah.

When you leave Malachi you have the Babylonians taking Judah into captivity. When you get to Matthew you have the Romans in charge. How did the Roman's get involved and how did Herod get to rule?

With the close of Malachi there are no religious and political parties. But in Matthew you find a number of opposing political parties: the Pharisees, Saducees, Herodians, Essens, Zelots, (of which James and John were members).

Also you had the Qumaram Community from where we get the Dead Sea Scrolls.

When you close Malachi there are no synagogues. When you open Matthew there are synagogues in almost every Jewish town. There are seventy in Jerusalem.

In the Old Testament all worship was centered on the Temple. In the New Testament the worship was centered around the Temple and the Synagogue.

With the close of Malachi you find one school of thought. With Matthew you have two main Jewish Schools of Rabbi Hilial, and the school of Rabbi Shama.

In Malachi the spiritual leaders are priests but in Matthew they are rabbis. The nation was divided internally through different parties. Externally they struggled with an old never-ending war. The Jews were descendants of Jacob—twelve tribes.

The descendants of the twelve Arab nations, the Palestinians, refuse to live in peace with Israel.

A Gentile came to power that Daniel had predicted. His name was Antiochus Ephapanes. He was an Arab and under his leadership he was determined to wipe out the Jewish religion altogether 168 B.C. Just like Hamon wanted to do more than 150 years before during the time of Esther the Queen.

Under Antiochus Ephapanes all Jewish sacrifices were forbidden. The rite of circumcision was to cease; the Sabbath and feasts were no longer to be observed, and disobedience carried the penalty of death. All books of the law were ripped apart or destroyed by fire. Jews were forced to eat swine's flesh and to sacrifice at idolatrous altars setup throughout the land.

Then to crown his deeds of infamy Antiochus erected an altar to the Olympian Zeus with an image of the god probably bearing the features of Antiochus himself, on the altar of burnt offerings within the Temple Court. That was not bad enough so he sacrificed a pig on the altar and splattered the blood everywhere.

(This was prophesied in the Book of Daniel called "The Abomination of Desolates" (Dan. 11:31)).

Jesus refers to this historical event as a type (picture) of what will happen in the future just before He comes again in Matthew 24:15. He calls The Abomination of Desolation.

It will be fulfilled in the middle of the Tribulation period when the Anti-Christ sets up his idol in the temple of Jerusalem and demands that all people worship it. (See Revelation 13.)

During the four hundred years of silence there was severe persecution in which many were put to death. (See 1 Maccabees 1:57–64.) This was a time much like Germany experienced under Hitler in which the government was hunting down Jews to kill them. They wanted to stomp Judaism off the face of the earth. Many Jews hid in small towns and in the mountains. But even there people betrayed them.

What can we learn from this review of historical events? What happened in these four hundred so-called years of "silence?" There have been two—from Joseph to Moses there was four hundred years where God did not choose to speak to his people through prophets. Again, this happened between Malachi and Matthew.

There is a word in Paul's letter to the Galatians that says, "When the time had fully come, God sent forth his son, born of woman, born under the law" (Gal. 4:4). The time of our Lord's birth was an appointed hour, the moment for which God had been long preparing. Some of the exciting preparations took place during the four hundred years of "silence," however you will understand the New Testament better if you understand something of the history between the O.T. and the N.T.

After Malachi ceased his prophesying and the canon of the Old Testament closed, the number of the books in the O.T. was fulfilled and the inspired prophets ceased to speak. God allowed a period of time for the teaching of the Old Testament to penetrate throughout the world. In about 435 B.C. when Malachi ceased his writing, the center of the world power began to shift from the East to the West.

Iraq had been the world power but was soon succeeded by the Media-Persian Empire as predicted by the prophet Daniel, who said that there would rise up a bear that was higher on one side than the other, signifying the division between Media and Persia, with the Persians the predominant ones.

At the height of Persian power there arose in the country of Macedonia (which we now know as Greece) north of the Black Sea, a man by the name of Philip of Macedon, who became a leader in his own country. He united the islands of Greece and became their ruler. His son was destined to become one of the world's greatest leaders of all time—Alexander the Great.

In 330 B.C. a tremendous battle between the Persians and the Greeks altered history for all time. In that battle, Alexander, as a young man of only twenty years old, led the armies of Greece in victory over the Persians and completely demolished the power of Persia. The center for world power then shifted farther west into Greece and the Grecian Empire was born.

A year after that battle, Alexander the Great led his armies down into the Syrian world toward Egypt. On the way, he planned to siege the city of Jerusalem. As the victorious armies of Greece approached the city, word was brought to the Jews in Jerusalem that the armies were on their way.

The High Priest at that time who was a godly man was named Judda (who is mentioned in the Book of Nehemiah) took the sacred writings of Daniel the prophet and, accompanied by a host of other priests dressed in white garments, went forth and met Alexander some distance outside the city. All of this is from the report of Josephus, the Jewish historian who tells us that Alexander left his army and hurried to meet this body of priests. When he met them he told them he had a vision the night before in which God had shown him an old man, robed in white garment, who would show him something of great significance. According to the account, the high priest then opened the prophecies of Daniel and read them to Alexander.

In the prophecies, Alexander was able to see the he would become the notable goat with the horn in his forehead, which would come from the West and smash the power of Medio-Persia and conquer the world. He was so overwhelmed by the accuracy of the prophecy and, of course, by the fact that is spoken about him, that he promised that he would save Jerusalem from siege, and sent the high priest back with honors.

Alexander died in 323 B.C. when he was only about thirty-three years old. He had drunk himself to death in the prime of his life, grieved because he had no more worlds to conquer. After his death, his empire was torn with dissension, because he had left no heir. His son had been murdered earlier, and there was no one to inherit the empire of Alexander.

God used this period of Greek rule to prepare the world for the Gospel:
1. Universal language
2. Road system to travel everywhere
3. Soldiers stationed on the road to provide safety for travel
4. Safety on the seas—no pirates

The events that took place prepared the way for us. The Roman Empire came on the scene and declared peace around the world and developed a great way for all to travel and communicate. Now we have a common language, Roman peace, and improved transportation. This set the stage for the "New Testament."

Jesus is born and he launched a church—on the move! God was positioning the world state so the Gospel of Jesus Christ would spread across the world.

What God is doing in the silence is setting the stage and re-arranging the stage so his purposes and will can be accomplished. If you are in this period he is re-arranging the stage so your life will be positioned to accomplish His Will.

We cannot afford to be silent, but must turn back to God in repentance for this nation!

Purpose To Know God In Changing Times

In the midst of changing times, God never changes. We must keep seeking Him through reading His Word, praying, and having times of waiting in God's presence. We must seek to know Him and find out what He says in His Word.

Take a few minutes to think about the next few questions. Do you seek God or simply want what He can provide? Are you in pursuit of knowing God? Or, do you seek His gifts only? Does your life portray the love of Christ on a daily basis, or is it only evident on Sunday? When someone hears your conversation during the week, whether in your office or while you are out in public, do you reflect the image of Christ? These are very viable questions because our life is a sermon.

At the end of life, we will receive rewards from God. After the Olympics a few go home with trophies while others go home having participated in games but some never finished. America is much the same way now, it seems. America has fallen to the depths of sin much like Sodom and Gomorrah. The main sin of Sodom and Gomorrah was not perversion, but rather idolatry and materialism. America started out with a foundation in God and Christian principles. What has happened? When the spiritual climate of a nation declines, it is not long till sin abounds.

We know God's hand is upon us, but we can certainly tell it seems to be lifting from the devastation we see across the land from our wrong choices as a nation. Our nation has asked God to leave through removing prayer from schools and now the threats of prayer being removed from events and meetings.

Remember what happened right after September 11? For a few weeks, everyone was flocking to church and praying. People were standing together on television praying to God. What happened shortly thereafter reveals the heart of this nation.

We live in a fallen world and sin is very real. Evil is very real. Once the bad news report is over and life seems to go back to normal, people forget. Many get blessed and forget the blessings come from God.

Business partners walk out on their responsibility like a bunch of rats running off a sinking ship, to children stealing from their own parents in business, robbing their own parents' homes, to compromise in the house of God. Teenagers walk into schools and shoot teachers and students. Rage and violence is on the increase. Devastation is leaving a trail across the nation and abroad. Marriages are struggling. People are betraying one another and devouring one another. Sound familiar? It sounds to me like the discourse of Jesus found in Matthew 24 and 25. He revealed what would happen in the end times leading up to his Second Coming.

We are living presently with signs of the end in view. We must know our identity in Christ and purpose to know God. Our purpose is to know God and make Him known. We move from living earthly minded to eternity minded at all times.

I receive calls and have meetings with people who have experienced theft from their adult children stealing from them personally and their corporations. Teenagers and adult children are breaking into their own parent's homes and robbing them of possessions. Mass shootings have been all over the media. People are angry and in need of help but don't seem to know where to turn. Report after report of angry hearts to people who are mad at the world is on the rise. Anger is rooted in fear.

People are afraid, desperate and making bad choices in crisis. One bad choice can leave a trail of destruction. The world can be caught up in seeking things, rather than seeking God. It can be a new job, a new home, more money, to more prestige in your business—or even church platform. The world is filled with many who have fear and live trying to control everything.

> *"For false messiahs and false prophets will appear and perform great signs and wonders to deceive, if possible, even the elect. See, I have told you ahead of time"*
> —Matthew 24:24–25, NIV

Brokenness: The Power of Surrender to the Holy Spirit

We have been warned by God of things to come and we see them now. We see division in the government, what is wrong is called right, and we have a leadership crisis in America.

Life has changed everywhere. People are in a hurry going nowhere. It seems everyone is on a time constraint and living in a rush. It is evidenced by road rage, right on down the line to any pastor (man or woman of God) who tries to control the atmosphere in the church by not allowing the worship to rise into true worship.

When any minister lives in fear or is caught up in "census" as David was in the Bible to performance rather than a church filled with the power of God, there will be no revival—but confusion, competition, and backbiting. When God is not the one who fills the house—we experience little or no power.

People seek to fill the void in their heart through things, larger homes, attaining wealth and properties, to being caught up in people pleasing and their own personal agendas, to power and control—making sure their livelihood is set for years.

There is nothing wrong with having things as long as they don't have you. "Necessity or luxury?" you might ask yourself. The Bible says: "'And these are they which are sown among thorns; such as hear the word, and the cares of this world, and the deceitfulness of riches, and the lust of other things entering in, choke the word, and it becometh unfruitful.'" (Mark 4:18-19 KJV). *It is the control of and the lust for those things that chokes the word in our lives.*

Jesus wants our hearts to be soft and pliable so that when we hear the Word, we accept it, and we bear fruit. Then Jesus said to them, *"Is a lamp brought to be put under a basket or under a bed? Is it not to be set on a lampstand?"* (Mark 4:21 NKJV). We are not to hide our faith in God but to share it with others.

What stories of Jesus' love and His involvement have helped you through some storm in life? My nephew wrote an essay and shared his message on what he has been through at a very young age in life and the teacher had to start handing out tissues. You have a story that can help someone else. Dare to step out in these changing times and share a personal testimony. As the crowds followed Jesus, there will be many drawn to you through your transparency and your testimony of hope in God.

The crowd that followed Jesus to the lakeside was so large that He absolutely had to get into the boat on the lake to minister as the gospel records. During that day and age, there was no indoor plumbing and there were no cars. Very few people even had a donkey and they certainly didn't have a TV.

Something I remember from a trip to Israel is quite interesting. The first time I went to Israel was in 1992, we saw Bedouins who had a TV hooked up to an energy source in the middle of the desert. That was the funniest sight—to see a TV screen in the middle of the desert as we passed by on the tour bus.

Did you know that right in the middle of whatever desert or storm you are facing personally, you have a power source? The Holy Spirit of God is our power source. He enables us to see the big picture much like the TV screen I saw out in the middle of the desert.

There is nothing wrong with owning a television, as it is a tool God uses to spread the Gospel of Jesus Christ. It is what you do with the TV that can cause a problem. There is a button on it or a remote where you make choices. Choices are part of daily life.

We must all take inventory, not only of our hearts but our families and homes. I hear men and women talking about storage units where extra stuff is stored. Homes are filled with things and yet we go out and buy more.

You may be shopping and constantly spending money on all kinds of face products to the point of it being ridiculous and reaching the point of vanity, to the person who buys an RV and has three homes that collect dust. There is nothing wrong with owning properties—many do it as a business investment. There is nothing wrong with shopping and making purchases. As a matter of fact, most women like to shop and some men do as well. But there does come a time when we must all take inventory. *God will speak to you about yourself where you need to change.* He is not going to speak to you about your neighbor and friends. He speaks to you as an individual. He will show you things so you can pray for others.

Sometimes people strive due to covering pain. What is it that we are covering when we are obsessed with the next new car, bigger house, new outfit or the latest new phone or piece of technology? Is there a place of sadness or an unhealed place in our heart? Are we competing with our elder brother or next-door neighbor? Have we experienced great loss or abuse? Are we covering pain? Are we just doing it because everyone else is doing it?

Are we giving secret tests to family members to see if they really love us? Are we disappointed in adult children? Are we buying things with money we don't have to give to people who don't care about us at all? Are we buying things because we can now and couldn't years ago? Areas of pain manifest in covering. The same thing happened in the Garden of Eden. Adam and Eve hid from God.

Healing is needed and balance is the key. People are desperate for relationship so they seek to please people instead of God and resort to buying stuff for people that expect it—while forgetting the people that really have needs.

What are you chasing after now? Or, are you chasing after a person, the Great "I AM?" Who are you following? The disciples followed Jesus and had relationship with Him, but really no fellowship until Jesus was resurrected and the Holy Spirit touched them.

Judas was also a follower but he was lost. He betrayed Christ. He loved the things of the world more than Jesus. He was obviously not broken. We all have to move from salvation to brokenness through spending time in the presence of Jehovah. In the presence of Jesus is where we find real peace and joy.

Brokenness is a place we must all come to where we are empty of self. Only then can we be filled with Christ. When we are filled to overflow by the power of the Holy Spirit, we become a river of life to others.

A great book to read is *Brokenness, The Forgotten Factor of Prayer* by the late Mickey Bonner. You will be blessed to read it. As a matter of fact, make sure to have a box of tissues when you sit down to read it.

You can find refreshing by reading God's Word, a book that God has called someone to write, or just soaking in His Presence. You might be asking now, "How do I do that?" You can find a quiet place in your home to a walk in the park. Listen to "soaking" music. Soaking music is worship music that brings you into the presence of God by quieting your soul (your mind, will and emotions). At first, this might be tough when life can seem like a rat race on occasion. We must all learn to ascend to the mountain of God and find a place where we can truly worship and fellowship. We need to do this individually and corporately, as the body of Christ.

I remember a conference I had one time and I was totally silent at first. People began to squirm in their seats. Then I asked everyone to turn all cell phones on silent. It was interesting to see how long it took for each person to become still and learn to be silent for a few minutes.

At some point in life, every person will come to a place where he or she needs Jesus. He will be the only one who can fix a particular problem, heal the heart, or intervene in a time of crisis. We must be broken to the point of all we want is Jesus!

Our hearts must be soft and pliable to be touched by God. I thank God He allows just enough heartache to move us to tears so that we remain soft and pliable in the Hand of God. We can be moist with the Water of the Word of God to be a witness to others.

America needs help, my friends. America needs to humble herself as a nation and ascend to the holy hill to meet God in prayer. God is our creator. He loves people and desires that none should perish.

America was founded upon Christian principles but has fallen to extreme depths of sin just as God has warned us about in Scripture. Rather than recognizing Truth between right and wrong, it seems America has been desensitized to the point of no return *unless*

Christians take a stand for God's Word and the foundational principles America was founded upon.

We need revival and for God to ignite the passion and zeal in our hearts for HIM again. Revival can only come when we are empty of self. You cannot fill a container that is already full of something. We must all choose to lay down our preconceived notions and "stuff" to get back to the basics in God. America has way too many false gods—idols.

I hear people speak about other nations with many gods, but America has her own multitude of gods as well. Two of the largest are technology and sex. Instead of running to the phone or your latest new I-pad or I-phone, wouldn't it be a change if we would first run to the great "I AM?" Can you imagine how much different our world would be? Instead of being consumed with the world's operating system we could finally come to understand the Kingdom of God and His ways.

BACK TO THE BASICS

We must get back to the basics of God's Word and relationship with Him first. We move from relationship to fellowship in God. Is there really much difference in us today and Adam and Eve in the Garden of Eden? It is interesting to note that it was a tree of the knowledge of good and evil that God told them they must not eat from or they would surely die.

If we choose to stay consumed with technology, rather than developing a relationship with the Lord, we too, will surely die. People need each other. No man is an island. We have to live rightly and according to God's ways.

Where is the honor and integrity? What are you teaching your children by the way you live? Do you compromise in any area and then move to justify your actions by reasoning? Would you guard your brother or sister's back when you see them being harmed or would you be so envious and jealous that you would rather take a bite out of them rather than working for success yourself?

Do you think people owe you something? Do you mistreat people that need you and try to get close to people that don't? Could anyone sit outside the door of your office and hear every single conversation and still believe you are a born-again Christian? Would they be shocked to learn you lie, cheat, or compromise your own beliefs because you are deceived?

You can choose to pray and ask God to remove anything that is not like Him out of your life and surrender to the power of the Holy Spirit. He will lead you, comfort you, and fill you with the river of Living Water.

We have to move from an outward show of religion to an inward heart of relationship with God. The one thing I have learned that is a common denominator in all religions is to honor your parents. Isn't that interesting? It is honor. We must learn to honor God by a heart that is empty of self and be filled with Him through living out of His Word—the Bible. This comes through spending times of waiting in His presence and listening for the still small voice of God.

HEART CHECK

The Bible says, *"If you curse your father or mother, the lamp of your life will be snuffed out. An inheritance obtained early in life is not a blessing in the end. Don't say, "I will get even for this wrong." Wait for the Lord to handle the matter. The Lord despises double standards; he is not pleased with dishonest scales. How can we understand the road we travel? It is the Lord who directs our steps. It is dangerous to make a rash promise to God before counting the cost. A wise king finds the wicked, lays them out like wheat; then runs the crushing wheel over them. The Lord's searchlight penetrates the human spirit, exposing every hidden motive. Unfailing love and faithfulness protect the king; his throne is made secure through love. The glory of the young is their strength; the gray hair of experience is the splendor of the old. Physical punishment cleanses away evil; such discipline purifies the heart"* (Prov. 20:20-30 NLT).

The human spirit is the Lord's searchlight. People may think they are actually doing right, but the Lord examines the heart. (See Proverbs 21:2 NLT) God's Word says that wealth created by lying is a vanishing mist and a deadly trap. (See Proverbs 21:6 NLT) He goes further to say, "Because the wicked refuse to do what is just, their violence boomerangs and destroys them" (Prov. 21:7 NLT).

Unfortunately, in this world, the net is tossed out to catch the bad guys and takes innocent people's lives as well. This is why we must learn not to tolerate the slightest sin. If we don't deal with sin it can bring great harm. If we see a brother or sister living in sin or going down a wrong path, we must choose to confront them in the love of God.

If we tolerate sin in our own life, it will have the power to bring about destruction. If we tolerate sin in an employee or choose to ignore it because of who we think they are, it may have the power to bring about devastation. Satan has a plan for every single person's demise. Don't kid yourself into thinking you are above sin.

Check your own heart. Ask yourself this question, "What is God speaking to me through this chapter?" Allow the Holy Spirit to soften any hard places that have been made through sin and rebellion.

Patience Reveals Purpose

"....be not slothful, but followers of them through faith and patience inherit the promises."
—Hebrews 6:12

Patience comes when we learn to abide in God and trust Him no matter what circumstance we face. Patience undergirds and sustains faith until the answer comes or the end result is manifested. Patience is concentrated strength. We gain pearls of revelation and wisdom through hardship and difficulty, conflict and irritation as we turn to God and hunger for more of Him. We are unable to enter into revelation without the leading of the Spirit of God (See 1 Corinthians 2:6-8). The Bible says, "Call to Me, and I will answer you, and show you great and mighty things, which you do now know" (Jeremiah 33:3).

After you have meditated on the promises of God's Word, you will find they get down into your heart. They seem to maintain a calm assurance in your spirit till the answer comes. Patience encourages you to keep trusting God, rather than man. Patience is actually power and gives you the courage to resist the devil and his lies about God's Word at work in you or your circumstances. After you have learned to wait, patience knows that God never lies. God's Word always works. Neither does patience draw back in fear, but it empowers you to move forward in faith in God.

It is during the time of waiting where patience does her work in each of us. I have personally experienced lots of waiting. Waiting teaches us to be still and know God.

Never give up. Don't choose to quit. Trust God till the answer comes and it will. God's promises never fail. Continue to put the Word of God first in your life, and with patience you will receive the promises of God if you faint not. Keep the faith and trust God in the waiting. Patience is just as important as faith.

I don't believe most people are very patient. Most people have the "I want it now" mentality. Unfortunately, the last generation has produced a generation that is somewhat like that with the spirit of entitlement. I have never heard of such stories of adult children shafting their parents, stealing from them, and choosing not to be responsible while leaving the parents and step-parents holding debt they owe. It is happening in business and personal lives across the nation as well. *God have mercy on America.*

When a person does not want to be responsible, he will begin to justify and entertain reasoning. This is still a lie from the pit of hell and will produce unwanted consequences somewhere in the future. Wrong choices *always* leave a trail of unfortunate consequences. (Study Hebrews 10:32-39 for further study)

I don't believe success happens accidentally. Victorious living comes with a price. Winning in life comes through deliberate plans, purposes, and action. Probably the number one principle I have learned is everything is about attitude. Most of you have heard the phrase, "Your attitude determines your altitude." I don't know who said that first, but it is true.

Having a positive attitude does not mean you praise God *for* the bad things that happen, but your life is lived in an attitude of gratitude, praise, and worship in all things. We are to praise God *in* the midst of all things.

Purpose in your heart to know God and do the right thing when no one else is looking and you will be a success. God is with you. He delights in those who seek Him and want to obey His Word. Joseph in the Bible went from the pit to the palace and no matter where he was God was with him and caused him to prosper.

In the pit Joseph had to make a choice; in Potiphar's house he chose to flee sexual temptation, in the prison being falsely accused he shared his gifts (dreams and interpretation), and in the palace he shared his resources. The story ended with forgiveness and sustaining the people of nations, and our story only ends well with forgiveness and doing what God has put in our hearts to do with Him.

What is an opportunist? An opportunist is a person who exploits circumstances to gain immediate advantage rather than being guided by consistent principles or plans. Opportunism is the conscious policy and practice of taking selfish advantage of circumstances—with little regard for principles or consequences.

Rather than being like Joseph's brothers, why not be on the lookout for lost souls? Learn to invest in people and make a difference.

Any time you invest in people, you change their lives. Choose to do something and make a difference. Choose to be nice and give others hope! You can make a difference! Take the time to start being nice to people—one person at a time. Be a life changer on a daily basis.

At the end of the day, no one is going to take any material things with them at death. It will be only people that matter. Begin to live eternity-minded, choosing to help others along their journey even in the midst of your times of waiting. Learn to meet the needs of other people when it is in your power to do so.

Choose Life

"For to be carnally minded is death; but to be spiritually minded is life and peace" (Rom. 8:6).

You might find this to be a strange question, but I am going to ask it anyway. If you had the choice between life and death, which would you choose? You might think that the majority of people would obviously choose life, but I don't believe that is the case. Most people are blinded by sin and carnality and don't realize what they are doing in the natural.

It is not necessarily choosing to jump off the Empire State building, but rather learning to look at life a little differently with choices and consequences on a much broader scale.

The Bible reveals that being carnal-minded is being tangled in the world's system. To be worldly minded is death and to be spiritually minded produces life. When a person is first born again his spirit is alive in God and will produce tears and sadness when he or she chooses to go back into the world's way of doing things or old habits that go against God's Word.

God has placed a GPS system that I call "God's Positioning System" in each of us. It is God's warning system. God wants us to choose life in Him. I talked about this in my first book, *God's Priceless Treasure*.

Don't choose to get so unnecessarily entangled in the business of living that you miss God's best for you through living life in the Spirit of God. It is the most amazing way to live.

You can actually choose death by default. You can also choose death by not making a decision when you know you are in a situation and you stay in denial. Deal with the issue at hand.

In the story of Martha and Mary in the Bible, you can see how Martha got caught up in preparing a meal and missed a time with the Lord herself. You can read the account in Luke 10. Mary had set aside everything else just to sit in the Lord's presence. The seemingly important business of living overtook Martha's life, rather than allowing the Word to have priority.

Martha was consumed with fixing a meal. Did she not remember Jesus fed the multitudes? Did she think she had to help God out? Or, was she just so busy being busy that she forgot the best part? Sitting at the feet of Jesus! What about you? Do you feel overwhelmed with life? Do you feel overwhelmed with business, finance, health issues, relationships, or even life itself to the point of exhaustion? Do you find it hard to find balance in life?

You can actually get more done in less time when you commit your day to God and give him the first portion. You must choose to learn to rest in God and learn to trust Him, even in the most adverse circumstances. You can learn to rest in God through abiding in Him.

The Bible tells us, " Come to Me, all you who are weary and heavy-laden, and I will give you rest. Take My yoke upon you and learn from Me, for I am gentle and humble in heart, and you will find rest for your souls. For My yoke is easy and My burden is light" (Matthew 11:28-30).

> "Can two walk together, unless they are agreed?"
> (Amos 3:3).

When we get into agreement with God and with each other, we can learn to rest in Him. This is the place of abiding.

Abiding in Him

If you don't know God's Word, you won't know how to activate the power of God in your life. The enemy wants us as a nation to be blind and ignorant. As long as Satan can keep us distracted and ignorant of Truth, we will be a powerless nation.

As we confess God's Word we activate the power of God in our lives. When we have wrong thinking, we separate ourselves from God's provision. Learn to have right thinking by renewing your mind. You might be thinking, "What does renewing the mind mean?"

Start reading the Word and confessing the promises out of your mouth by saying them. When you get the Word of God from your head to your heart and back, you will begin to have right thinking. Wrong motives come out of the heart. Separate yourself from wrong thinking. Go back to the Father God like the prodigal son who came back and repented. The elder brother lived at home and had access to all but had evil and resentment in his heart toward his own brother. Both are clearly wrong. Anyone can get out of balance on either side!

As believers, we must have a heart of compassion for the lost. People are drawn to Jesus by the love of God the Father. I don't know many who have been drawn to God by a rod or stick. I do know of a few cases where God was drawing for years and then the young man or woman was so afraid of going to hell that he or she repented.

If a person continually makes wrong choices, because of God's great love, He will bring correction. A good father disciplines his own children. If you are a parent, you totally understand. Can you imagine hearing the sentence being pronounced, "You are confined to prison for a life term?" Or, what about this one, "You have a one year jail sentence." Would you go out the next day and do the same thing again that brought about the consequences of jail in the first place? Let's hope not. Repeating the same patterns of behavior that brought death will still bring death. It is purely insanity to keep doing the same thing and for you to expect a different result.

People sometimes don't want to be responsible. Responsibility is the ability to respond properly in every given situation with what you know. It is a choice we all must make!

On a regular basis, I hear of a huge majority of teens and some adult children who expect their parents to pay their bills and give them what they think they want without paying for it themselves. This is ignorance on the part of a parent to continue giving to an adult child, except when it is a need or crisis. They will never grow up and take ownership or responsibility for themselves and their own actions.

On another note, parents sometimes want their kids to have better than they had themselves. If a person doesn't work for something, he will not appreciate it. You must continually train your children with age appropriate consequences.

You can actually set your own children up for failure. It would be like buying your daughter's diamond for her engagement just because her fiancé didn't have the resources to buy what she thought she deserved or wanted. That is a marriage that is doomed to fail from the onset.

It never stops with just the ring. Then it is the cell phone bill, gas bill, and later a house because they can't afford where they want to live. It will always be something. Cords must be cut.

There is nothing wrong with helping your kids with a gift to get started, but it is clearly wrong to set them up for failure by giving them something too early that they can't even afford to maintain or take care of themselves. Oh, and let me continue with the next excuse you will find—it will be the grandkids. As a parent, you will begin to figure out ways to go against God's Word to pay for stuff and justify it for the grandkids. Or, worse yet, you will choose to override the parent's boundaries for your grandchildren. It is a trap of Satan. The enemy will always tempt you through reasoning, blaming someone else, or a circumstance to ensnare you.

There is nothing wrong with helping or even assisting in a time of tragedy, but sometimes we are playing God in the area of finance. Adult children must learn responsibility themselves. Otherwise, they will live a life always blaming others.

Blame Game

Adam blamed Eve for what happened in the garden. Most people like to blame someone else for what happened to them or what they did. This has been going on since the Garden of Eden. We must each learn to accept responsibility for our part of sin, repent and move forward.

Think for a minute, "What is my mind set on?" Spend some quiet time and ask the Lord to reveal it to you. Excuses, rationalization, or justification are all means to simply prepare to do it again. Repentance produces change. Repentance means to take on a new thought and go in a new direction. Repentance means you change the way you think. You begin to hate what God hates. The blood of Jesus brings cleansing but we must choose to go in a new direction.

When you are truly born again or saved, you will have a heart change. You won't have the same desires. The hole in your heart that can only be filled by God is moved from being empty and barren to being filled by the Holy Spirit through the new birth. You simply must choose. It is a process of growth along the journey of life—and we have all fallen short in some area!

I have women tell me that God will understand if they have sex outside of marriage. I often wonder what a person is thinking when they share with me they are a Christian but still think like the world. People don't realize God is protecting them through boundaries and principles He has set in His Word. People won't know what God says if they don't read the Bible!

I recently met with a woman who shared her story with me. A man who used to be in ministry was trying to seduce her to have sex outside of marriage and had the audacity to tell her it was a desire of the flesh and God would understand. After hearing stories like this one, time and time again, I have come to realize many are playing church and blinded by Satan.

There is a war between the flesh and the spirit of mankind. We must choose. Whatever you partake of actually brings growth in your life. Much like exercise, studying God's Word produces growth and change of direction. Whichever is stronger wins the battle. Is it your flesh or your life in God?

People blame others for their mistakes and wonder why the chastening of God does not stop. We have all fallen short of the glory of God. It is time to get serious with God and be the church. It will be found in the last prayer Jesus prayed. It is in unity.

Unity

Unity is about the power of people moving from "I" to "us." Instead of being caught up in "I" we must move to "us" to be successful. It takes team effort to have a successful business, family, or even ministry. It is the power of "us" that brings about multiplication.

Isaiah actually prophesied that to "us"—not unto "me" and not unto "you." It is in the power of unity as a body of believers in Christ that we find hope again as a nation.

Scripture: Unto us a child is born.

Jesus gave us a blueprint for the Kingdom of God. In His model prayer, He also said "Our Father," not "My Father"—can you see we were in His mind? The pronouns used in this passage are plural showing the power of unity and revealing it is essential for the body of Christ.

As we come *under* God's authority and pursue wisdom, we find understanding of Scripture. This is a great part of the "u" in unity. We move from "I" to "us" and we find understanding in unity. We can also move to say the "n" in unity is networking. We must learn to work the net. Not only the net for fish in the Bible, but also networking—bringing people together and connecting.

People get all bent out of shape when people spend money to go away to spend time together. Unfortunately, this even happens in the church. The body of believers will start to gossip and assume, saying things about who is going on trips to the point of moving into dangerous territory with God. God is all about connecting and it is vital to get away. Jesus did it as He took His disciples alone to pray many times throughout the New Testament.

God will go to extreme measures for just one soul. He may send you on an extravagant trip just so you will be His mouthpiece to a person who is in need of salvation or direction. Money is nothing more than a tool here on earth.

Don't get caught up in small stuff. Begin to pray to God on your own behalf first. Sit and listen to what He has to say to you. He is for you and not against you. He is for us as a nation—and not against us. Pray that America will turn back to God before it's too late.

Let me ask you a question. If you have a son or daughter, would you choose to cut their arm off with a chainsaw? Of course not! However, that is what the Body of Christ does unknowingly in the church and it happens in the marketplace. It is sad. I recently stood in line at a tradeshow and I heard the people in front of me making comments about another minister. The Holy Spirit spoke to my heart to be still and listen. Interestingly enough, my message I was to share later that afternoon was partly about the same topic. God still got His message across without me saying anything personal to these people I did not know. He had it positioned already in the message He had given me to bring.

God wants us to connect with others and build relationships so we have the right to speak into their lives as well. He wants us to get so close to Him that we can hear Him at the slightest whisper at the door of our hearts! Take time to build a stronger and more intimate relationship with God! When we live in God's ways, we do not grieve the Holy Spirit within. We need the Holy Spirit.

Destruction Within

Could it be that Satan doesn't have to do much to destroy America? Could it be that Christians and even family members do it themselves? Could it be that people destroy themselves and their families from within? Could it be that we don't have to worry so much about terrorists for we have our own within America?

In the Old Testament, murder and adultery were sin. In the New Testament, Jesus let us know clearly that gossip was the same as murder; as well as lust in the heart being the same as adultery to Him. Are you starting to see the problem with America?

Any wonder we hear small kids repeating what they've heard their parents say at the dining room table, when they *think* the little ones aren't listening. What is wrong with America? What is wrong with the church? I can tell you. It is the heart. There is still an area of darkness in any heart that does this!

If you find yourself being in someone's presence and immediately, after they depart, you are raising your eyebrows and gossiping or saying unkind things, *you* have a serious problem. It is a heart problem. In order to have a cleansed heart, you must choose to spend time in the presence of God and study the Bible. You and I must take time to have alone time with God but we must not forsake the assembling together with other believers.

We must learn to keep our mouths shut. Just because a thought comes to the mind does not mean it needs to be released through the lips. Sometimes God reveals things to us so we will pray. He shares secrets with people He can trust to pray for the Body of Christ! Prayer is the desperate cry of the heart of mankind that initiates the beginning of divine revelation to the heart and mind. It is the spirit of revelation that opens up our knowledge of God, and from that comes forth the release of His power from heaven. Spending time in prayer gives us access to all things pertaining to life, will shape the world around us, and will shape the world through us.

The Body of Christ

When we come together as the Body of Christ, we have it all. When we are apart, we are in need. No one has it altogether. Trust me. We are all a work in progress. If you think you've arrived to some place of superiority, I can assure you there is room for improvement.

Joseph went through extensive training as you can read about in Genesis. He went from the pit to the palace in a short period of time. He spent years in training for his family and nation.

Joseph's brothers were in serious trouble. They despised their own brother. They threw him in a pit and tried to destroy him. We have all done this, either knowingly or unknowingly, at some point in our lives.

I was at a Christian event listening to a brother in Christ who has his doctorate make an interesting statement. He said, "Why are there so many calling themselves Dr. now in the body of Christ?" to "everyone is a doctor now." When I heard this Doctor of ministry say that, I thought to myself, "Why on earth would he say that?" I realized at that moment there must be a place of darkness, even in his heart. If someone continues their education and earns their doctorate, would it not be proper to honor their work? I don't know about you, but I can just imagine how any of us can become a stench in the nostrils of Almighty God.

When we choose to open our mouth to sabotage someone else, it is clearly sin and reveals the condition of the heart. We can arrive at a place where we think we are all that and a bag of chips. We are nothing without God.

We are called to build up the Body of Christ and not tear each other down. We need each other! We can't sing a duet divided against each other. We sound like we are in a duel if we don't learn to sing at the right time and together in unison.

Duel

I just watched two cats on television in a duel. The music that was playing even sounded like a war about to start—awaiting the dramatic outcome. There was a moment of silence and then one of the cats knocked the other cat off the podium. This is life my friends.

Many of you have seen westerns and duels where two people are at war with each other—and in most cases, one ends up dead or wounded. Families watch from the windows and live in fear and panic. There are people today who are in despair, gazing out the windows to see devastation in the family, business, or own personal lives.

Many get shocked into reality when their hopes and dreams have been shattered either for themselves or someone they love. Others fear they are losing control. Some fear losing the battle against their own private demons, drug dependence, alcohol abuse, gambling, lying, cheating, anger, violence, sexual abuse, divorce, or even sickness.

Families have experienced tragedies, people have lost focus, and ended up having massive heart attacks from the stress and worry. Many feel they can't seem to get ahead and live from paycheck to paycheck. What would cause sinful traits to be evident from family to family? It is environmental? It is genetic? Is it family baggage? It is a curse? Just because something bad is happening does not necessarily mean someone is living in sin. Satan won't roll out the red carpet for those who choose to step out in obedience—don't ever forget that! Read about the life of Paul and how he experienced adversity.

Seasons change and so do the times. America is changing almost as fast as technology. What is going on? What is God revealing?

"Do not be deceived, God is not mocked; for whatever a man sows, that he will also reap" –Galatians 6:7.

"God is no respecter of persons" –Acts 10:34 KJV

You may take everything personally and get offended easily. You might have even made an inner vow or public one stating something like this, "No one will hurt me again." When you do that, you actually open the door to a spirit of rejection, anger, and violence. The devil sets you up to be upset. There is a battle between the flesh and the spirit—what the enemy may tempt you to do and what you know is right in God.

Some of you reading this book may be dealing with uncontrollable rage and anger. You may be thinking, "Why on earth am I reading this book on revival and turning back to God as a nation?" The answer is simple. God wants you to be free. He wants to revive you and give you a new heart. He desires the best for you and has a great plan for your life. (See Jeremiah 29:11). He desires that every person on the planet know Him, live in freedom, and share the good news of the gospel of Jesus Christ.

Instead of walking in God's plan, you may realize that you have become everything you said you wouldn't become. Your parents may have abused you and you made statements declaring you would not be like them. Instead, you are now abusing your own children.

"The word of the Lord came to me again, saying, "What do you mean when you use this proverb concerning the land of Israel, saying: 'The fathers have eaten sour grapes, and the children's teeth are set on edge'? As I live," says the Lord GOD, "you shall no longer use this proverb in Israel. Behold, all souls are Mine; the soul of the father as well as the soul of the son is Mine" (Ezek. 18:1–4). Turn and live!

True Freedom

God wants you to live in true freedom. John 8:31–36 reminds us that as we abide in Jesus Christ, we receive His freedom. Jesus has set us free from the penalty and the ongoing curse of sin. Through the shed blood of Jesus Christ, we have a new and better covenant with God the Father. Through Jesus' blood, He forgives us our sin and delivers us from our iniquity.

God has redeemed us from the curse being passed on. Redemption occurs when we understand that the root of our problems is in the spiritual realm. The chains of bondage are broken as we apply God's Word and power to our lives, and as we choose to walk in righteousness and obedience to God. Freedom then has the opportunity to become reality in life.

Jesus is the Living Word. God and His Word are one. Together they are to be the object of our affection. Together they are what we are to keep—His whole counsel. For example, John 14:15 says, "If ye love me, keep my commandments" (KJV). God's commandments are His Word—so if we love God, we will keep His commandments. Here is the result: "..and he that loveth me shall be loved of my Father, and I will love him, and will manifest myself to him."

If we are going to keep God as our first love, we have to keep His whole counsel as a pattern for daily behavior—and not just a few select verses. God's manifesting Himself because we love Him wholeheartedly and His commandments—is Him giving us His divine presence.

True freedom comes when we live out of God's whole counsel. If you are ignoring the direction the Word brings, then you are saying that you either know better than God or that something else is more significant to you than He is in life. You can make a change—put His Word back on top—and fall in love with Him all over again.

John 8:42 is a fundamental principle of salvation. The evidence of being a true child of God lies in one's attitude and love of Jesus. You will live in an attitude of faith and obedience. Will you choose to love Jesus and live a life of obedience, or be like the Israelites that circled in the desert for forty years?

> *"Jesus said to them, "If God were your Father, you would love me, for I came from God and now am here. I have not come on my own, but he sent me"*
> –John 8:42

Circling The Lawn

Several years ago, we had something interesting happen in our lawn. We've prayed for God to protect our home and land and set a hedge of protection about us. We thanked Him for His anointing and thank Him daily that the Holy Spirit reveals all hidden truth. (See John 14-16 for details). We thank God for His angels that bring protection.

While we were away, a vehicle full of teenagers drove up in our lawn and circled, tearing up the yard and damaging the sprinkler system. Our neighbor saw them doing it and phoned the police. The police came out and while they were standing in our neighbor's lawn talking about what happened, the vehicle of teens came back with another vehicle following behind to show them what they had done. Apparently, they were bragging about it.

Needless to say, the police took them in and charged them. We went to mediation and could tell who was family by their similar attitudes. I was shocked to hear one set of parents ask us why we didn't call them first. I didn't know the teens, so how could I have called the parents?

If you have teens that think it is okay to damage someone's property, they don't value property or have respect for people in general. Did they think it was funny to reimburse for damages? I think not. I wonder why parents who have bad attitudes don't have a clue why their children pick up the same behavior patterns.

Like the teens that circled the lawn, the Israelites did the same in the desert. America is circling as a nation. We can circle as well when we don't choose to submit to God's Word and time tested principles.

We can become the very thing we hate. The Bible tells us there are generational curses that are passed from one generation to the next. Thank God for the blood of Jesus that breaks the cycle in our lives from passing to our children.

How many of you have faced things in your own life and now your children are facing the same? You can better understand what Paul wrote, *"For what I am doing, I do not understand. For what I will to do, that I do not practice; but what I hate, that I do."* – Romans 7:15

The first thing you must do is be born again by the blood of Jesus Christ. The Bible says, *"Do not marvel that I said to you, "You must be born again."* –John 3:7

I am not talking about turning over a new leaf or just deciding to be a better person. The Lord changes us from the inside out. When we are born again, Jesus gives us a chance to start all over again. It is not about religion, it's about a personal relationship with Jesus. The Holy Spirit resides within us. We come to God through Jesus Christ. The name of Jesus is above every sickness and disease. The name of Jesus is above drugs, alcohol, hatred and every thing the enemy uses to torment us. God forgives our sin and He sets us free.

He desires that we turn to Him and become a nation whose God is the Lord. When we turn, we will find hope again. Honor and respect will be evident across the land. Remember how God answered our prayer about our home and land. He will do the same for us as a nation when we turn back to Him united in prayer, loving our neighbors and honoring God above all else.

When we turn back to God and fully understand the believer's authority in Christ, we will see people healed, blind eyes opened, and begin to pray in power without one iota of doubt. We will say "No problem" to cancer, missing limbs, and other deficits and deformities. When we learn to see with our spiritual eyes, we will see more clearly than with our natural eyes and won't care if people think we are religious fanatics. We become God-pleasers and live supernaturally in our everyday life. Would you rather live in power or circle like the Israelites for forty more years?

Honor and Respect

Where did the honor and respect go? When both are lost, language changes. This is a huge contributing problem in homes across our land. It is the same in business. An employee comes to work and takes on more responsibility. It's not long before he or she thinks they know more than the one who started the business in the first place. Next, they have the audacity of wanting what you have without paying for it or even being responsible.

I firmly believe this is why God has allowed the financial crisis across the nations. God did not cause it—the nations have asked God to leave. Poor choices in government, right on down to all forms of leadership that have made wrong choices have resulted in devastating consequences. When we don't deal with issues and problems when they are small, we have larger problems on the horizon.

Husbands and wives do stupid things as well. I hear it all the time. People are hurting. Men are devastated because they have lost their jobs and sources of income. Women are in fear because of lack of security and the nations are in trouble. What is the answer?

The Great "I AM" is the answer. We must move to interceding in faith for the Body of Christ to being real, genuine and free from hypocrisy or pretense in order to move out to a world that is hurting and lost without Jesus. We must choose to embrace the world without judgment, but with grace and the love of God. While God loves us unconditionally, He also loves us too much to leave us the same way we are at present. He sends divine correction because He loves us.

We must choose to live a life of intercession. This is the "i" in unity. God will put something on your heart that is pressing to move you to prayer.

We must also learn to trust God and think outside the four walls of the church. That is the "t" in unity. We come to the understanding that God is for us and not against us, that He has a Kingdom plan where we have a purpose with Him in bringing it to fruition. We are His hands and feet in the earth. He may put someone on your heart and nudge you to send a particular message in a text that brings encouragement or even saves a life. It may be a simple phone call or a note of thanks. Whatever God puts in your heart to do, no matter how small you may *think* it is, simply do it and don't wait any longer. Learn to obey God immediately.

We move to see the bigger vision of God and we begin to put away childish ways and begin to walk in dominion or authority as we move forward growing into full stature in Christ. Finally, we move to the 'y" in unity. It is YOU! Yes, God has a specific purpose and plan for your life. (Read Jeremiah 29:11)

God called you with a divine purpose. You are part of the Body of Christ and are vitally important. Satan will try to keep you in drama (devil racing after my assignment) to keep you out of God's amazing plan. (You can read more about this in my book: *GOD'S PRICELESS TREASURE—How To Overcome Challenges, Be Transformed and Know Your Purpose*)

It's all about advancing the Kingdom of God and building up the body of Christ. You are part of that plan. It's about not being afraid of man, not being afraid to confront religious strongholds, doctrinal divisions and the like. It's also about not being afraid to confront unresolved issues or offenses between believers so you can move forward with answered prayer. It's about restoration and reconciliation. If we don't move forward when God instructs us, we will certainly move with divine discipline.

We must stand up in America and return to God in prayer and repentance.

Divine Discipline

Hebrews 12:5-6 tells us that when the Lord disciplines us He is acting out of His love. Parents discipline their children to teach them to obey. There must also be age appropriate consequences. Discipline is not a form of payment for wrong actions. Discipline is a method of correction. The purpose in discipline by our heavenly Father is to bring us back into His divine plan to not suffer future consequences. There are always consequences to poor choices. God disciplines us to move us away from areas where we don't need to go. God sees the big picture. He knows the end from the beginning.

He disciplines us to prevent us from suffering or harming others. As a parent, you are not demonstrating love if you fail to discipline (see Proverbs 13:24). You are actually setting your kids up for failure. You are setting them up to reap a harvest of disastrous consequences. (See Proverbs 19:18)

A parent who loves their children will apply discipline to prevent further rebellion. This brings about health and wholeness. Some parents make the mistake of disciplining out of anger, rather than love. This breaks the spirit of the child.

> *"There is no fear in love. But perfect love drives out fear, because fear has to do with punishment. The one who fears is not made perfect in love"* (1 John 4:18 NIV).

It is not God's motive to make a child fear punishment. The unconditional love of God and His discipline go hand-in-hand. They are not contradictory. When we choose to respond to His correction, He is already at work to help us with the circumstances and He turns all things out for our good. It may be hard to believe at first, but eventually you will see the good.

I have recently mentored a woman in another state who made some poor choices after her husband made a fatal mistake, had an affair and abandoned the family. The crisis brought her to a place of knowing she needed God and she and the kids were actually born again.

The couple later divorced and the children chose to live with the dad. She stopped going to church and starting spending more time with people who did not have a relationship with God. She began to act the way she did before she received Jesus. She started out great at first, renewing her mind and engaging in Bible studies, but chose to slowly pull away after her move. This is how subtle Satan is in his plan of demise.

When you go against God and make wrong choices, He will begin to correct you through divine discipline. It may be painful a first, but will bring about good in the end. In the midst of adverse circumstances, we must encourage ourselves in the Lord and inquire of Him.

America has separated herself from God and the consequences are manifesting on every turn. When we choose to sin willfully and rebel against God, He continues to love and forgive us. However, there are natural consequences to willful rebellion, one of which is broken fellowship with God, where we may experience an inability to pray.

Discipline is a reminder that God loves us (Hebrews 12:6). Discipline is never pleasant but leads to deliverance. You can see this principle operating in the children of Israel as they wandered in the wilderness.

Have you ever been on a jet that was starting to land but instead, all of a sudden, you realize you are circling? This is a holding pattern till other aircraft have cleared the runway or either there is a storm or some other reason for the waiting. Sometimes God puts us in a holding pattern till we choose to follow God, or till someone else gets into divine alignment. Sometimes he is waiting on others near us. I've been on numerous flights that were just about to land and all of a sudden, the aircraft was instructed to circle in a holding pattern. Life can seem that way at times as well.

You may feel benched like a new player on a baseball team, waiting for your turn. You may be thrown out of a game due to a penalty. You may be on the sidelines of what God is doing until you choose to get on with God's program. God may be waiting on someone close to you to obey the last instruction. Whatever the case, there is a reason.

It may be as simple as gossip, anger, rage or failing to forgive someone who harmed you, to calling someone and saying you are sorry for the things you've said about them. It is the small foxes that destroy the vines.

> *"Catch for us the foxes, the little foxes that ruin the vineyards, our vineyards that are in bloom."*
> —Solomon 2:15 NIV

The little things can throw anyone off course. Sometimes we are thrown off course from what someone else has done. God is with you even when you feel like you are "going through hell" due to circumstances.

I was with a woman a few days ago and she was sharing how she had to take stomach medicine when she was home, but when she was away on a trip she was fine and didn't even have the pain. The situation she was in was causing disruption to her soul and producing anxiety. Pain is a clue something is out of order. It is our body's warning system.

When we walk through discipline, we must remember God is with us. He wants us to succeed in life. He wants us to obey Him so we can step into His divine plan for us. God also gives us emotions to warn us of something being wrong. We must stay in-tune with God and live out of His Word to know which way to turn in any given situation. Sometimes, life can seem to go off course. Have you ever felt that way?

You may have left your spouse and abandoned your children, but God still loves you. He hates your sin, but He loves you. He is longsuffering and is waiting for you to return to Him and receive His forgiveness. The price has already been paid. You may have abandoned your relationship with Jesus and be living outside of God's plan for your life. You may be sleeping with your significant other outside of marriage and justifying it in your mind. It is sin, no matter how you look at it.

You may have shafted those that raised you up from a child and think you are getting away with it, but God sees all. Nothing escapes His all seeing eye. You will reap a harvest of consequences from wrong choices. Joseph's brothers thought they had gotten away with their plot of demise but many years later found out they hadn't and were in need of the very brother they had sought to kill.

People make wrong choices due to fear and sometimes due to pure rebellion. Sometimes, people *think* they are born again but have had *no heart change.* If you can still sin and think it is okay, you most likely have thought about it in your mind but never made a choice to receive God's forgiveness in your heart. A person who has truly been born again does not *want* to sin. He or she does not want to displease our heavenly Father.

You may be caught in the trap of sin and are trying to justify what you did through reasoning but God sees the sin. It is a trap from the pit of hell to ensnare and enslave you. It will produce bondage and destruction.

God won't leave a child of His on the sidelines forever. He will never leave you alone. You *may reject* Him through your own free will. However, God does not desire that any should perish and is moved with compassion for the lost.

God will pull you back to deliver you. Just like the aircrafts that are commanded to go into a holding pattern, our commander and chief will send us into a holding pattern to protect us from harm and for our deliverance. Could it be that America is circling? Could it be that America is in a holding pattern?

We were in a restaurant some time ago in Florida while I was ministering at a Christian tradeshow and we could not enjoy our meal for the noise and crowds that were eating and joking, enjoying their food and drinks. The majority of people were drinking alcohol and the more they had, the louder their voices rose in volume. I was sitting there thinking to myself about all the people who are missing out on a relationship with God doing the same thing in life spiritually.

My heart was breaking for the lost. What if the Lord had called us home at that moment? What would the people in the restaurant think that were not born-again? Would they panic when people are suddenly missing? Would they even notice? Of course they would. That is what will happen when Jesus calls us home. The Left Behind movie and book provide a fresh revelation of what that day will be like.

What if you are on a plane and the captain is a born-again Christian and the rapture takes place and you are not saved? You might not notice people missing in a loud restaurant, but I can assure you that you will notice if the captain of a plane disappears when Jesus calls us home.

As I thought about the people in the restaurant drinking and being so loud and disruptive, my heart was moved with compassion for the lost in the place. That is the love of God that is being shed abroad in our own hearts when we feel what He is allowing us to feel.

I watched the servers dealing with the people and the way they were dealing with all the noise. I couldn't help but notice one man that had a twitch as he walked from the back to the tables. I thought to myself, "No wonder! Could it be he had worked in the place so long with all the noise that he had developed a nervous twitch?" God help us all.

I was at peace in my heart but was certainly glad when the meal was over. None of us enjoyed that meal. The food was wonderful, but the atmosphere was horrible. Thank God for the fresh outdoors as we walked out in peace.

You must remember a few things when going through hard times or what may be divine discipline. Three things of utmost importance: God is with you, even during discipline. God never gives up on you. Lastly, discipline is your deliverance. America is about to go through divine discipline.

There are nations that have millions of gods of idolatry. Two in America are technology and sex. There is nothing wrong with technology as God gave people wisdom to create. Satan has no creative power. He simply thwarts purposes to allure people into sin. Sex in marriage is godly and for our pleasure. Sex outside of marriage is sin. Abuse and sex trafficking are sin.

Since America has had prayer taken out of schools, we have seen a drastic change—one of violence. Our nation chose to ask God to leave. What on earth is wrong with America? What about the Ten Commandments? Why are people so bent on trying to rise above God and show their ignorance? It is proof of ignorance and hardened hearts. We are seeing natural consequences to mankind's poor choices.

America is in a crisis whether most want to believe it or not. Having a nice home, cars, and bank accounts will not save you from going through discipline to a nation when it comes. If you have not read the books: *The Harbinger* and *The Four Blood Moons;* now will be a perfect time to read them both. I highly recommend the books.

Our nation must turn back to God to receive forgiveness and for God to heal our land.

Forgiveness

One of the greatest errors in the church has been to mix Old Testament requirements with New Covenant truth. God gave His Only Begotten Son that we might live free through the gift of righteousness, Jesus, knowing we are 100% accepted by God because of His Son and the finished work on the Cross at Calvary.

Our standing with God is not based on tradition, doctrine, rituals, or on performance in any capacity. People who focus on obedience or outward holiness miss the point that we're already perfect in our spirit and through trusting God we live that out in our daily life. Holiness is not a standard we live up to. It is a fruit of righteousness. Sin has already been judged in Jesus so we can be free from it. God sees us through His Son.

Our part is to grow up and mature in Him. We do this through renewing our minds and knowing His Word. Once you study the Word for yourself, you receive knowledge and understanding. It is a process and it moves you to a place of responsibility. We are all on a journey with God—and all at difference places. We learn to be patient with ourselves and help others. We also learn to receive instruction from people that have greater wisdom. Ultimately, our wisdom comes from God.

Responsibility is your ability to respond to what you know. We must choose to be responsible and learn to forgive. I have already mentioned the findings in Luke 17 earlier in this book that will give you great incentive for obeying God. Remember the facts about the sycamine tree.

The Midnight Hour

When you know you are forgiven, your life radically changes. You realize where you might have been had it not been for the mercy and grace of God. You are able to see clearly as you have your focus on Jesus.

Choose to forgive, mature in Christ, and expect God to intervene! Pray for those you have forgiven. You won't be able to dislike people for whom you pray. God will open your eyes to see the why in any given situation—if you ask Him in prayer.

Instead of being prejudiced by the past, we must deliberately exercise our faith in the promise of God for this nation and relationships. Don't allow the mistakes of others to predispose you to the same attitude toward them rather than employing our greatest tool—the expectation of faith—to lift them up. Paul prayed that the church of Ephesus would have a revelation of the hope of God's calling and of the exceeding greatness of His power toward those who believe (Ephesians 1:18-19). When you choose to pray in faith and believe your prayers are going to bring results, you elevate your expectation. Expect God to move on behalf of your prayers for this nation.

America needs to receive forgiveness and understand her God-given destiny. Every child in America has a right to live. What makes a person think they can destroy another? It is a person who has never understood the Kingdom of God through childlike faith in Him.

Through the Eyes of a Child

"Let the little children come to me, and do not hinder them, for the Kingdom of God belongs to such as these" (Mark 10:14).

Do you trust the Father? The art of innocence seems to be lost to most in our generation and it's relatively easy to see why. Fathers have abandoned their children and families; childhood years have been stolen away through poor adult choices and problems. Children have to become adults long before their time. Children who are abandoned have a sense of loneliness and rejection like no other. Children have learned how to survive the calamity of divorce and abandonment.

Childhood has a sense of innocence and vulnerability that is taken away early through the trauma of abandonment and absentee fathers. Have you ever wondered why the Bible says the Kingdom of God belongs to the childlike? That is because children know how to trust with total abandon and joy, even when they don't have the capacity for understanding.

Think with for a minute about a typical day in the life of a child. The door opens, the sun rises and either Mommy or Daddy says, "It's time to get up." The child does not normally worry much about what he or she will eat, or about clothing to wear. Children normally live in a home of some type and do not wonder if the home will ever be taken away. A child assumes that everything that belongs to Mommy and Daddy is okay and is his or hers as well. The heart of a child has trust in their parents like no other, and in most cases it comes without hesitation.

Even when the heart of a child does not want to obey rules in the home, the child realizes his or her dependency on them for survival and success. They don't really imagine life any other way. There is a certain comfort level in this childlike trust and dependence on the parents.

> *"Whoever then humbles himself as this child, he is the greatest in the Kingdom of heaven"* (Matthew 18:4).

When a person is born again and becomes a follower of Christ, he or she who is able to come to Jesus through the heart of a child will experience an abundance of peace, love, and joy in life. I find that most do not come to the Lord in this manner. Either they have been hurt by life, shafted by someone they never expected, lost respect for people that were supposed to protect them or provide for them, and have lost a certain level of hope and trust in mankind.

When a person has been hurt in this manner, he or she will go into what I call "survival mode" and stop trusting; and fully commit to providing and protecting themselves on their own. When a person comes to Jesus that does not trust, he or she will receive forgiveness but not have full understanding of the provision and protection we have in God through Jesus.

A person may know Jesus but live in the world's system, not realizing there is a better way. It is the Kingdom of God. To know the abundant life in Christ, you must let go of your control. You must choose to stop protecting yourself and recognize Christ is your defense. You must learn to realize God is your provider and begin to put your trust in Him, rather than in the arm of your flesh.

How do we get back on the path of innocence and trust in God through the eyes of a child? We turn to God with a heart that desires to please our Father God. It may seem a little awkward and frightening at first. It begins when you take a step of faith, even if you feel fear, and choose to let down your guard and learn to trust God for provision.

It is also being willing to receive from whomever or however God provides. This takes humility as well. Some people are big givers and at some point in life have to learn to receive as well.

This doesn't mean you don't work or do your part in maturing. The Bible is clear about not being slothful. You and I must continually trust God in every area of life and step out in immediate obedience.

God, the most loving heavenly Father has made provision for you and I every day—provision in grace and mercy. God has already provided all you and I will ever need for life—our part is to learn how to receive.

Hearing that might sound odd to you because many often demand that God lay out His plan and provision in sight *before* trusting Him. After our experience of God's divine intervention at Mercy Hospital from February 24th through March 20th of 2012, I can assure you I know the sweet childlike trust we can experience in God, if we choose to step into faith and have the heart of a child to *simply believe God at His Word*.

You can read the entire account in my book: *A Leap f Faith (25 Days at the Mercy Seat)*. It is an amazing story of how God goes to extreme measures to get our attention and the fact that He is divinely at work in the details of our lives, even if we are unaware.

You might be saying, "I would feel better *if* I could see provision or a glimmer of hope." I understand that thought pattern—and most do as well. It is one thing to actually know the truth, but it is yet quite another to actually believe it wholeheartedly. There is a sweet rest available to the believer in Christ that surpasses all human understanding. Once we come to the place of understanding the truth that God provides for us, we no longer need to see proof to believe it is true.

I don't have a problem trusting God. I do know that people are not always trustworthy. This is why it is vital that we learn to listen to the Holy Spirit and follow His leading at all times.

I must tell you something else very important. God is intimately involved in your life and it will amaze you if you will ask Him to open your spiritual eyes to see. I know because I live it. There is a sweet calm that comes over you when you live by faith and trust in

God. I remember what happened after hearing the news about Dan from the cardiologist, "He has about one week to live without surgery." God had me notice a Stop sign outside the hospital on the corner of Randolph Road and Vail Avenue that had a sticker underneath the STOP on the sign so it read: STOP worrying.

That is totally God. This will increase your faith to believe for yourself. When you begin to recognize the small things that God is doing in your life and the life of those you love, you will begin to stay amazed at the fact that the God of the Universe not only loves you, yet is also actively involved in each ordinary day. He delights in doing extraordinary things through ordinary people. The powerful testimony in my book: A LEAP OF FAITH will open your eyes to new levels of understanding in faith. There is a great deal of rest when you have faith in God.

Most adults do not want to believe like a child. The flesh will always resist the life in faith. This is simple because believing requires us to lay down our control. It also requires us to lay down taking credit for our own victory. Victory is in Jesus.

What we do with God is all the work of God and the power of the Holy Spirit. It is a supernatural work. It is all to the glory of God.

He searches to and fro to find someone to stand in the gap through prayer and obedience to His instructions.

God requires your surrender to His Will and His ways through continual obedience, and a faith that compels you to keep your heart intensely focused on Jesus. You actually have a heart after God, a heart that is enlarged and filled with Jesus, and your focus is entirely upon Him. You live eternity minded at all times.

When they looked up, they saw no one except Jesus.
—Matthew 17:8, NIV

When you believe in Jesus and learn to abide in Him, this opens the door for His life to manifest through you. That is the beautiful work of God. You must learn to look upward toward God, keep your focus on Him, and off your circumstances and others.

When we learn to live in Christ and obey Him, He will manifest Himself to us. Most of Jesus' final discourse to His disciples consists not of commandments they were to obey, but of promises He would fulfill on their behalf. John 14:15-26 is the heart of His message of comfort—that after His departure—the Holy Spirit would come in His place. Jesus died and rose again. He sent the Holy Spirit to reside within us, and Jesus is coming back again.

Much like the disciples looked up and saw no one but Jesus, we have to see God in everything. I love how God works, don't you? He is the Master Teacher. I believe it is the heart of the Father God to structure life in such a way that we may truly become wise only by choosing to live as children in total abandon and trust in Him.

Whatever God tells you to do He has already made provision. This brings great assurance and a peace that calms the soul. This moves us to childlike faith and trust in God because we believe Him.

You must resolve to have endurance. You and I actually gain strength for each day as we keep our focus on Jesus—as a child looks to a father. God desires that we love Him in that same way. He desires that we learn to walk with God, imitate His Son Jesus, and live with eternity in mind. He wants the best for us and for us to look to Him like Jesus always did in childlike faith, expecting God to intervene on our behalf.

Pray: "Lord, help me to have childlike faith to believe you at your Word. Help me to see through your eyes and to have all my trust in you, Lord."

Jesus didn't tell the apostles to remain like children—He told them to become childlike! Children know where to turn when life is beyond their control, they ask questions, and children are not controlled by race and socio-economics—they are inclusive. The heart of a child is moved to tears in response to pain and brokenness, they are pretty simple and don't usually hide their emotions—they tell the truth, even if you don't want to hear it.

We must learn to take a leap of faith and learn to trust God totally in childlike faith!

Not a Walk in the Park

Our walk with God is not exactly a walk in the park. There will be trouble because we live in the world. Our sacrifice is that we stop living according to our old fleshly ways. It would be like walking in the sand and turning around to pick up old skin that has fallen off your heels as you walk in hot sand. No one who is in their right mind would go back and pick it up. But that is what many Christians do in life.

We can choose to turn anything around for God by living eternity minded. You can choose to take a phone call that is a wrong number and turn it around in God. I received a phone call asking for FURNITURE NOW. My business number used to be a company that sold furniture and lighting. The man that called from New York asked me if I was Furniture Now. I said, "No" and then he asked if I sold lighting. I thought to myself, "I don't sell lighting, but I can point you to the light—His name is Jesus." We can take time to talk with people and connect for a moment. Are you starting to see how you can respond to life through an eternal view? God opens doors for us to walk through and point others to him, even sometimes with a sense of humor.

Start obeying the Word today. Choose to come to the Lord each morning, present yourself, and make a decision to do what God's Word says. Make a determination. You will no longer be conformed to the world as the pressure rises, but you will become more like Christ.

The real battle is all in the mind anyway. You make a decision in your mind and your body will follow. You can be transformed into the image of Jesus. It starts on the inside and later shows on the outside.

Your struggle may be deciding whether or not you are going to have an affair with that person you are secretly attracted to while another person's struggle is gossip. You may be the one that is tempted to lie to save yourself and throw someone else under the bus. No matter what the case, you must choose.

This is where the rubber meets the road. You choose rigorous discipline by renewing your mind in the Word of God, much like you would choose to exercise on a daily basis. You must choose to replace the void in your life with the Word of God. Get up, get out of bed, shake off the lethargy, get dressed in whatever suit of clothing and get out in the world to share the message of hope and make right choices that line up with God's Word! We learn to live out of God's Word like wearing a new suit of clothing—dressed in His love and truth.

What Kind of Suit Are You Wearing?

Getting the Word of God from your mind to your heart is like putting on a new suit. On any given day we are enjoying the benefit from someone else's glory, and the great majority of the time we are totally unaware. We don't even think about it. For example, in order to wear a suit with a skirt or pants, you will need a zipper. Someone invented the zipper and we use it for our benefit. This changed the world of fashion forever. The zipper serves as closure and forms a protective barrier.

I was also reading about birds and realized the zipper functions in a similar manner as a bird's feather functions. Did you know that God designed the individual strands of the feather to interlock tightly to form a waterproof barrier for the bird? I have never seen a bird on a limb having a nervous breakdown. If God cares that much for the birds of the air, how much more does He care for us?

Whenever you buy a book you are purchasing someone else's finished work. Lots of seemingly endless hours are spent throughout the night, writing, editing and rewriting. That book represents a step of obedience to write what God has put in their heart. The book is a product of someone's precious time, effort, energy, and passion. A finished book is the result of an author's obedience and can be a tool to encourage others.

Will your life ever be on display for others to read? Do you know who you are in Christ? The ignorance of identity and purpose tends to lead people astray and pervades every society and culture across the globe.

When a person obeys God and the calling on their life to write, they are pouring their heart out to others in hopes of bringing life and wholeness to help someone else. Testimonies and miracles turn into books of encouragement that will lead many to pick up the Bible for themselves—some for the first time. The Holy Spirit uses whatever He chooses to lead people to Jesus.

Jesus used testimonies of encouragement, hope found in Him—the Living Word—to bring each person to encounter with Him. When we are willing to share what God has done in our lives personally, others take notice. They realize there is hope for them. There is hope for America—if she will turn back to God.

God can use whatever He desires to lead someone to Him. It is a religious spirit to think God can't use a book someone has written to encourage others. Don't be like a Pharisee and have a critical spirit. If God can use a donkey—He can use anybody and anything. Don't put God in a box.

God may have placed a dream in your heart to partner with a ministry, start a new business, or even open a bakery that has Christian materials for people to read. Whatever God puts in your heart to do, He has equipped and empowered you to do with Him.

God puts gifts and talents in each of us to be used for His glory. When you don't choose to follow after God, the enemy can use you to lead people astray. One of the greatest expressions of the value, dignity, worth, and position of mankind in the earth was a humble shepherd-king from the hills of Judah in ancient Israel. The Bible tells us David was a man after God's own heart (see 1 Samuel 13:14; Acts 13:22). This simply means his heart and mind were in tune with God. He was sensitive to divine revelation because of his intimate relationship with God.

As individuals, we must choose to turn back to God in intimacy. We must choose to stand up for Christ in all we say and do. We must choose to pray and ask God to revive us again, as individuals and as a nation.

Requirements for Revival

Many Christians are praying for spiritual awakening and revival to sweep across the nations. What does it take to experience revival? How does God interrupt your day to spur your heart toward Him?

Spiritual revivals are only produced by the Holy Spirit of God and not by the hands of man. Despite our well-planned services and hours of studying, it is the Holy Spirit that sparks revival. Despite the extreme advances in technology and media, revival is not a phrase or prayer that says, "The show must go on" to "lights, camera, and action."

Man made programs do not necessarily generate or produce revival. Revival is a work of the Holy Spirit in the heart of mankind. They are the product of the sovereign work of God. God will move in response to just one man or woman who cries out to Him in sincerity.

This book is a product of a deep heartfelt cry God placed in my heart for America to turn back to Him. From the warnings He has shown me to the news that lines up with the Book of Revelation, we can see we are in a world of change and need of repentance and revival.

The world has yet to see what God will do through one man or one woman who is wholly consecrated to Him. Ask yourself the question, "Do I really want revival?" "Am I willing to avoid compromise in every area?" Whenever we compromise we come between God and His promise to us.

God looks at our heart to see us. He does not view as man does. He sees the motive and intent of every heart.

We know that the love of money—greed, and sex outside the boundaries of marriage will destroy any nation, any family, and any person. Lying and compromise, covering up sin, covering grades to promote your favorite team in sports, or whatever it may be that has brought about compromise in your life, will destroy you.

It is time to stop playing church. We must move from *having* church to *being* the church. We have come to a massive contest between good and evil. It's about rising up and being the church of Jesus Christ and loving people right where they are in life—helping them come out of the shadows of their past. Everyone has a past and there are no perfect people.

It's time we stand up and learn to operate in the gifts of the Spirit of God. The gifts of the Spirit are the weapons God gives us to fight and win our battles. Never underestimate their strength, power, and usefulness. Spiritual gifts are given to equip each of us for God's service. It is much like being trained in military with boots on the ground. We move into action through the power of Christ.

Gifts show up when we confront sin and face the people. (See Luke 8:26-39) It doesn't matter if you show up at church dressed to the nines or dressed in jeans, tennis shoes and a t-shirt. It's all about the heart—not the outward appearance of man. It doesn't matter what you have attained in life, if you've got a bigger business, larger church, or *think* you have arrived at some special place in life. The most special place we can be is at the feet of Jesus, worshiping Him, and leading others to know Him. Extreme worship exposes religion in everyone. It is time we move into worship in Spirit and truth.

Jesus is coming soon! We must be about the Father's business—souls and advancing His kingdom. God gives us wisdom in His Word. He tells us if we will humble ourselves and pray, and seek His face and turn from wicked ways, He will hear from heaven and extend His hand of mercy and grace.

Will America turn? Dark nights can be illuminated by one small candle. Will you turn the light on for Jesus in your home, in your neighborhood and business? Will you choose to be a light in the darkness?

The Spirit of God has moved in times past in incredible ways. He responds to the desperate cries of God's people to His heart. It's not about having another conference *about* prayer, but rather beginning to pray on a regular basis for churches and in the marketplace. It is time for the leaders to arise and take their rightful places.

When we come together and pray as a family, as a body of believers, a business or church team, we experience the joy of transformation in the presence of Jesus Christ with other believers of the same heart—a heart after God!

The Answer: God's Conditions

"And (if) My people, who are called by My name humble themselves and pray and seek My face and turn from their wicked ways, then I will hear from heaven, will forgive their sin and will heal their land" (2 Chronicles 7:14).

Let's ask the following questions: Whose 'people' is God speaking to? How are these people described? What are God's four conditions? What are God's three promises?

The context of this scripture is the just completed Temple that was built by Solomon in direct response to God's Word to his father, King David. Solomon prays on behalf of the nation, crying out to God to be merciful to them during future trials as they pray with a contrite heart toward the city and Temple of God in His name. God appears to Solomon in the quiet of the night and gives him the conditions for spiritual healing of a nation:

God's conditions are limited to His people, the Israelites in the Old Testament and through His Son, and Christians right up till today. God is telling us as believers in Him to humble ourselves and pray for healing for the nation. If we fail, healing will not come. What does humility look like in the natural?

Prayer without humility is futile and a waste of time. God is moved by a sincere heart cry from His people. Only when we recognize our need of God and our helplessness without Him are we truly humble. Humility is actually a posture of the heart. Humility is represented in people who are totally committed to God with the

The Answer: God's Conditions

understanding that without God, we are nothing. It is an attitude and posture of the heart.

As a nation and a people, we can choose to humble ourselves under the Mighty Hand of God. We can make the choice to be kind, compassionate, and live a life of giving sacrificially, while standing up on God's Word.

No one can make you humble. However, they can humiliate you both privately and publicly. Humiliation produces anger and resentment, not humility. We humble ourselves *when* we choose to obey God and His Word no matter what the outcome. Jesus humbled Himself as He obeyed His Father and gave His life up for us (Philippians 2:8).

Humility is when we are convinced of our helplessness and God's resurrection power. Pride is what keeps anyone from humility. Pride is an attitude of the heart and a personal belief that a person thinks they don't need God and that they can do whatever they want without Him.

You might be familiar with hearing someone say, "I will do it my way. It is my business and my money. It's my life, my way, or the highway." These are all significant warnings of pride at work in the heart.

We wouldn't even be able to wake up in the mornings if we didn't have the breath of God filling our lungs. He is our sustainer and a very present help in time of trouble. It is He who created us and gives us life. He is the one who gives us strength to make it through each day. We need God.

We must learn that temporary setbacks are not permanent failures. In the midst of extreme adversity, we must make corrective actions and step back for a minute to take a closer look at life. America is in such a place right now. Our nation has created laws that make sin legal. If we don't take corrective actions, we will fail.

In the midst of doing a second turnaround edit on this book, my husband had the football game on between Seattle and Green Bay. At half time, it looked like Green Bay had already won the game. At the final hour, down at the wire, Seattle came back with an amazing victory. This can happen for America—if she will turn.

We can see as the whole world is looking at what is happening in the Middle East, the Bible is unfolding before our eyes. It all began and will all end in the Middle East. Jesus is coming back no matter whether we believe it or not in this life.

We are being trained to rule and reign with Him in the Kingdom of God. What a glorious time that will be. While we are still here, we are called to occupy till He comes. We are to be about the Father's business. We are called to stand up for Jesus Christ.

In Egypt, multitudes of Christians stood up in the streets against terrorism. People on a flight on September 11, 2001 chose to stand up and stopped another attack on another place. They lost their lives but ultimately stopped that planned attack.

If America doesn't choose to stand up on God's Word like Franklin Graham spoke out about the recent news of the allowance of chanting at Duke, then we are fast approaching destruction. When we stand up we can make a difference. Freedom of religion means just that. When America chose to open gates and borders and allowed people to come in without proper papers, it was a vital mistake.

We all know this nation didn't really turn back to God on 9/11 but merely experienced about a three-week cry due to pain. It wasn't really about repentance. True repentance is choosing to turn back to God that produces a lasting heart change, and a turning from sin with experiencing the mercy of God.

Every person is in need of God's mercy. We all need divine intervention from God. We are nothing without Him. As a nation, America must realize her total depravity and need of God. We need to cry out with a deep heartfelt cry as a nation for God to bring revival to every heart across this land.

It is a personal choice to seek God on a daily basis, and to live a life of prayer. We must humble ourselves and seek God's face like never before, both personally and corporately as individuals in need of God.

Seek My Face and Turn From Their Wicked Ways

Are we seeking God or His blessings? Are we seeking to cover and do whatever we want without thinking about the eternal consequences? Are we a nation that is alive or experiencing death?

The nation has become occupied with vampires, mediums, monsters, *walking dead,* and occult movies and books that seem to dominate the media. God is greater than all. We must rise up as Christians, dead in our sin but alive in Him, to walk out the divine call across this nation. We are called to share the Truth about Jesus Christ.

People are seeking whatever and wherever because they are desperate and deceived. Jesus is the answer to every problem we face. He is the revealer of God the Father (see Colossians 1). God is not dead. I loved the movie too. You might have seen it yourself. God has not been caught off-guard or by surprise by anything. He has not left us as victims. We are victors in Christ Jesus.

He calls us to stand upon the Word of God. His divine purposes are always accomplished, even when it doesn't look like it. The Spirit of God produces boldness in us as Christians when we really know who we are in Christ.

Instead of bowing down to adversity, we must remember we are not *under attack,* but rather we are seated with Christ Jesus in heavenly places. We will experience attack and tribulation, but we are not *under* it. We must learn to have bulldog faith and not budge off of God's Word. We must rise up in His power and boldness to seek God's face and stand upon His Word.

When a person is born again and reads the Word, their eyes are opened to the Truth of the Gospel. When you read the Bible, you can see that God does exist. Let's take a look at what David wrote in Psalm 14: "The fool has said in his heart, no God." You have to be foolish to actually believe that God does not exist.

We have a choice to make if we want to see change. We must pray not only for the needs of our families, but for our friends, co-workers, and neighbors across the land. Pray for revival, strong marriages, godly parenting, and honest leaders who walk in the fear of the Lord. With the present crisis across the globe, not just in America, we have good reason to cry out to God as believers, with confidence in God that He desires to work on our behalf. (See Psalm 34:17, 19.)

We must humble ourselves, seek God with all our hearts, and turn to Him in prayer. We must turn from our wicked ways for God has conditions for when He will respond to our prayers. The word "wicked" includes all deliberate, willful disobedience—not just violent crimes such as murder. If we want our prayers to be heard, we must not only confess our sins, but repent of them as well. We agree with God and choose to turn from sin and obey His Word.

What will God do in response to our prayers? He will hear our cries, forgive our sins, and heal our land. He will restore our nation and makes us into a nation that honors Him again.

If we love our nation and want to continue to enjoy the land, we must turn to God in prayer and repentance. I challenge you to kneel before God and ask God to revive us again, both personally and corporately as a nation.

Family and the Family of God

I love my family. I love the family of God—the Body of Christ. God has great people doing work with Him. The Bible tells us that the gates of hell shall not prevail against the church. (See Matthew 16:18.)

The church is the Bride of Christ and Jesus died for her. He loves her, and gave Himself up for her. When we get connected to a church and begin to serve, we have less time to be critical of the people that actually go there—they are our family. We love and support family, or at least most do.

I will never forget a dream someone shared with me on one occasion. This pastor called me to share that another pastor had a dream about him and his wife. He said his pastor friend lived in another state and had called him that morning. We were all having dinner that night as friends and he wanted to share the dream so I could pray and ask God for the interpretation.

The man that had the dream told him that he saw him in a casket and his wife standing at the door—at a distance. She did not know that he was actually still alive in the casket, with his heart beating, because she would not get close enough to see.

I sensed the Holy Spirit revealing the message was this: The pastor represents Jesus—the pastor's wife represented the church. If we are unwilling to come close to Jesus, we won't be able to see the heart of any matter, we won't know the heart of a person, and we will stand at a distance and miss out. As believers in Christ, we must have hearts like Jesus where we are moved with compassion, not only for the lost but also for those walking through seasons of adversity, calamity, tragedy, health issues, and whatever else may come.

We are here on earth to stand beside each other, help when it is in our power to do so, squeeze a hand and listen intently to someone who is grieving, and to be a person who is so empty of self, but alive in Christ, that we feel the other person's pain and are moved to tears and action like Jesus. Remember, Jesus wept. Live a life of prayer, but don't use prayer as an excuse not to help someone in a time of need when you have the resources to do so.

We are here to help the hurting, feed the hungry, encourage the brokenhearted, and hear the countless stories of pain and help others walk through to the other side of healing. I wouldn't be alive today if it weren't for Jesus.

We are not here to manipulate and finish people off. We are here to encourage and spur people on to seek God and find their destiny. We are here to connect with others in the Body of Christ that we might fulfill our role and advance the Kingdom of God together. It is all about Jesus and people coming to know Him.

God saved Saul from Tarsus, a man who was having Christians murdered. He saved Moses and used him, even after he committed murder. David committed adultery, had a man murdered to cover his sin, and was called "a man after God's own heart."

There is hope for all. God doesn't give up on anyone. We must not either. Don't give up on your family. Choose to turn to God and ask Him for a new heart—a heart filled with His love so you can love others.

We are here on earth learning how to love others with God's agape love. That is the supreme test of all time. Don't allow anything to pull you out of your walk with God—no matter what problems you face.

The church is full of people and where you have people, you *will* have problems. No one is perfect and as a matter of fact, if you don't like the church where you worship and are serving, then when you leave and find another one—you will find something you don't like there as well.

We must learn to renew our minds in greater measure by spending more time with God and reading His Word. It is not the primary job of your local pastor or teacher to fill you up for an entire week with a spiritual meal. In the natural, if you only ate one meal a week, you would eventually die from malnutrition.

We love people and use things as tools. We don't use people. No one likes to be manipulated.

Computers are tools that can be used to spread the gospel and encourage the family of God. Computers are only as good as the person working with it and entering the data. You can have a virus on your computer and it will run slowly and irritate you to no end—until you clean it up. I have heard that computers and technology make life easier. Have you heard that? We still have the same amount of hours in a day and we get to choose how we use them.

As I have reflected over the week, I began to think about how Jesus never got in a hurry. I had a pastor call me who told me he had a minute, as he was jumping off a plane and after we finished our two minute conversation as he ran through the airport to get his rental car, his voice sounded like a person who had just ran a marathon. He was totally out of breath and winded. He took the time to return my call.

I had another lady text me and then call to tell me she was feeling squirrelly and asked for a verse in the Bible to help her. I immediately sent her a Scripture. Next, I received a call from a lady who saw a woman frantically park in a handicapped parking space as she darted out of her vehicle to drop off a grandchild while the mother was sick in the car. Then the phone rang, and my cousin informed me of an aunt that was dying from a stroke in the hospital.

Next, the dog I was babysitting saw me from the grassy area just behind the pool and having no fear at all, or either he has seen too many Superman movies and proceeded to be so excited just to see me that he came running right off the wall behind the swimming pool into my arms. Yes, I raced from the door to catch him just in time. Next, I learned that the tax department and new tag system had overcharged my mother on her vehicles, so I had to make that phone call and straighten that out. Shall I go on?

Another friend calls to say her well has dried up at the mountain house and the inside of the home has been flooded. Oh, and let's not forget the bee either. A friend's dog saw a bee and the dog accidentally rolled out the door, breaking her leg and ended up having surgery that cost them about $7,000. Not sure if it was a bee but whatever the case, the dog got hurt.

Oh and let me share this. If you live in Gastonia, you can have your pet neutered or spade for about $200 less than if you live in the Lake Norman or Concord-Kannapolis area. Gas is 24 cent less a gallon on the same tank of gas four miles apart. President Obama is having problems in the White House. A woman with a child drives her car right into the gate and she is killed on the spot with her child in her car.

People call to ask how you are and they start talking immediately about themselves and dumping everything they can think of in a matter of a few seconds. It is because they are in pain. Guess what? We are here to be a light in the darkness and it is our choice to take time to stop and bring encouragement.

We have to take time to spend with people. Sometimes people call us because they need someone who will listen. A listening ear is important. We have to take time to spend with family and friends. If we don't take time to connect, we drift apart in life like a ship lost as sea. We have to take time to spend with God. We have the ear of the King!

The art of communication and respect have been lost to some degree. Adults and children alike are playing games on their cell phones while surrounding the family table to celebrate someone's birthday in their presence. Teens decide to shoot someone who is simply running down the road because *they* are bored. Have you heard enough yet?

The days of Tigger and Pooh are long gone. The days of *Leave It to Beaver* are in the past... and I pray the days we are seeing now do not last the way they are—for America and the nations are in serious trouble. What went wrong?

Could it be that when you are running so fast that you don't know which end is up, that you have lost your way? Are you like the dog running off the cliff that doesn't know about the five-foot drop and the steps below? Are you like the woman who received the news about her dying relative?

I recently heard the true story of a struggling family who had lost connection due to greed. Distant relatives came to visit. The man brought milkshakes to the entire family, but didn't know the husband was not at home. This man decided that rather than waste a shake, he would drink two of them. It was to his surprise, that something else began to shake. The two shakes put him into overload and you can figure out the rest of the story. His wife was embarrassed and ran toward the door, fell out over the steps and went face first into an anthill. Yes, she was his aunt but I don't think she thought it was too funny.

These are what you call embarrassing moments or have we lost the art of family? Have we gotten so caught up in acquiring that we have forgotten people? When anyone gets derailed in their thinking and focused on life's problems, we can have family chaos. Life happens, doesn't it? People have problems. We all do.

Jesus looked out over the countryside and saw multitudes, but He saw people—people that mattered as individuals. How do you see people? Do they matter to you? Does America matter to you?

When things become more important than people, chaos begins. When schedules are more important than people, chaos increases. When sin comes through cracks, the enemy slings the door wide open. Welcome to family in America. It is time we take back families and our nation. How do we breakthrough to the other side from chaos to peace? The answer is turning back to God and the Bible and reconnecting with the family of God.

The Body of Christ is radiant even on her worst days. Dare to connect with the family of God and find out that your life really matters. Jesus wants us to tell all people that He loves them, He died for them, and He is coming back again!

Breakthrough will happen when we return to our first love—Jesus Christ, love our family and the family of God—the Bride of Christ. Will you pray for America to turn back to God? Will you reconnect with friends and family? We need each other.

Breakthrough

Breakthrough happens when we choose to stop and rethink life. We gather the family and establish a family altar and time of prayer with devotion. We actually allow the family to be a part of the conversation and listen to people when they talk without interrupting them.

Jesus sat down with the woman at the well in John chapter 4. He talked with her and told her about her life. He met her where she was in life, didn't condemn her, and engaged her in conversation. He brought her to a place of encounter with Himself. This moved her to a decision and action. She turned back for an entire village to tell them about this man that knew everything about her.

The Good News of the Gospel is simple. There are steps we can take for spiritual breakthrough. We must choose first to humble ourselves by admitting our own personal sin. We cannot see our sin unless we first humble ourselves before God and allow the Holy Spirit to convict us.

Second, we pray to God, asking His forgiveness for the sins He reveals in our lives. Third, we seek His face continually. Begin to pray and decide you are not willing to settle for anything less that *seeking His Presence,* while passionately pursuing a new encounter with Him. We must turn from our wicked ways: God will hear our prayers for America and the nations *if* we turn to Him in true repentance.

True repentance is more than talk—it is also action. Whether we sin individually, as a group of people, or as a nation, following the requirements in 2 Chronicles 7:14 is the only way for breakthrough. God will not bless our nation if we continue to dishonor Him.

As we become closer to God as individuals, the Body of Christ (or church collectively) will grow much stronger and we will sense more of His Presence and experience personal revival. We will experience an outpouring of the Holy Spirit in our midst.

Prayer For Rescue From Difficulty, Hardship, and Destruction

Practice your faith and ask God for a greater hunger and thirst for righteousness. The PRAYER in Colossians 1:7–14 has the power to rescue someone when facing destruction, difficulty, and hardship.

Pray and ask God to be filled with the knowledge of His Will; in all spiritual wisdom and understanding (that we would mature); bearing fruit in every good work (leaving an influence for all eternity); increasing in the knowledge of God (DRAWING CLOSER TO GOD daily through reading His Word and applying it through practical steps of obedience); being strengthened with all power (by the HOLY SPIRIT); while joyously giving thanks to the FATHER (with an attitude of trusting God while developing GODLY character through the trials and hardships). Commit yourself to intercede for others. Pray it for yourself as well.

"So the king gave the command, and they brought Daniel and cast him into the den of lions. But the king spoke, saying to Daniel, "Your God, whom you serve continually, He will deliver you" (Dan. 6:16). God will deliver America if we will turn back to Him in repentance.

The alarms have been going off. The news is filled with violence and unrest. We must choose to operate in faith. Faith brings strength—God's way of hope and direction. Storms are everywhere and we must learn to lighten our loads. Storms have the ability to clarify what is important in this life.

God has to be our anchor of protection (see Acts 27:23). We can lie down in peace with God (Psalm 4:8). Even with the whole world on edge, we can still have peace in God. We have to purpose to know God and learn to hear Him. In the midst of battle, we have to know His voice. In the midst of war zones, military are trained to obey instructions immediately. It is to save their very lives. We must learn how to hear God and obey Him.

HEARING GOD

I was recently talking with a friend and we were sharing about hearing God and what people need to know. This might help you as well.

1) God is our Deliverer on a daily basis, but we don't like what we hear and therefore don't obey and don't get delivered as a result.

2) God is our Judge, too. No one wants to hear that. If we continue to refuse to hear and obey, then we cannot really be surprised when we don't get what we ask for.

3) People need to learn *how* to hear and what it means to obey in practical words and ways. God is always speaking—we must simply learn to tune into God, learn to receive and turn aside to see Him in the details. Could it be most people want the big words from God often before they are willing to obey the smaller things?

4) God loves you and I, and longs to deliver us, but He is the perfect Father and knows just what it takes to capture our attention and the discipline needed to work things out for us when we refuse to hear.

5) Don't seek riches or *expect* riches in this life or for everything to go perfectly for you. Be grateful and live with an attitude of gratitude for what God has already given. Ask God to help you be a better steward. This is for all of us. We can expect God to bless our obedience.

God is good and he desires to bless His kids. He rewards those who diligently seek Him. We have to be willing to turn aside and sometimes that means new friends and new connections, doing things differently, and learning from others.

TURN ASIDE

In the Old Testament, Moses turned aside to look at the burning bush. He realized the bush was not consumed by the fire and ultimately caused him to take notice. Moses experienced God himself as he turned aside to look.

How did the bush ignite? Was it God in the fire? Was God in the bush? Or, was it God that set the bush on fire with His holy presence just to get the attention of His servant Moses? What will it take for you? *Whatever it takes* is a great phrase. Some of us would do well to pray that prayer, "Whatever it takes Lord, I want to know you and experience you."

Life is too short in a world with people starved for compassion and the love of God to stay stuck in drama. God has a great plan for your life, but you have to move forward with God to see the revelation. The Israelites wandered in the desert for forty years on what was actually an eleven-day trip. God knew if they got too close to Egypt, they would want to go back to what they knew and "thought" they missed. It is the same today. Not much has changed.

We have to turn aside and learn to listen for the still small voice of God and read His Word. Then we act on the Word of God! We learn to apply God's Word to every situation. We turn to God for His perspective in all of life! Then we move forward with God leading the way.

We hate the things God hates, but love people. When you have been delivered from an area of bondage, you will begin to hate that same sin. When you are delivered from negativity and complaining, you will hate to be around people who are negative.

Choose to step out of situations that prevent you from your potential in the Kingdom of God. Don't allow things from your past to hinder your destiny. Don't get so caught up in your career, raising families, and the financial demands of this world's system that you never make time for God's blessings in your life.

Choose to trust God and ask Him for help to get out of the rat race and begin to walk with God in greater things He has prepared for you to do. God is able and willing to help you make any changes as you surrender your will to His.

Great leaders have to first surrender to the will of God in order to lead. The best way to lead is from your knees in prayer. Nothing happens without prayer first.

Are you willing to ask God to help you, empower and equip you to take positive steps rather than staying stuck in bondage? Whether you need to make radical changes or slight adjustments, God will help you as you surrender to Him. What will it take for you to turn aside?

Inspired by God

"All Scripture," says the Apostle Paul in his second letter to Timothy, "is inspired [breathed-out] by God and profitable for teaching, reproof, for correction, for training in righteousness" (2 Timothy 3:16 RSV).

All of Scripture, therefore, has an amazing practical application to our lives today and also great value. As we apply Scripture from Nehemiah, we can see where the first seven chapters tell the story of rebuilding the walls of Jerusalem. We must learn to close the gaps where the enemy has a place to attack through some outward practice or perhaps an inward attitude that has been destructive and potentially damaging our relationship with others. It may be an inward desire for secret promotion through manipulation.

We must learn to change our outlook, renew our minds, to be reinstructed in the truth, to correct our own thinking and learn to think like God thinks. My friend, that involves a careful hearing of the Word of God. All Israel stood before the Water Gate and listened, hour after hour, to the reading of Scripture. That is what changed the nation. *And get this—they stood up the entire time.*

As we choose to carefully apply this to our own personal lives, it also involves, as it did for the Israelites, acknowledging our past failures and confessing to God; as well as praising Him for His goodness.

The outcome of this produces commitment to a new lifestyle. They were willing to put it in a binding covenant, sign and have it sealed by their Levites and priests. This is an amazing display of the need many people feel to put into verbal form the new direction or change they want to make in their life. Many do this at the beginning of the New Year and some never follow through. The memory of the commitment wanes as the year passes.

We are inspired at the beginning of each New Year to write out a plan, start an exercise program, and perhaps change our daily habits. We have to commit to change and follow through to see results.

One day as I was talking to a physician, he shared about his new grandson who was born early and only weighed four pounds. His name is Niam, which I learned means commitment. He had to stay in the hospital for longer than normal, as he needed extra help to live. His parents had to entrust their newborn baby to the care of the hospital in order that he might have a *chance* to live.

We must entrust our lives to God in order to live—yes, really live. We must choose to commit to honoring God's Word above all else—especially our selfish wants and desires. We must all choose to commit to something. Not making a choice to move forward is settling in defeat.

When we choose to turn to God and let His Word sink deep within, we are inspired by God to change. When we commit everything to God we step into a deeper truth and new place of trusting God. We have different wants and desires. We care about people and are moved by the pain and hurting due to broken down places. We are not only inspired by God, but also moved to action.

Deeper Truths

Let's take a little deeper look at Nehemiah and see what we can learn. Take time to read the first few chapters in the Book of Nehemiah. There are several things we can learn.

First of all, Nehemiah has concern and is moved in his spirit to go to Jerusalem. He then inspects Jerusalem's walls in secret and keeps the plans in his heart for a while, but he does rebuild the wall of Jerusalem. The enemy sent opposition and Nehemiah defended the oppressed. *The same is happening in America.*

Directed by the Spirit of God, Nehemiah obtained permission from King Artaxerxes of Persia to return to Jerusalem. He rebuilt Jerusalem in spite of the opposition from those who had remained behind during the exile and were local residents. We know from Scripture that the Levites led the Jews in prayers of confession, which also acknowledge the absolute leading of God's Spirit through the cloud of His presence in the wilderness. They also acknowledged God's miraculous provision of bread and water given by His Spirit in Nehemiah chapter 9.

After the people confess their sins, they agree to obey and sign a document. Nehemiah signs this, and with him a company of priests whose names are given. Then a group of Levites, those who serve the temple, signed the agreement as well. Then a group of leaders, the rulers or nobles of the land, sign it as well. In verses 28-29, we have the common people. A commitment is made and the Spirit of God leads. When we choose to commit, the Spirit of God will lead us. When we commit anything to God, He promises to take care of it.

HEART CHECK

Ask yourself this question, "What have I not committed to God?" Whenever we do not listen to God, He will send His Spirit to warn us about our sins. He will reveal the broken down places. He will use people that He brings people across our path, to giving us a Scripture that is illuminated by the Holy Spirit. Because of His great love for us, He patiently endures our sins while seeking our repentance. Because of God's mercy and grace, He does not abandon us. Our part is quite simple: Hear and obey!

In what particular area of your life have you not obeyed God whole-heartedly? What warnings are you receiving from the Spirit of God? Will you hear what the Spirit of God is saying today or will you harden your heart to the sound of God's voice? Will we turn back to God as a nation and commit to follow after God?

The Spirit Leads

Led by the Spirit, Nehemiah has the walls dedicated and we also know temple worship and praise continue under the leadership of Ezra and the priests. (Study Nehemiah 12.) We can surmise from this passage, that God's Spirit still directs His leaders to rebuild every area the enemy has destroyed in order that God be glorified, praised, and worshipped.

God's Spirit takes the lead in yielded, submitted, worshipping lives. We find in the Book of Ezekiel that the Spirit comes, lifts, takes hold, sets one upon his feet, and speaks—yes, speaks. Learn to listen and He will speak. Learn to worship and He will move you to the place of intimate worship where you need to be. Choose to enter in to His presence and invite the Spirit to lift you up in praise. (See Ezekiel 3:12, 24.)

I remember one Sunday morning during worship the Lord opened my eyes to see the Lord Jesus walking down the aisle of our church and stand before the pulpit in a cream linen cloak. This is an open vision where God opens our eyes to see into the Spirit realm. The Holy Spirit spoke to my heart to read Psalm 63:2. The version I read said: *I have seen the Lord in the sanctuary.* My pastor at our home church also had a vision or dream that same week and saw the Lord standing in front of him at the podium. Pastor said he saw the Lord open his robe and there were leeches on His body. *God is coming to cleanse the Body of Christ—His church!*

The Spirit of God moves us from glory to glory. He continually lifts us up to see different places. Wherever Ezekiel was taken, the Holy Spirit had a vision or revelation for him. He does the same today. He has not changed. However, the Spirit cannot take us where we are not willing to go. Are you willing? Or, are you so comfortable in living in worldly sin that you choose death over life? God forbid. He cannot show us what we are unwilling to see. Are your eyes closed to the Truth found only in God?

The Holy Spirit is our teacher and comforter. He leads us and instructs in which way to go. (See John 16:12–14.) The Holy Spirit also teaches us about the goodness and grace of God. He has given us the Bread of Life (John 6:35) that satisfies every longing and hunger. He has given us Living Water that quenches all thirst. (See John 4:10–14.)

We must choose to keep our eyes on Jesus—the Author and Perfecter of our faith (Heb. 12:2).

HEART CHECK

Are you willing to be lifted up to praise Him? Are you willing to stop living in deception in every area?

Where is the Holy Spirit leading you? Are you willing to stay on the course even if the journey is unpleasant?

Attack—Big Surprise

When we choose to see what God sees and move to action, we experience divine alignment, we recognize our assignment, we are anointed and empowered by God to do it, we experience attack, and we advance the Kingdom of God. Is there any wonder Nehemiah was experiencing attack? Nehemiah was experiencing attack because he chose to obey God and rebuild. In Nehemiah 4:1-6, the enemy attacked by trying to bring confusion to the mind. Sanballat's initial attack was to confuse that mind: *Now it came about that when Sanballat heard that we were rebuilding the wall, he became furious and very angry and mocked the Jews. And he spoke in the presence of his brothers and the wealthy men of Samaria and said, "What are these feeble Jews doing? Are they going to restore it for themselves? Can they offer sacrifices? Can they finish in a day? Can they revive the stones from the dusty rubble even the burned ones? Now Tobiah the Ammonite was near him and he said, "Even what they are building—if a fox should jump on it, he would break their stone wall down!" Hear, O our God, how we are despised! Return their reproach on their own heads and give them up for plunder in a land of captivity. Do not forgive their iniquity and let not their sin be blotted out before Thee, for they have demoralized the builders. So we built the wall and the whole wall was joined together to half its height, for the people had a mind to work.*

For a man whose name means "a secret hatred," Sanballat (Satan) didn't keep much hidden this time, did he? He was furious and openly said so. This is the very nature of Satan and his hatred is against all mankind, but for the unsaved it is so well hidden that most don't believe he even exists. Blinded to the fact that they are captive, bound by the power of the evil one (1 John 5:19), they refuse to become Christians because they don't want to give up their so-called freedom. This all changes as the wall starts going up and it enrages Sanballat because it is symbolic of walls of salvation and Satan hates righteousness.

It is the most common attack—the attack on the mind, especially to new believers. This attack is common to all Christians throughout their lives. The Apostle Paul, fully aware of Satan's ways, wrote "For we walk in the flesh, we do not war according to the flesh, for the weapons of our warfare are not fleshly ...We are destroying speculations and every lofty thing raised up against the knowledge of God, and we are taking every thought captive to the obedience of Christ" (2 Cor. 10:3–5).

In Ephesians 6:17, we receive instruction "to take the helmet of salvation." We are given two passages that reveal the constant need to protect and renew the mind. In Nehemiah 4, the enemy used fear, depression, mockery, and doubts to demoralize the builders. Ask anyone who is building walls of salvation in their life or who is marching forward to lead others to Christ. See if they don't experience attack. As a matter of fact, if everything is going great, check out your course.

Satan comes to steal the word before it can take root inside of us. (See Matthew 13:4 and 19.) Nothing has changed in life. Satan comes with the same mode of attack. Satan wants to capture our mind and emotions in order to throw us totally off course. Satan will come and say things like, "You will never amount to anything." "You can't be used by God." "You are nothing but unpaid clergy." Oh, and what about this one, "You will lose all your friends." Satan will even use well-meaning Christians at times.

The greater your pursuit of God and doing His Will, the greater the attacks will come. In the case of Nehemiah, we can see that Sanballat prompted the attack from Tobiah. This doesn't really come as any great surprise. "The flesh" (Tobiah) sets itself against the Spirit (Nehemiah), and the Spirit (Nehemiah) against the flesh (Tobiah). They war against each other. Satanic forces come to demoralize the Christian.

Attack—Big Surprise

As soon as you start to move forward in whatever God has called you to do, the enemy sends out assaults. Big surprise? In Romans 8:6, the Bible says: "For the mind set on the flesh (Tobiah) is death, but the mind set on the Spirit is life and peace."

What are you facing personally right now? Look at America as a nation. God, help America turn back to *You* as a nation.

In Nehemiah 4: 7–15 we find the second attack was physical persecution: *Now it came about when Sanballat, Tobiah, the Arabs, the Ammonites, and the Ashdodites heard that the repair of the walls of Jerusalem went on, and that the breaches began to be closed, they were very angry. And all of them conspired together to come and fight against Jerusalem and to cause a disturbance in it. But we prayed to our God, and because of them we set up a guard against them day and night. Thus in Judah it was said, "The strength of the burden bearers if failing, yet there is much rubbish; and we ourselves are unable to rebuild the wall." All our enemies said, "They will not know or see until we come among them, kill them, and put a stop to the work."*

Everything began in the Middle East and everything will end in the Middle East. The enemy wants to stop people from praying and building. Prayer is our communion with God. A guard represents prayer. Prayer builds guardrails for our protection. Prayer brings protection and provides wisdom. We pray God's Word and He dispatches angels to bring it to pass (see Psalm 103:20). The strength of the burden bearers failing—could that be prayerlessness in America as a nation?

Nehemiah and his people survived the first attack on their minds. Now a new attack was being devised and it involved sticks and stones, not just words. The first thing we might note in this passage is that all of their enemies are engaged in this attack. Sanballat is at the front of the list. Tobiah and Geshem's people—the Arabs are also in the group. *Does this look like what is happening again today in the Middle East?*

Satan uses both to persecute and destroy God's people. In church history, we conclude the attack came from the Roman Empire, who threw Christians to the lions. This is Satan's strategy—using the world and its system (Geshem) to do what he wants. Satan opposes the work of Christ and seeks to kill (verse 11). The Roman Empire became the Roman Catholic Church (Tobiah –that "good" religious system that says Jehovah is good, but hates God's true people) and the persecution and deaths continued.

Now physical attacks are here in America. God is refining our faith through the fiery trials. America must turn back to God and stand up for Israel.

What's Next?

Don't allow your mind to spiral out of control. God is still sovereign and His purposes are playing out in the big picture of life. Let's read about Nehemiah's response.

> *And it came about when the Jews who lived near them came and told us ten times, "They will come up against us from every place where you may turn," then I stationed men in the lowest parts of the space behind the wall, the exposed places, and I stationed the people in families with their swords, spears, and bows. When I saw their fear, I rose and spoke to the nobles, the officials, and the rest of the people: "Do not be afraid of them; remember the Lord who is great and awesome, and fight for your brothers, your sons, your daughters, your wives, and your houses." And it happened when our enemies heard that it was known to us, and that God had frustrated their plan, then all of us returned to the wall, each one to his work'* (Neh. 4:12–15).

Nehemiah reveals his secret. They set up a guard and prayed to God both day and night. They had a deep love for God, leading to dependency upon God, and obedience. Nehemiah was not complacent and he did not underestimate his enemy either. He stationed guards in the lowest parts, yet gave credit to God that He would give success.

The Midnight Hour

There are weak places in all of our lives where we have to build and strengthen through God. Sanballat (Satan) attacks the exposed places, where the wall has not yet been built.

Nehemiah's prayer and attitude was always, "The God of heaven shall give us success; therefore we His servants will arise and build but you (the enemy) have no portion, right, or memorial in Jerusalem" (Neh. 2:20).

We must remember the Lord our God and stand against the opposition with trust in God. What was the result of Nehemiah's faith? The Lord frustrated the enemy's plan (verse 15).

It is a divine and golden moment in time when you hear God and move forward to answer the call. The Body of Christ is crying out for leadership now. We need to allow the Spirit of God to move us like Nehemiah was moved. We don't need another message where the whole place is so loaded up with bondage and condemnation that no one can smile. Jesus came that we might have life.

We need strong leaders in America and in the church. We need God-pleasers and not man-pleasers. The fear of mankind will destroy any person and any nation. I love God and His people. I love the church—the body of believers. I have a strong passion for souls and want all to hear the message of Jesus Christ.

I love people but I don't always like what they do. No one is perfect. Every person has an opinion in life. One thing we would all do well to remember is this: *there is something you don't know in every situation.*

We are in a leadership crisis today—right here in America. It stems from the same problem in the family and very fabric of the nation. Husbands sometimes don't want to lead for fear of offending. Parents are afraid to discipline their own children for fear of being accused of child abuse. Teachers in schools are having problems with standing up and taking authority because someone might say they have violated their so-called rights.

Why are people afraid to stand up for what they believe? Or, could it be far worse, that people don't really know what they believe? People are afraid to take a stand for fear of hurting feelings or separating families. What on earth is going on?

When someone won't take a stand and speak the truth about a situation, life does not go on as normal. We move to a place of sitting back and tolerating things that should never be tolerated—in family, in business, and even in the church. It is not really normal though, is it?

We must choose to elevate our thinking and renew our minds in the Word of God so that we have the mind of Christ and think what He thinks about any given situation. Whomever you fear will determine the decisions you make in life.

If you fear the opinion of man, you will be ruled by people's opinion. I believe God wants to bless His people and this nation again. However, we have to know what God says in His Word. With all the attacks against Christians and preachers who have become known through media, is there any wonder our nation is in peril? People have opinions over statements and look for everything to criticize. What has gone wrong?

When a person gains recognition, people will have varying opinions. If you have the fear of man, you will be moved by whether people are rejecting you or not. There will always be crazy-makers. There will always be people the enemy uses against you to make you begin to question what God has put in your heart to do. The enemy uses this to attack your mind and to make you doubt.

We need to rise up in boldness in Jesus Christ and the truth found in the Bible. With a nation on a moral decline like we see in America, this same pattern existed in classical Greece and the Roman Empire right before their fall.

Joseph found himself in a pit after a fall. He didn't fall in it by himself. His brothers threw him in the pit because they grew envious and jealous of his relationship with their own father. Could it be that America has a similar problem? The enemy of our soul hates God—our heavenly father!

The enemy tries to stir up strife and dissension between families and friends. We must remember we are not in a battle against people, but the enemy works through people unaware. We see a much bigger version in America and across the globe.

We are a light and hope for reconciliation when we share the love of Christ and get into His divine plan for our lives. Move past any pain, don't waste any sorrows, get out of any pit of despair, and step into faith in God to do what He has put in your heart to do with Him.

The Pit of Bitterness

Have you found yourself recently in a pit of despair, wallowing in bitterness of your heart? Have you found yourself in utter turmoil, only to find yourself in a place you never wanted to visit in the first place? You must learn that the Holy Spirit does not lead by feelings. He leads us where we need to go. His plan is vital and perfect for us.

The Bible says, "The Spirit lifted me up and took me away. I went in bitterness and turmoil, but the Lord's hold on me was strong. Then I came to the colony of Judean exiles in Tel-abib, beside the Kebar River. I was overwhelmed and sat among them for seven days" (Ezek. 3:14–15, NLT).

Have you ever been in a place where you felt overwhelmed, or like Job, you were weighted down like the sands of the sea? It is not fun to be in such a state, is it? Life can sometimes not turn out exactly as we might have planned.

I have heard many stories of parents intervening in the life of their child to save them from ruin. One such young man had fallen into an area of sin and his parents called him out on the carpet, you might say and helped turn him around.

This young man's father loved him so much that he went overboard to help him see the light of God even in the midst of his wrong choices. Sometimes, like David, when we get out of position, we fall prey to the temptations of sin.

This young man responded properly and is now happily married with a family and is in ministry. That is the love of our Heavenly Father as well. He has great plans for His children but He desires that we know Him and obey His Word. His Word is perfect and He brings discipline because of His great love for us.

Sometimes, we have to end up flat on our backs or in a pit before we get tired of crawling around in the pigpen. I call the pigpen anything that does not line up with the Word of God because that is where the Prodigal Son ended up and recognized his need.

When we are born again, if we get into mud, we immediately want to be cleansed. If we have not been born again, we think the mud is natural and normal. Ask yourself, "Have I truly had a heart change?"

God used that young man's parents to assist in setting their son on the right path. He was set on his feet again. God wants to set us in correct position and in divine alignment with Him. He has great plans for you and *the best is yet to come.*

At times the Spirit stands us up to be still and listen to His voice. Sometimes he gets our attention in such a manner that we suddenly stand at attention. It is in this place where we can be still and listen carefully to the words of our Father. In this place of waiting and listening for instructions, you don't move till He moves you.

Don't open your mouth and speak until He has spoken. Don't move ahead into action until He acts through you. The Spirit of God will stand you up so that you can abide in Him. There are times of waiting, preparation, and a time where we must stand up! Deborah had to stand up with Barak in Judges 4–5 to win a battle. She was a judge, prophetess, and a woman of wisdom who stood up and told the most able military general what he must do to win the battle.

Ezekiel had such a time as this in Ezekiel 2:1-2: "Stand up, son of man," said the voice. "I want to speak with you." The Spirit came into me as he spoke and set me on my feet. I listened carefully to his words."

Ezekiel had a call and a commission. God commissioned him to go to the nation of Israel, a nation that was rebelling against Him. The Bible tells us the nation of Israel and ancestors rebelled against God from the beginning, and were still in revolt to this very day. God said they were hard-hearted and stubborn people. Whether they listened or not, they would know there had been a prophet among them.

God sends people to warn us of sin and destruction. He sends people to nations to warn as well. God wants to bless us as a nation

The Pit of Bitterness

and as a people. He wants to bring our God-given dreams to fulfillment. Our part is to hear and obey His instructions.

HEART CHECK

When has the Spirit of God made you stand at attention to listen to Him?

Have you obeyed? If not, go back to the last instruction and choose to follow hard after God.

God has a great plan and purpose for your life. He desires that you are saved and made whole so you can bring the good news to the poor. Both those who are poor spiritually (Matt. 5:30) and poor naturally (Luke 6:20) desperately need the good news of Jesus Christ. He is the secret ingredient.

He desires that you be set free to comfort the brokenhearted. Those that mourn and grieve over sin and its consequences will be comforted by the Holy Spirit—the Comforter—God's Spirit. (See Matthew 5:4; Luke 6:21; John 14:16; 2 Corinthians 1:3–11.)

His plan for you is to announce release to the captives and freedom to the prisoners. The Holy Spirit brings liberty and freedom into our lives. "Now, the Lord is Spirit, and wherever the Spirit of the Lord is, he gives freedom" (2 Cor. 3:17).

The Bible says, "For I know the plans I have for you," says the Lord. "They are plans for good and not for disaster, to give you a future and a hope. In those days when you pray, I will listen. If you look for me in earnest, you will find me when you seek me. I will be found by you," says the Lord. "I will end your captivity and restore your fortunes. I will gather you out of the nations where I sent you and bring you home again to your own land" (Jer. 29:11–14, NLT).

God-Given Dreams

Before we talk about dreams, we must address dream destroyers. 1. Divine delays —when it doesn't happen quickly (example of my first book *God's Priceless Treasure* that took fifteen years to birth and only thirty days to write) I haven't written another one quite that fast again. There is more to writing books than just writing.

If you are not careful, you will try to make something happen in the flesh rather than waiting on God. The prophets of old did this with dreams and visions. They were expected to have them often and if they didn't, they would say anything to save face.

2. Temporary circumstances – 2 Samuel – (Example: Thenias giving birth – Philistines took the ark – she looked at present circumstances and named her son Ichabod (meaning God's spirit has departed). When we walk through adverse circumstances and tragedies in a row, we can sometimes have negative thinking. Don't name your future by your present circumstances. Call things that are not as though they are—live in faith and decree and declare God's Word over your life and circumstances.

Don't buy into lies. Don't assume what everyone tells you is true— look to God and His Word. Trust God and run everything by Him.

Joseph of Arimathea was willing to loan Jesus his grave. He believed Jesus would do what He said he would do (in three days)— why would you need to buy something you were only going to use for three days? Don't buy into depression for joy comes in the morning. This man believed Jesus at His word.

3. False evidence appearing real: Joseph's brothers hated him for his dreams in the Old Testament. You can't kill someone who

God has given a dream to in life. When they tried to kill Joseph they failed – they dipped Joseph's coat in blood and took it back to their father – They thought without a doubt that Joseph was dead. (Without a doubt means perfect faith – they had perfect faith in a lie – false evidence appearing real. The ones that tried to kill the dream had to bow to the dream many years later.)

(Brothers go to the father—they buried his coat—while Scriptures said He was given proof—He has given us His Word but sent wagons of provision – miracles–When the father saw – he said it is enough – I believe he is alive.) You can take time to read about the life of Joseph and see the amazing ways God prospered Joseph everywhere he was—because God was with Him!

You must start saying powerful positive words about your future—what God says about you in the Bible.

There is much in life that you and I can't control from the economy, the weather, gasoline pricing to the rise and fall of the stock market, and you certainly can't control the choices other people make that affect you. When someone makes a bad choice, unfortunately, it not only affects that person but everyone connected in some way or other that is involved or not involved.

When American leaders make wrong choices, the nation suffers the consequences. One wrong choice leads to a series of consequences. No one person is to blame. We must choose to turn back to God and make corrections.

Today, my husband phoned me as I was driving to an appointment and said, "We have a problem." He then proceeded to tell me the sewage pump light was on—which meant a warning. I told Dan the company that checks and maintains it sent a representative out on Monday. It was the owner of the company's son. I immediately called him to inquire about it.

After inspection, he learned the twenty-amp breaker snapped in the control panel and they thought perhaps there was a power surge. I explained that we have a generator. Since they were out anyway they took the lid off, cleaned the inside, and found oil within. The Father and the Son both came out. We need the Father, the Son and the Holy Spirit. God will allow an alarm to go off to get our attention.

God is doing a breaking in the Body of Christ and in His chosen people. Breaking means we are being emptied of self to where we recognize our need of God. He is allowing all hidden truth to come to the surface. We need to know things that are hidden because *sometimes what we don't know can hurt us.*

God is exposing wrong attitudes and false beliefs where people think they can hide sin and not be found out. There can also be people around you, in your business or in your own family that think they are getting away with hidden sin as well. It can show up in any organization, any family, and in our own personal lives as well. Sin is always found out and God sees all. The Holy Spirit reveals all hidden truth.

We need the oil of the Holy Spirit applied to every situation and the blood of Jesus. America needs God. There is power in the blood of Jesus. There is power in walking with God. We have a direct line to God when we abide in Him. The greatest wireless connection is prayer. It is not a new cell phone or any other form of technology.

The Remedy For Mind Problems

The mind can give you all sorts of problems. That is actually where the battle is in life. It all starts in the mind and can send anyone down a path of destruction, or can send you into victorious living.

There is good news—you have a choice. There are some things you can control. Have you ever heard of a bucket list? I have determined the mind is also like a bucket. It is either a water bucket to bring refreshing or a bucket filled with anger, rage, unkind words, negativity and so forth. It is our choice. We must fill our minds with good things. It is important what we watch and hear. If you don't believe me, listen to your kids and grandkids.

God gives us family to manage. We are to manage our families in such a way that we grow and flourish like a beautiful flower garden. When we choose to elevate our thinking by renewing our minds in the Word of God, everything changes. Problems become opportunities and serious issues can be eliminated through process.

We don't think clearly when we focus on problems. We must choose to focus on God and His purpose for our lives as individuals and as a nation. We are called to manage what we allow inside our mind similar to Adam who was to manage the Garden of Eden. He made a wrong choice that brought about disaster for all mankind.

Thank God we have the Blessed Hope—Jesus Christ. There is hope for all mankind. There is hope for that particular area in your life where you are struggling.

God promises that if you will faithfully manage one area of your life, it will have an amazing impact that is positive on the quality of your life. This one simple choice has the power to release joy in your life, as well as contentment with your life no matter what your circumstances. It is simple but it is not necessarily easy. When you have true God-given joy, it can't be disturbed by your circumstances... or by your emotions. It doesn't mean you won't experience problems, it simply means your problems won't have the power to take away your joy.

You won't be moved by the news that someone is pregnant out of wedlock. You won't be moved by the news that a family member doesn't want to honor their responsibility financially. You won't be shocked when the call comes about an emergency, because you will have your hope and trust in God. The Bible says that it is foolish to trust in man, but through the Lord, we will do valiantly and He will trample our foes. (See Psalm 60:11-12)

We learn to manage our mind by surrendering to the Holy Spirit, renewing it through the Word of God, and abiding in Him.

Trumpet or a Trap

When news comes, do you declare what God says like a trumpet announcing the return of Christ or do you have a trap that brings a snare? Do you live by your feelings and allow your mouth to get you into all kinds of trouble? It is a choice.

People never cease to amaze me. I don't understand why people don't heed the warnings when they are small, but instead wait till they have proof or a brick? Why on earth would someone need proof to obey God's warnings and instructions? Why would you wait till a problem gets bigger before you choose to deal with it? I don't understand this at all. But we have all done it in one area or another.

How much grumbling and complaining comes out of your mouth? Can you make it through one day without complaining? You must choose to stop murmuring and complaining. When you choose to live this way, incredible fruit will be produced in your life.

Choose to be desperate for God and listen to His voice at the slightest whisper. He will give you the power to renew your mind and manage your emotions so they do not fly all over the place and run wild.

We don't really need to tell people they have messed up—they pretty much know it. We don't need to heap more condemnation on them. We do, however, have to confront in love and deal with real life situations.

We have all made mistakes and wrong choices. When you choose to complain and get aggravated, you lose your joy. Is it really worth it? No, absolutely not.

Nothing good ever comes from whining and complaining or speaking negatively. It certainly does not move God. Only faith moves

God. Actually, a negative mouth is like swallowing poison. You will soon find yourself in a bad mood. While complaining feeds a spirit of dissatisfaction and unhappiness, it also puts you in agreement with the enemy rather than what God's Word says about a particular situation. It can make you feel miserable and leave you having a headache. The Bible encourages us: "Do all things without grumbling or faultfinding and complaining [against God] and questioning and doubting [among yourselves]..." (Phil. 2:14, AMP).

It's important to note that the Apostle Paul wrote these words to one of the healthier churches in the New Testament. We learn from Scripture that the Philippians were generous, they loved God, and they were supportive of Paul's ministry. However, they still needed to be reminded to choose joy. We still need to be reminded today. Paul knew just telling them to stop complaining wouldn't fix the problem. They still had to learn joy in the midst of every circumstance.

We have to choose to live in joy and pursue peace. God is the Great "I AM" so therefore we are to be joyful in our fellowship with Him. Because of who He is we are regenerated through the new birth. Because of who He is we are able to have the mind of Christ through the renewing of our minds by the power of the Holy Spirit.

Because God is the Great "I AM" we are able to live in the Sabbath rest. We are refreshed and our hopes and dreams are restored. Because of who He is, we are restored in health, family, relationships, and finances. Because of who He is, we are able to reach the lost. We are the repairers of the breach through our constant abiding in Jesus Christ.

It is time to have revival as ONE—so that it spreads like wildfire across America and to the nations. Ignite America by choosing life in God, by living in *joy* with the sound of your voice reflecting the joy of salvation, and by letting your life shine like the light in the darkness to spark a flame in others no matter what lies ahead.

Because God is the Great "I AM" therefore we are...regenerated, renewed, refreshed and receive rest, restored, and we can reach others to repair the breach as we stand in the gap. We must choose to stand up like the passengers did on 9/11/2001 on the flight that crashed in the field. We must choose to keep building like Nehemiah! We must choose to stand.

The Fields Are White With Harvest

People may attain great wealth and success, but still not be full of joy. Rich and famous people experience depression too. Success and wealth does not make anyone immune to depression and other life issues.

What exactly does that tell us? No one, no matter what status, finds true joy in individual strength. Joy doesn't come from external things; it comes from within. We know what it is like to experience need and we also know what it's like to experience plenty. We have learned the secret to being content no matter what the circumstances. We also know we can do all things through Christ who strengthens us. (See Philippians 4:12–13.)

Real joy that is unwavering is exhibited when we are truly in love with Jesus and we love what He loves—people. He knows exactly what we need and knows how to bring change. If you catch yourself complaining, you are not living the quality life that Jesus paid for on the cross at Calvary.

In a world that is filled with chaos and hurry, you must choose to lift up your eyes unto the Lord and choose joy. It is far too precious to give away. Satan makes it his business to destroy you and steal your joy. God gives us strength through joy, but we must choose it.

You must choose to be committed to the highest level of excellence, choose to seek God with your whole heart, and choose to respond like Jesus. In any given situation, inquire of the Lord and ask this question, "What would Jesus do?"

Don't look at your problems, look to Jesus. Don't talk about the problems, but pray the answer found in God's Word. Call things that are not as though they are. Look at the life of Abraham and how he believed God. Lift up your eyes unto the fields, for they are already white unto harvest. Look for people in need of God and turn to God in everything.

God is greater than your greatest need and His love is deeper and more rewarding than life itself. Purposely choose to live in contentment because this opens the door for true and authentic joy that only comes from God. Make the choice today, my precious reading friend.

Remember, even though you may not always see it presently, God is working things out for you. He is currently taking the pieces of your life and turning them into something great for you. He takes the broken pieces and gives us a fresh, new start.

Perhaps, you've thrown in the towel and called it quits on your marriage, your career, or on what God is calling you to do. You may feel like Joseph did in a pit of despair. You may need a gentle reminder from God to go in a different direction. You may be pregnant and in limbo on what to do next. Make it right. Choose life. Repent and move forward in God. Pursue God with all your heart. Inquire of the Lord and expect instructions.

Choose not to be a control freak, but learn to relax and encourage those around you to do the same—the fields are white unto harvest. Invite God into your marriage, your finances, your health, and every aspect of life. Ask God to start a revival in your own heart and family.

You might be the person saying, "I'll be happy when I meet the right person" to "when I get that job I will be happy" to even "when I get that big break, I will be happy." Money won't make you happy. It certainly helps as a tool and gives you easier access to certain things in life. However, it won't make you happy.

Families in America are hurting—and around the world. Fatherless homes produce teens that are looking for purpose and someone to affirm them in life. When we choose to deal with the real problems in America such as the breakdown of family and fatherless homes we will decrease the population problem in prisons and realize the enemy comes to steal, kill and destroy. Satan is dividing homes and the nation through everything from race to status. Stop the divide and realize people are loved by God and have a divine purpose. We can make a difference, one person at a time—to the nations.

God is extremely interested in the details of your daily life. He is concerned for America and the nations. He wants to bless America. He wants us to lift up our eyes and look at the fields, for they are already white for harvest! (See John 4:35)

With revelation from God that overrides the natural order of things, every day is a harvest day. Choose to dive into the Word of God and hunger for more of Him. Spending time with Jesus brings increase in the anointing on your life and the natural order of things turns to supernatural. Jesus was anointed without measure which defied the natural principles that illustrated spiritual truths.

The more we are empowered by the Spirit of God, the more our lives will defy the natural principles where we see God's divine intervention and divine appointments on display. What a way to live! We will begin to see accelerated growth and more people come to know Jesus in unusual ways and settings.

Turn to God and pray. Choose to turn to God and stand up for Christ in the land. Stand up against hatred—and stand out in God's love. Be nice to people—starting where you live. What the world needs is Jesus and a church on fire spiritually for God. Blessed is the nation whose God is the Lord! Lift up your eyes unto the Lord—look to the fields—for they are white with harvest!

The Great Divide

We have division in politics and right on down in the family. I recently had a person call me that was unaware their phone had dialed my number. I answered but realized it was a mistake. What I heard was interesting—a few people were apparently having pictures taken and I heard one say, "…From this side only, I don't show my other side." We may think no one notices, but people do.

No one is perfect but the other side shows up. This other side has shown up in America. God is involved in everything and we better come to believe it.

The greatest example of God's divine involvement in the political affairs of any nation is made evident through Israel. God established the nation's constitution, legal structure, and the laws to be followed by other nations. (See Deuteronomy 4:5–7.)

God is active on every scene throughout the Bible, whether seen or not. His name is not mentioned in the story of Esther, but His hand is made evident through the saving of a nation by one woman's courage, divine position set up by God, and choice to stand up and come before the King. She chose to stand up and do what God put in her heart to save her people.

There is no escaping God's activity in life—whether personally or politically. What this means to me is that we can't divide our personal life from our public life. We can't put God on one side and politics or any other matter on the other.

We can't pretend to be someone we are not. We can't live one way at work and another way at church. We can't live one way at church and another in the marketplace, and not expect people to notice. We have to be real and let people know we are saved by God's grace, but we do experience problems in life.

People are hurting and in desperate situations. People are experiencing attack like I have never seen in my life. People are experiencing attack across the nations from Islamic extremists and for the first time, the church bells are not ringing in Mosul. A prominent speaker and head of an organization shared that Islamic extremists have infiltrated U. S. political and security institutions and she had come to America to ring the bells—to be a voice of hope for her people. We must wake up in America. People need to know their life matters. God cares personally about each and every person on earth.

God was very personally involved in the life of King Nebuchadnezzar of Babylon. He was a great secular ruler during the height of pagan rule. God protested his unrighteous government and we can see throughout the pages of the Bible one common thread: When a nation turns to God, she is blessed. When she turns her own way, things do not go well. Bottom line.

Let's read what the Bible says in Revelation: *And He has on His robe and on His thigh a name written: KING OF KINGS AND LORD OF LORDS* (Rev. 19:16).

When Jesus returns to earth to rule and reign, He will come as "King of kings, and Lord of lords."

We have an obligation to build again in this nation—building people up in Jesus Christ and coming together for the sake of family. We owe it to the generations in the past to occupy territory where a great price was paid to bring it to us. We owe it to all those who have gone before us and we owe it to our children, and grandchildren. Let's turn back to God as a people who love the Lord, redeemed through the precious blood of Jesus! We must choose to walk in our authority and divine influence as we take back enemy territory.

My Walk

My walk with God includes walking, attacks, loving God and loving people, and the Kingdom of God. We are called to outlive our life in this world. We are to be about the Father's business—advancing the Kingdom of God.

In our walk with God, we must learn that we wrestle not against people, but evil powers, principalities and rulers of darkness. We must choose to align ourselves with God's Word. We must learn to walk together.

While walking our son Landon and his family's puppy named Ollie one day, I took time to spend with him and thought about the ease of walking with him. I began to think about how God must feel with us. I noticed Ollie was easily distracted by the wind blowing the grass to the sidelines, and even the trash containers that were in a row to be picked up. He noticed other dog's business that someone failed to pick up and discard as well. As I thought about this, I realize people are no different today. People are interested in trash and other people's business. If we are not focused, we may find we are easily distracted as well.

Ollie was veering off the path and paying attention to the wind blowing rather than being able to walk in a straight line with me for a short distance. I would reach down and pick him up to carry him. As a matter of fact, I carried him more than he walked because he was like a baby then. When a person receives Christ as Savior and begins their path in the Christian walk—a relationship with Jesus, sometimes they must be carried as well.

My Walk

I noticed Ollie as he rather quickly learned to follow the leader. He stayed on the straight path for a short distance. Just like God does with us, we need to be picked up and carried for a distance. We can see things from a different perspective and can feel our Father's heart as well.

Ollie was watching my feet and started to do a small run on one occasion with me—I do mean small since at that time he was only a little over 3 pounds. I carried him most of the walk since he was small. He wanted to go his own way a few times, but was excited to be lifted up and carried. These are reminders in life—to help others when they need to be lifted up and have someone to walk beside them with struggles in life, or even when failing.

We all need people in life. We are created for relationship. We all need each other and someone to walk with us. Who has God placed in your life that you can walk beside through a new season of life or struggle? God desires that we walk together in unity. When we move from knowing about God in our head to receiving Him in our hearts, life begins to change. We learn to walk with Him. Many people know about God, but don't know him in their hearts and their lives are going down wrong paths. They are in need of God to fill the void in their lives that only He can fill. *America must get back to the basics and learn what walking is all about again. America must turn back to God. Will you turn and believe God again?*

Believe God

Believe God and live in the light of His Word. Allow God to do surgery in your heart so you may see with His eyes and from His point of view. When we are unhealed at some time or other in our own heart, we can have blind spots that prohibit our sight. Life can also have a few bumps along the way and for some, tragedies, disasters, and extremely tough times may come.

If we are not careful to keep our focus on God, we can develop calloused places in our heart from hurts. Hurting people hurt others. It is time to ask God to heal any area in our own heart that may need healing. We all need spiritual surgery. In order to be all that God says we can be, we must choose to believe who He is—the GREAT I AM. His light shines brightest in the darkness. We must choose to run everything in life by the light of God's Word.

Instead of quitting or giving up, ask God to ignite the spark of love in your heart for people. Jesus could see the harvest in John chapter four when He sat down at the well. The Bible reveals that Jesus knew He needed to go by Samaria in John 4:4. He could see the fields white with harvest. How about you? Your neighborhood, business and workplace are great fields that are white with harvest. Ask God to open your eyes to see what He sees.

Learn to look for the best in others. You can't ignore the bad and live in denial, but you must learn to be who God has called you to be and see what He sees in people. Christians are the hands and feet of Christ on the earth today, the visible manifestation of HIM in the world (1 Corinthians 12:27). Ask God for a listening heart that hears what He hears. People are grieving over loss and tragedy in America and the nations. Sometimes the greatest thing you can do for someone who has faced a tragedy is to listen and be present—not necessarily to have all the answers, but we know who does—God.

We live in a fallen world where sin is very real and evil is on the rise. We can find hope in God. When a person is walking through a hard place, they can only see today. The families in New Town faced extreme loss through the reality of evil at work in the heart of a man who chose to kill innocent children and adults. There is no tomorrow for them at present. They are grieving loss. This happened on December 12, 2012 and everything as they knew it changed forever.

America is in serious trouble! You can see the headlines and news reports that fill the airwaves. Scandals, terrorist attacks, and evil are rampant *but God is with us*. We must choose to believe in God!

The Bible tells us that Jesus is called "Immanuel"—God is with us. He is a very present help in a time of trouble. (Read Psalm 46:1.)

Evil is present in this world because of the fall in the Garden of Eden. It is not God's fault. We all have choices just like Adam made a choice. We make choices every day. Parents buy their children games that are nothing but killing little figures and competition. Children play with them for hours filling their minds with violence. Violence is on every form of media, and we wonder where the children, teenagers, and adults get ideas?

The mind is like a computer that can be programmed. Whatever you think about yourself, you will become. If you hear that you are a failure long enough, you will eventually begin to believe it. If you believe you have no hope, you will lose all hope.

I have heard countless people tell stories of how someone of importance spoke death over them, told them they would never amount to anything, or something even worse. People can flat be mean. The people that are mean are in need of Jesus too.

One of the greatest problems people have is thinking that no one else has suffered what they are suffering! The Christian life is not floating on some glory cloud and singing all day long! Every committed Christian will find warfare to be a part of his or her total experience in life. Life is a battle and we must choose to trust God.

There is hope in Jesus and the fields are white with harvest. With tragedy in New Town, CT, lives ended before they had really begun.

I can't begin to imagine the loss these parents are still living with and the families with heartache and grief. The overwhelming sadness can leave a person devastated in sorrow. Sorrow and grief can linger when we've had hopes and dreams that seem to be dashed forever. Countless lives have been taken out early because of evil across the world.

REMEMBERING HELPS US TO BELIEVE GOD

Let's review the life of Abram whose name was changed to Abraham. This was a man who believed God. You might find a different viewpoint as you read along with me. God told Abraham he would make him "the father of many nations" as well as make him the "father of our faith." Most have heard the story of how God promised Abraham a child and how Sarah laughed because of her age. God promised Abraham that he was to have a child, and from that child's lineage would come kings and rulers of "many nations" as well as the Messiah—"the Seed to come." (See Genesis chapter 16 through 18.)

I can only imagine the disappointment Sarah must have felt in waiting that she chose to take matters into her own hands by telling her husband to sleep with her maidservant to produce a child. Abraham and Sarah were of old age and childless when God gave that promise. Sarah tried to help God out through having Abraham sleep with Hagar that produced Ishmael.

It is obvious that she doubted the promise of God. She chose to take matters into her own hands and we know the rest of the story. Years later, God came again and told Abraham of His promise and just like God said, nine months later Isaac was born. We can see the promise, the struggle of taking matters into their own hands and trying to help God out, and then the divine manifestation.

Sounds like life today, doesn't it? Don't you think people get tired of waiting? They get discouraged, believe the lies of the enemy and then try and figure out how to help God out. This is how we end up in a mess.

Parents decide what their adult children should do based on their thoughts and try to help God out in setting the stage to bring about the will of God, or is it man's? How do you know what God wants

Believe God

when it comes to specifics? How do you know you have heard the voice of the Lord or received a word from God? Keep reading and you will learn.

Recapping the events in the life of Abraham, we find in Genesis 16:15–17 Abraham was actually eighty-six years of age when Hagar bore Ishmael. When Abraham was ninety-nine years of age, the Lord appeared to him and reiterated the promise. (See Genesis 17:1–22.)

You may have eyes to see, but no vision. Let me explain. Take a look with me at the number of years between the promise and the provision of manifestation. Abraham, at the ripe old age of ninety-nine, received the promise. At the age of eighty-six, Abraham tried to help God out and bring about the promise himself. We see thirteen years between the promise and the manifestation. The promise involved both God and man. We see circumstances, seasons, and times operating in the life of Abraham. Both God and man must participate. We don't have a problem with God; it is always mankind's obedience that is the issue.

The promise is always initiated by God and changes the world forever. I know, in my own life, God changed my name and changed my life forever. He has used a small town girl to go the nations and do things with Him that I could never have done on my own. God gave me a promise and an instruction each time. It is our choice to obey or not.

There is no way I could have ever accomplished what God spoke to my heart on my own. It is God who empowers us to do greater things for His purpose in His kingdom. It is only God who can bring the promise to fruition. One thing I know for sure, I have been in places and circumstances where I knew it would take God to pull it off. I believe God allows us to be in seasons and circumstances where we know our only hope is in God. If it happens, it will be the doing of God. I have a deep underlying knowing that only God can accomplish in my life what He has called me to do with Him. My part is to simply listen, trust Him and obey.

It was the same for Abraham and Sarah. It is the same for you. It is the same for America as a nation. Based on my own life experiences with God, I know if God says something, it will surely happen! Don't give up in the waiting and don't try to help God out. There is a vast chasm between what man can do and what God can do. God has the best viewpoint from above. He sees it all. We only see in *part*.

It is also pretty obvious there is a season where man tries to bring the promise to pass himself, rather than fully trusting God. My husband was talking to me yesterday about a specific matter and I heard him say he had asked God to help him get something straight. When I heard it, my spiritual antennae went up and I thought for a minute or two before I responded. *That is a good thing to do women!*

I asked Dan if he had thought about asking God to bring it about Himself. I shared he might just want to tell God, "I can't fix this at all. I need you to bring it to pass and tell me what to do."

There are times, much like the children of Israel, when we are in a position or a place where it may feel like the Red Sea is in front, the enemy behind and mountains on either side. We are put in this position where we have no place to go but forward in God. We have to make a choice. We learn to obey when we are in a crisis where we have no control.

There are times in all of our lives when we are clueless and powerless in and of ourselves in situations. If it gets fixed, it will surely be God. Do you understand what I am talking about? You may be in a similar situation where you realize if there is going to be change, it will be totally God's divine intervention. You may be at a place where you need a miracle. His timing and our timing are never the same.

America is facing the same. She needs help. She needs to turn back to God in repentance and prayer. Our part is to pray and turn back to God.

God desires that we live in abundance in His Kingdom. You have to learn how the Kingdom operates in order to live under it and in it. Abundance is God's design. Our part is to mature in Him and live surrendered to His will in order to live supernaturally in the natural — no matter what.

If you have lost all hope, stop and turn back to God. Even with what you might have done in your own strength and circumstances you have created through disobedience or not heeding God's warnings, God will use it all to bring His promise to pass. Even if you are in a crisis that was created by someone else, God is still in control. Remember the story of the life of Joseph. He was falsely accused and mistreated. His brothers meant it for evil, but God meant it for good. (See Genesis chapters 37 through 47.)

Listen to God and obey Him. He knows everything in life. He knew Sarah would laugh and take matters into her own hands—as well as Abram. He knows all. The consequences that were set in motion, when Abraham and Sarah tried to help God out, continue today through the crisis and unrest we see in the Middle East. There are always consequences to disobedience.

We all experience times of unrest and crisis and will eventually come to a place where we need God to intervene. I know from experience, you will get to the place where there is no hope, except in God. You will find excitement, hope and ultimately desperation for God to intervene. Have you been there?

SEDATION OR SURRENDER

Both 2013 and 2014 have come and gone. We are in another new year. *Four* blood moons are coming to pass in perfect alignment. Warnings are everywhere. The alarms are going off for this nation to turn back to God. Take time to read the book: *The Four Blood Moons* by John Hagee. (Visit www.daniel11truth.com and see for yourself.)

It may seem like this nation is in a place of extreme crisis with unfavorable circumstances beyond all hope in the natural, but God will use the past and present to give way for the birth of His promises to be fulfilled. Put your hope and trust back in God and believe Him!

I remember on a drive into Charlotte, I was on the phone with a lady who was sharing a praise report. She was talking about the difference her father-in-law had noticed in her in the last year. He told her that even her attitude had changed. Guess what had changed most in her life, her associations. Who we associate with in life matters. People have influence on us whether we realize it or not.

I looked up and saw a billboard that said ATTITUDE BY BUSHEL—BRANCH OUT while I was on the phone with her. I love how we can see God revealing He sees right where we are in life. God desires that we mature and help others along on their walk with God. Instead of being infected by negativity and lifestyles of disobedience, we choose to impact others through our own life. Others will notice the difference in us as we choose to pursue God and become more like Jesus. God wants us to branch out and touch others.

I believe it is wisdom to always be mentoring and helping others, to have people in life we can run things by alongside us, and to be receiving from others who have more wisdom than us at all times in life. We are called to make an impact and be an influence for Christ.

God wants us to grow and mature in our knowledge of Him and in our understanding. We learn something new every day as the Holy Spirit equips and empowers us to help others along their way. This only comes through a life that believes God, inquires of Him, and chooses to turn to God in everything.

We must turn to God in surrender instead of using sedation or other forms of relief to cover rebellion. We find ourselves confronted with rebellion inside us, rebellion in the world around us, rebellion against government, rebellion against God, rebellion in children against parents, rebellion in students against teachers—and the list goes on.

The real answer is total submission to God—where He is Lord over all! Give every person over to God. Give every situation over to God. Trust God to make every single thing right in your life and believe Him.

Let's take a look at Psalm 60:11-12. A few weeks ago, God spoke to my heart to read these two verses and when I did, I knew God was letting me know He sees every detail and He will make every crooked place straight. He will avenge us from our enemies. He was also reminding us not to trust people, but to trust God only. We are called to trust God and love people.

I believe God wants us to participate with Him in greater measure than ever before. There is more to be seen in life when we participate with God. He has greater things for us to do with Him.

Enter the unknown, knowing God is with you. "The name of the Lord is a strong tower; the righteous run to it and are safe" (Prov. 18:10). After we run to God, we inquire of Him and choose to obey because we believe and trust in Him!

Inquire of God

Decide to pursue God and *inquire* of Him before making any decision. This will bring great change in your life and your life will impact others. The greater the impact of any decision, the more time we must spend with the Lord, asking Him to direct our thoughts and help us make wise decisions. After making a decision, we must move hastily and determinedly to do what we are convinced God wants us to do.

Nehemiah waited four months before action. In the larger scope of things in all that Nehemiah accomplished, those four months before God he spent much time planning and praying about what he should do, represented the most fruitful time of all. In this time of waiting, Nehemiah cultivated character and conviction he would need when confronted with opposition that threatened to level the walls even while he was still in the process of building them.

God still trains us the same way today. It is in the times of waiting where character and conviction are cultivated in our own life as well. Nehemiah 1:4 shows how this man of God chose to respond to the devastating news that the crumbled city walls had become a reproach: "So it was, when I heard these words that I sat down and wept, and mourned for many days; I was fasting and praying before the God of heaven." (Read John 7:38)

He was moved with compassion to weep and mourn over the ruins before he could rebuild the fallen walls. America has fallen walls. America has opposition. Christians have opposition. Notice the five key points from the passage in Nehemiah: sat down, wept, mourned, fasted and prayed.

Dealing with his own personal grief in a righteous manner, he made a wise choice and turned to the *only one* he knew who permitted the calamity. God did not cause it. He turned to God and humbly asked for mercy to forgive the sins of a nation and restore their former glory.

The sin of the nation was the real issue at hand, not the ruined walls. Nehemiah saw the truth. In his prayer, he never once mentioned the walls of Jerusalem but that her people had turned from their God and were living under His judgment. This was and still is the bottom line. Here we are again today in America.

Put on a new attitude and begin to praise God that He is still a God who loves us. Praise God that He is still the God of the entire universe. He is our Creator. Pray for America to turn back to God before it is too late.

Thankfulness

We have grieved the Holy Spirit here in America. We have grieved God by asking Him to depart. Much like a church that was once thriving with people coming in and out, when the Holy Spirit is grieved the blessing of the Lord is no longer present. Just as we can see empty buildings that used to be thriving, we too, can be thankful.

Choose to celebrate family and friends because you never know what minute might be your last. Develop a spirit of giving and generosity. Do this on a daily basis, even if all you have to offer is a smile or a kind word. You may be the one God uses to save someone else's life. He may use you as a key player in the saving of an entire nation like He did Esther.

Be thankful you have homes to take shelter in, clothes to wear, and food as many do not have basic necessities. Pray and ask God for more *joy*. Joy doesn't come through willpower or even external blessings…it comes directly from God Himself.

Stay full through a deeper walk with God! You will be glad you did. The choice to strengthen your relationship with God will bring far greater joy, adventure, transformation and breakthrough for anyone who dares to pursue a deeper walk with God. You do it by pursuing intimacy with God and having a heart of thankfulness.

The fields are white with harvest but I don't believe the world wants to be like most people that profess to be Christians. We have a pastor at our home church that does a great illustration of Eeyore—moping around with a sad face. He uses the illustration to give us a clue we need to put on joy. From a long face, to moping around like the cartoon character Eeyore, to the one who blows a gasket because someone got their seat; is there any wonder why so few people are running to find a church? Think about it. Do you have joy?

God is pleased when we walk into corporate worship and actually worship Him. His heart is moved by what hurts us—and He is touched by our desire for more of His Presence. He is moved by our faith.

Instead of staring at your circumstances and worrying yourself into despair, why not trust God? Elevate God above your problems. Begin to thank Him in advance for making every crooked place straight.

When we get our hearts right, we will begin to see the fields of people that are lost and on their way to hell. They are searching and don't have a clue what they are actually in search of at all. God wants to use you to turn the lost to Him.

Resurrection Power

We all need CPR on our own heart at some point in life. Christ was crucified and resurrected for people. (Christ crucified – People – Resurrection) Always remember God can resurrect what we think is dead. Christ's power resurrects. Jesus Christ is seated at the right of the Father at the Mercy Seat in heaven. Through our authority in Christ, the manifested presence of that power is made available in the life of every believer.

He is not caught off-guard or even surprised at what is going on in America or across the globe. He knows the beginning from the end. He knows the full story and has already won the victory.

Paul prayed, *"May God reveal to you not just the past greatness of Christ but his present greatness."* Paul's prayer was: *"that ye may know...what is the exceeding greatness of his power to usward who believe, according to the working of his mighty power"* (Eph. 1:18–19, KJV). It wasn't just for one—it is for all who choose to believe and receive.

Jesus was a miracle worker as he walked the earth. He was the Son of God, the teacher, and Messiah. Jesus opened the eyes of the blind, healed deafness, healed paralytics, restored withered arms, and healed lepers. He turned water into wine, looked at two loaves and five fishes, looked upward and gave thanks, and served a banquet to multitudes with leftovers. He also raised the dead on more than one occasion.

In this present day in which we live, people believe that Jesus can forgive sins and relieve guilt. He can give us peace and eternal life after death on earth. While many believe Jesus for all this in

The Midnight Hour

the unseen world, few believe him for their everyday affairs. Many do not commit their marriage, family, career, finances, and circumstances to God. Many may sense there is no hope for America.

We need a fresh revelation of Jesus' power since the time Christ was raised from the dead. He is seated at the right hand of the Father in Heaven. "God hath put all things under his feet" (Eph. 1:22). We must do what God says in His Word—turn back to Him as a nation.

While many are searching for a relationship, many in the Body of Christ are living together outside of marriage and going against God's Word. Many are sleeping around, having sex outside marriage, having affairs, and destroying their souls. Some women become wounded, lonely, and so desperate they resort to living in sin and will stoop to the level of seducing men who are single or married. Some men fall for the trap of seduction and destroy their marriages, family, career, and personal lives and live in regret the rest of their days. Any man or woman caught in this trap will end up in destruction unless they turn back to God in repentance.

God loves the lost and He desires they come to know Him, not just *about* Him, but have a born again experience that leads to fellowship with Him in constant communion. The Spirit of God will move you from glory to glory. You will begin to experience more of Him and become addicted to Jesus. God desires to teach you Himself. He is The Master Teacher—and delights in your coming to Him.

He revealed Himself to me as the God who created the heavens and the earth. He revealed Himself to me as the God who split the Red Sea as He intervened at Mercy Hospital for my husband Dan. He had two open-heart surgeries and two strokes, but God made him live again through His resurrection power.

God revealed Himself to me as the God who fed the children of Israel in the desert with fresh manna from heaven. He healed the blind and the maimed. He revealed Himself through the life of Jesus, His Word, and through the signs and wonders in the Book of Acts. He reveals Himself by going to extreme measures to make Himself known in the lives of ordinary people in extraordinary ways. He goes out of His way to make me aware of His presence in my daily life. He is speaking to us all—we have to turn aside, look for Him, and expect Him.

To receive fresh manna daily, I believe you must be hungry. You have to cultivate hunger for God. This is where true power is found in prayer. Deep calls unto deep. We must have such a desire to know Jesus that every other thing and every other desire begins to fade away. You must yearn for a sanctified life—a life that pleases God.

When each individual in this nation decides to turn to God, one by one, we will see revival across this land. There is hope in God! Don't every forget that. Satan is real and a powerful enemy—but we are already victorious in Jesus Christ. We have to learn to stand upon His Word and do whatever He puts in our hearts to do with Him.

When God's Spirit Moves In Your Life

I remember seeing what I thought was a shadow of a person in my home many years ago, approximately 1993 or so, and I sensed an awesome peace as I noticed I had no fear. I had been praying to God to know Him at the slightest whisper at the door of my heart. The presence of the Lord filled my room. My life took on new and more profound meaning as I began to grow expediently through God's Spirit and His Word.

God began to make Himself known to me in ways I had never experienced before. I began to realize He had been there all along, throughout the younger's years of my life, but I did not fully recognize His presence then. Does this sound familiar?

In 1975, I remember being in a car accident when my car hit a solid sheet of ice as I topped the hill driving the speed limit, but due to the ice my car came down at a high rate of speed, overturned down an embankment with gas pouring out of my car. I was still alive and breathing. I remember seeing my Bible I kept in the car—it had fallen out of the glove box. The car was upside down—but I was alive. What a God we serve. He is for us and not against us.

I realized that the Holy Spirit was with me and angels had to be surrounding me, as I was definitely alive. What you did not know is that the Holy Spirit had spoken to my father to call me and warn me about the black ice but his supervisor wouldn't let him use the phone. It is obvious that my daddy prayed and even though I still hit the ice, God's angels were dispatched to protect me.

The Holy Spirit is God's agent here on earth. Jesus is seated at the right hand of the Father. Before the Son left...in the gospel of John... when the disciples were getting full of anxiety...then Jesus said, "It's better for you that I go, for unless I go the Holy Spirit won't be able to come" but the disciples didn't understand.

Out of our hearts come the issues of life. The Bible defines us as someone who believes in Christ and filled with the Holy Spirit. The Holy Spirit is the main person here on earth that we need to get to know. The only way we have power is through the power and presence of the Holy Spirit.

As we study the person and work of the Holy Spirit, we must realize He is the most neglected person of the Trinity. The church was born and the Holy Spirit was sent down in the Book of Acts, and they were all filled with the Holy Spirit.

Peter was stumbling, argumentative, questioning if he was the greatest, and he had the best teacher, Jesus. He had the greatest model, the Son of God. What did it do for him? On the night Jesus was betrayed and arrested, Peter fled through the crowds.

People still run from God today. People run the opposite direction. They turn away from God and are entangled in sin through wrong choices. America has turned away from God as a nation.

Peter denied that he knew the Lord three times. Why did none of the outward teaching work? Only the inward power of the Holy Spirit brings about change. Jesus' promise and prophecy is coming through the preaching of Peter. We see him acting with wisdom in courage in the Book of Acts. Jesus walked with the disciples...but when he left, the Holy Spirit would come and reside in them. The Holy Spirit resides in the inner court of a Christian and gives power to witness and bring change. Christians have been changed because they have the Holy Spirit residing inside them producing power.

The Thief

Let me tell you, Satan follows you and knows your weakness just like a mob follows someone when they are out to kill. Satan comes to steal, kill, and destroy and is trained as a contract killer to destroy. Some of you are crying out to God in your present circumstances, "Lord, I need you now!"

Satan sometimes attacks people of God not because of what they are doing wrong, but because of what they are doing right. Satan can also come through an open door of sin from yourself or someone else.

There is a battle over souls. When you trust the Lord as Savior and have the Holy Spirit you have inner strength and power to be bold and live above fear. I want you to learn to love the Holy Spirit and get to know Him intimately. Learn to trust His instruction and the inner witness that protects, teaches, comforts, and leads.

The Holy Spirit inspired the writing of the Word of God. (See 2 Peter 1:21.) The Holy Spirit was hovering when God spoke the Word. Christianity is centered on Christ. The Holy Spirit does not draw attention to Him self but puts the spotlight on Jesus Christ and makes the things of Christ very real to us and applicable to our individual hearts.

We need the resurrection power of the Holy Spirit to walk in victory. We witnessed this in extreme measure at Mercy Hospital. God saved my husband from early death and raised him up after his heart had stopped. I believe many today are in heart failure. Without a right heart, you won't live long. You won't live, or truly live, without a right heart in God either.

The thief comes to steal, kill and destroy but Jesus defeated Satan and won the victory. Jesus took care of the past on the cross. God

The Thief

has promised he will remember our iniquities no more. What about today and tomorrow? How am I going to reproduce the life of Christ through my own self-effort? I am not unless the Holy Spirit resides in me and flows out of me.

The Father sent the Son, but the Son sent the Spirit. He teaches us and makes the Word of God real to us when we read it. He makes the New Covenant produce power in our life. The letter of the law kills because my sinful tendencies override my conscious until I have the power and grace of the Holy Spirit flowing from my life. The New Covenant is a born-again experience and our sins are forgiven. The Holy Spirit lives inside us and empowers us to represent Christ.

Have you had an encounter with the Holy Spirit? Do you still operate in fear, anxiety, and hatred? Only the Holy Spirit can produce God's love in your life to those who have betrayed you. It's easy to love loveable people. The test comes when we've been hurt by people we least expect and feel God's love toward them as He empowers us.

God will send people into our lives to help us grow. He will position people who have gone before us and have walked in the places we are presently walking. He goes to extreme measures to make His presence known in personal ways.

Have you felt the touch of the Holy Spirit? Have you had a fresh encounter with the Holy Spirit? The Holy Spirit has saved you from death and tragedy many times in the past and most of us are unaware.

Just as the wind blows through the wheat in a field, the wind of the Holy Spirit is blowing today and He wants us to know Him. The Holy Spirit gives us boldness and power to be witnesses. We need a return to the power of the Holy Spirit and the gospel of Jesus Christ in our individual lives and churches. The power of the Holy Spirit is stronger than any sin or circumstances. America needs this power again. We need revival. What will it take to turn America back to God?

Nothing with God is impossible. Are you tired of just going to church? Is the church you attend a Holy Spirit hospital? Does the Holy Spirit move in your life, family, and church? Let's return to the simple power of the early church—preach the gospel of Jesus Christ and return to the power of the Holy Spirit.

The Holy Spirit—The Power Source

I remember being in a church many years ago and the Holy Spirit opened my eyes to see a vision of the Lord walking down the aisles. The pastor stood up and said he saw the Lord walking the aisles of the church. That was totally God. Then on another occasion, all the lights went out but God's presence was real and strong.

A few months later, I was listening to a pastor in a church who spoke against what he heard had happened and the power of God quickened my body in such a way that I couldn't stand up and knelt down quietly. I remember feeling the fear of the Lord as I heard this pastor tell what he heard in disbelief.

On my drive home, I was passing exit 25 on Interstate 77 and all the lights went out across the area. I arrived home and checked my mailbox. I had a letter from David Wilkerson and the title read: "The Night God Turned Out the Lights In the City." You see, my precious reading friends, God was letting me know He did turn out the lights in that service that I experienced myself. God can turn out the lights and turn them on again. He is the Great "I AM."

Just because someone does not believe something doesn't mean it is not true. Jesus is alive! He is coming back again and we must be watching for His return! We are called to live out the Great Commission—advancing the Kingdom of God.

The Kingdom of God Mentality

Jesus talked about the Kingdom of God and gave direction to the disciples for their future. As a Christian, we live in this world, but we are not of this world. In Acts 2, Peter preached the first sermon and the church multiplied. He was bold and did amazing things. Philip, tax collectors, zealots, and others had no formal training but were being taught by the Holy Spirit and were endued with power from on high. Jesus had told them to wait in Jerusalem prior. Jesus had risen from the dead and they now knew that their Savior had died on the cross, risen from the dead, and was giving them instruction. His blood was shed for the remission for sin for all mankind. The disciples now understood the good news.

The Holy Spirit is our power source. When Jesus walks in a room or a church, even if the lights go out, the power source is still there. The Holy Spirit is our divine agent here on earth. The great need of today is the power source –The Holy Spirit. We are going to face spiritual warfare, persecution and all sorts of attack, which is why we need the power of the Holy Spirit. We don't need more praise and worship choruses, nor do we need more Bible translations; we need power.

We need to stop rearranging furniture and putting on shows, but live with the blessing with God's power in our lives and our churches. Have you experienced the Lord's touch in your life? Is His power operating in your home? Do you live with eternity in mind? Are you kingdom minded?

Jesus promised power of the Holy Spirit. When the church is not operating with the flow of the Holy Spirit, the services can feel barren and empty. When faithful souls pray and seek God for the power of the Holy Spirit and hunger for righteousness, we have revival. Revival comes when we get tired of barrenness and realize God has more for us in Him. We humble ourselves and confess our sin. We confess the sin of grieving the Holy Spirit. We surrender and submit to the Lord. This kind of prayer and humbling preceded every former revival. Ruth's humility is what caught the eye of Boaz in the Book of Ruth as well. He said, "Come hither."

No matter what you have walked through or experienced, the Holy Spirit wants to help you. If your business, marriage, or family is failing, the power of the Holy Spirit can resurrect and heal.

First Corinthians 12:7 teaches us (KJV), "But the manifestation of the Spirit is given to every man to profit withal."

John 14:21 says, "He that hath my commandments, and keepeth them, he it is that loveth me: and he that loveth me shall be loved of my Father, and I will love him, and will manifest myself to him."

You will not be able to escape the love of God. He loves you and me! He loves the sinner but hates the sin. He opens our hearts to receive Him. He brings change in our lives. The only thing constant in this life is change. God never changes—He is the same yesterday, today, and forevermore.

Change

Everything that brings change is not good. Sometimes when we change we are moving toward fads and novelties, when only the preaching of God's Word and honoring the power and presence of the Holy Spirit will bring proper change. We must start with self; humble ourselves; seek God and pray, and begin to call on God. He will not turn away from us.

When we want more of Him, He turns toward us and fills us so others can come to know Him. We need to confess our lack of ability and God will send new rivers of power in our lives. Amen.

When Jesus spoke to the woman at the well and revealed her past to her but did not condemn her, she heard Him and received revelation that touched her heart. Is God using you to touch the heart of people? Her heart was changed and God used her to share her greatest tool of evangelism, her testimony, to point others to Jesus.

One encounter with the Word of God, Jesus in the flesh, changed her forever. She came to the well empty and barren. She left full and left her water pot behind. She left what represented her past behind and left excited! Have you experienced an encounter with Jesus?

This is why I have shared stories within this book—in hopes it will help you to see that God is real and that He will do the same for you. The Holy Spirit is our helper and our comforter. He teaches us, reveals all hidden truth and shows us things to come. (Take time to read John chapters 14 through 17.)

America needs change—she must turn back to God!

The Greatest Teacher—The Holy Spirit

If you will open the Bible and ask the Holy Spirit to open your eyes and heart to receive revelation, the Holy Spirit will teach you Himself. If you read the Bible and receive revelation and obey the Word you will grow spiritually. No matter what your I.Q. is or no matter how bright you are, the Bible can only be explained and understood if you are taught by the One who wrote it: The Spirit of the Living God. Pray: *"Spirit of the Living God, break me, mold me, fill me, and teach me. Spirit of God, come and teach me your Word."* The Kingdom of God is revealed Spirit to spirit.

A minister called me out of an assembly of thousands of people at a Christian conference where I was seated in the nosebleed section of the bleachers—way up in the balcony. I will never forget that day even though it was many years ago. It seems like it was just yesterday. I was listening intently to him share how he was nearly aborted in his mother's womb and could feel when his mother was upset after her husband, the unborn baby's father, walked out. She took a coat hanger and tried to abort him, but God, because of the Great "I AM" caused him to live.

God had a plan and a purpose for that man. He has a plan and a purpose for you. He has a plan and purpose for me. This minister called me out and shared a few words with me. He asked me if I knew how much God loved me and spoke very encouraging words of life over me. He said the Lord had a Davidic anointing on my life and that I would be like a cheerleader for Jesus. Take time to read

Jeremiah 29:11 and study the Bible daily. Choose to turn to God and ask Him to open your eyes and turn America back to Him. The Holy Spirit is our teacher and comforter.

Jesus was called teacher or rabbi. Before Jesus left the disciples, He made some specific promises about the Holy Spirit. He talked about the Holy Spirit and called Him the Spirit of Truth. John 14:16 tells us the Holy Spirit will teach us all things. The Holy Spirit moved upon man to write the Scriptures.

The Bible is my favorite book and is the Living Word of God. The lessons and truth that God wants to convey to us can only be understood by the Holy Spirit's revelation. The Truth God wants to get in your heart only happens by the ministry of the Holy Spirit.

Have you ever read a verse and just did not seem to understand it? You might be doing devotions but it is not being deposited in your heart. Ask the Holy Spirit to open your eyes of understanding.

Have you ever read a verse and you've read it twenty times or more? All of a sudden, a light bulb goes off and you see it in a totally different light for the very first time. This is the power of the Holy Spirit to bring revelation. It is the most exciting way to live.

First John 2:27 John says, "You have an anointing that teaches you all things." You can think you know the Bible and have no spiritual change. In the 1840's and 1850"s slavery was going on and there were Bible thumpers defending slavery; using the Scriptures to enslave hundreds of thousand of slaves, to propagate slaves to be torn apart from their families. Ministers were using the Scriptures to enforce their wrong beliefs. The tender revelation of the Holy Spirit is imperative. In the name of Scripture, they crucified the Lord Jesus Christ.

We all need discipline. God will reveal Himself in a way that you will recognize Him. That's the love of God, my friend. God revealed Himself to the Woman at the Well in such a way that she was moved to tell an entire town. God changed Saul of Tarsus through a Damascus Road experience, changed his name to Paul, and empowered him to be the first major missionary to preach the Christian gospel to the non-Jewish people.

We must desire to be like Jesus. Read and study the Word and allow the fresh revelation to come from the Holy Spirit within. Pray,

"Lord open my eyes, teach me things from You Word—teach me your ways" (from Psalm 119).

The Holy Spirit will open our eyes if we ask Him. Don't simply read the Bible to get ammunition. Diligently study the Scriptures to know God. Don't fall for the trap of religion where people study to build up prejudices and traditions. We must learn to lean upon the Holy Spirit and walk in God's love.

Search the Scriptures and ask for the help of the Holy Spirit so you can understand what God intended Christianity to be and to understand love and prayer.

God will position you in a place where it is just you and God. This way He will get you grounded in the Word of God so you can come to understand His plan for your life. Keep your heart tender and ask Him for a childlike heart. The Holy Spirit begins to work in our lives when we get to the end of ourselves and are desperate for more of Him.

> *"For the eyes of the Lord run to and fro throughout the whole earth, to show Himself strong on behalf of those whose heart is loyal to Him. In this you have done foolishly; therefore fro, now on you shall have wars"* (2 Chron. 16:9).

We have all experienced pain, heartache, and consequences of sin. We have all failed deeply. However, when you truly start to live in Christ, you suddenly realize you can't do one thing apart from Him. It takes God breaking us to a place of dependency upon Him to walk the Christian life in fullness.

The Spirit of God is trying to teach us to depend on the Lord. He will teach us what we need to know. We can't find our way without Him. We need the Holy Spirit. We have grieved the Holy Spirit as a nation here in America. Ask Him to empty you of self and fill you with His Presence to overflowing.

Don't be an empty shell or an empty shell of a building. The Spirit of God who brings the blessing has been grieved and is not welcome in many families, churches, and organizations in America. Church is impossible without the blessing and power of the Holy

Spirit. Jesus Christ can change anyone through the power of the Holy Spirit. He can change this nation.

He will go to extreme measures for just one person. He will do whatever it takes to turn the heart of a king. He will do whatever it takes to turn a nation back to Him. We need the Holy Spirit to revive us all again.

Jesus walked with the disciples and did miracles, but He told the disciples they needed the Holy Spirit who was coming. The disciples could hear the inflection of Christ's words. Out of the heart come the issues of life. Jesus could not get inside them but the Holy Spirit could after Jesus was resurrected and seated at the right hand of the Father.

The Holy Spirit is God's agent here on the earth. Change comes through the power and presence of the Holy Spirit. People will be enamored by the love of God that is exhibited through and in our lives.

If the apostles came back today, do you think they would recognize the church today? No outward teaching can replace the inward power of the Holy Spirit. Peter acts with boldness, wisdom and courage due to the power of the Holy Spirit in the Book of Acts. We need a new day of emphasis of teaching on the person, work, and move of the Holy Spirit. Christians are inhabited by the Holy Spirit and are more different than anyone on the earth.

According to Jesus, the Golden Rule of God's Kingdom is a simple twofold curriculum, love your maker and love your neighbor. Jesus' self-sacrifice—the cup of His suffering was exhibited on the cross of Calvary. He died once and for all for all mankind.

God has built a bridge between Himself and mankind. A bridge is a natural manifestation of crossing over. Hundreds of thousand of people cross over daily on bridges. We must be in love with Jesus and in tune with the Holy Spirit to see people in need of Jesus—the bridge between man and God who gives eternal life. Jesus is the only way to come to God.

SYMBOLS OF THE HOLY SPIRIT

In the Bible, God gives us a number of symbols of the Holy Spirit. You can't define nor can you explain it; but when someone is on fire with the Spirit of God and fire, it is contagious. Because of the fire of the Holy Spirit, the message of Jesus Christ and His love is being spread to others.

Wind or breath is really the same word in the New Testament. Water and oil represent the anointing of the Holy Spirit. The water and oil were put on almost everything in the Old Testament; and dew—was another form of Water.

Water was a representation of life in the Old Testament. If there was no water there was no life as well. As believers, I believe we can become dried up or like stopped up wells—where we have to dig them out again.

Unless the Spirit comes, there is no life in us and no life in our churches. Doctrines can be right but there is evidence of death and no power. There is no fruitfulness where there is no water. No water tends toward death. Jesus cried out, "If anyone is thirsty, let him come and drink from me."

Salvation is the life giving quality of the Spirit of God living within us. Without the Spirit of God, we try to produce something in our own weakness. When the Spirit comes, there is hope, joy, and peace.

The Power Source—Refreshing From The Holy Spirit

We need a river or a foundation flowing to see life. Notice it wouldn't be just a trickle but rivers of living water. Do you live off of a trickle or do you have a river? We can quench the Holy Spirit in the things we do and say.

We are very much aware of what Jesus did on the cross but sometimes we grieve him and miss out on the abundance of the river. He satisfies my needs and your needs, producing Christ in us, and fills us so we can have the overflow of the Spirit to others.

What is flowing out of you? Are you angry? Do you fight with people with no reason? Have you ever gotten dried out or arid in your Christian walk? Perhaps, even the harder you try the worse it gets. If you run around in life you will eventually get run down.

The Bible tells us that God will be like dew to Israel in Hosea 14:5. We will blossom like the lily. The dew comes in the quiet times of night – layer of refreshing water on the grass and flowers. The dew will help you blossom like the lily – when we just sit in His presence, with the Bible on our laps in times of reading and waiting in His presence.

You can get so beaten down from storms in life, whether they are financial, emotional, or physical that you can lose hope and need refreshing. You may be angry and tried of hearing someone breathing or even coughing. You may have reached a point where you don't want to hear any noise at all. Have you ever been there?

We need to experience refreshing from the Holy Spirit. He will come like dew and settle on you so you can face the challenges of a new day. He will give you new hope for your personal life, your marriage, your business, your church, and this nation.

Have you ever been in someone's presence and sensed a presence that made you feel refreshed? Try coming into God's presence and experience His refreshing. He brings lasting change that fills the void of the heart.

Our God is also a consuming fire and is often used as a symbol of the Holy Spirit. Fire penetrates. You can put water on a piece of wood and it will be wet. Oil will make the same piece of wood wet, but fire penetrates to the very core of anything.

The prophets in the Old Testament spoke a word of fire. When God deals with us, He doesn't deal with surface stuff but deals with grit in our life. Fire also illuminates. Thousands of years there was no electricity. Most of our years in the world have been by the light of a fire and not a light bulb.

You can avoid traps and pits by light. If you are in the dark, you normally fall or bump into objects. That is what happens in life when we are not following the leading of the Holy Spirit as a Christian. He illuminates our life and our choices so we know what to do. The Holy Spirit was sent to guide us.

It would be similar to getting up in the middle of the night and forgetting your spouse had rearranged the furniture. In the darkness of the night, you would bump into things that were out of position. We must choose to turn the light on and depend upon the Holy Spirit.

Just think how little the Holy Spirit is depended on to make decisions. People sometimes depend more on natural thinking to make decisions, rather than waiting for the Holy Spirit to give direction. It is imperative that we learn to listen to the Holy Spirit and make godly decisions, not selfish or emotional ones. Is your local church governed by natural thinking or can you sense the fire of the Holy Spirit and His power within as the guide?

Fire is contagious. When the Holy Spirit is moving in a person's life it will set other people on fire. When the Holy Spirit is moving in a church, His presence sets hearts on fire or ablaze for God. When the fire falls, you will lose your anger and depression. You will be able to smile again. It cleanses as the fire burns and it sends impurities to the surface so the Great Physician and Surgeon can remove them from our lives. It is not a one-time experience but daily experiences.

God sends the fire to burn the dross from our lives. God is like a refiners fire to make us the people He wants us to be. Let's pray for a new descent of the fire of the Holy Spirit to bring revival and a turning back to God.

We must turn back to God and pray for the fire of the Holy Spirit to burn anything out of us that does not line up with His Word. God's Word is full of verses on how He wants us to grow spiritually. He wants us to become more like Christ. God can use parenting, relating to each other as husband and wife, parent and child, to become more like Him. God can use our kids to teach us as well.

Our world is changing politically, socially, and financially. Life seems very different when you can see with spiritual eyes. Join a journey of a lifetime and pursue God, the God who never changes. We must choose to embrace the God-filled life to live abundantly and fulfill our destiny, both personally and as the Body of Christ.

Truth or Consequences

The Lord is coming back for a church without spot or blemish. The Lord is going to judge the earth and He is going to start with the House of God, His own house – the church. Judgments are not always condemnation, but they are the last call to repentance before condemnation comes. We may know the whole Bible, cover to cover, and attend church regularly, and even know the truth. However, we will not be judged on how much we know; we will be judged on how we lived and our deeds.

Paul warned us to "behold then the kindness and severity of God" (Rom. 11:22a). While many are deceived because they only see the kindness of God without seeing severity, others are deceived by focusing on severity and do not understand kindness. Reflect upon the kindness of Boaz in the Book of Ruth. To know the truth, we must come to understand both His kindness and His severity together.

Many think they can go on willingly sinning because we are in the dispensation of grace and that God will just overlook it. That is not the case. While it is true we are in the age of grace, we are also in *truth*. (See John 1:17.)

Our salvation depends on God keeping His Word. God is never the problem. It is also fundamental to the purpose of the church that we become a people of our word. I mentioned a bridge earlier and in every relationship there is a bridge; it is the bridge of trust. Without trust you may have forgiveness and love, but there will be no genuine relationship.

Are you an employee that can be trusted? Are you honoring your commitments or are you just in whatever you are doing at present for the money? Is the money more important than your word? Would you dishonor your word for money? Will you honor your word above God's word when it doesn't line up with the Bible?

I understand there are problems in the world today with the change in the world's economy. People have run off and left others responsible like a bunch of dead rats running off of a sinking ship in business. While things were good, people were standing with you, but when times got tough they chose to dishonor you and God.

The strength of trust is the determining factor in every relationship. The church needs to be the bridge that helps restore the relationship with God and mankind. In order to do so, we must be trustworthy.

We may experience attack and persecution, but we are still in Christ. He will avenge us. He says so in His Word.

We are forgiven because Jesus was forsaken. We are accepted. Christ was condemned. I am alive and well because the Spirit resides within me. God's amazing love was exhibited on the cross of Calvary. A King died for me. He died for you. He died for the sins of the whole world.

Broken Bridges

God is calling us to bridge the gap between the lost and Him as we share the love of Jesus Christ. Broken bridges are appearing in families, in business, and even in churches.

With the recent changes in economy, every family has been touched in some manner. People have been unfaithful in business and personally. People are desperate. Desperate people do desperate things.

America and all nations will face a major test in the area of economics at the end of the age. We are seeing it right now. People are doing horrific things to others financially and in other ways as well. People have gone mad and Satan has entered the heart of many like Judas. There is nothing new under the sun. This same type of evil has been going on since the beginning of time.

Trust the Spirit of God inside you. Even the slightest warnings mean something—if nothing else, wait. Always follows His leading.

Before the end of the age, I believe the world will look at the church and see a family that can be trusted because they walk in love and their word is their bond. The world will start to trust God when they recognize this trait in people in the church. The strength of our witness will be determined first by how much we trust God's Word and then by how much our own word can be trusted. We must become a people that care more about honoring our word to God than man. What I mean by that is this: We must choose God's Word over man's way.

Sometimes the very test we are walking through has been totally ordained by God because people will see and witness the power of

God to withstand the battle that rages. Reflect on the life of Joseph and remember that God is for us and not against us.

When we want to do the right thing but have been put in a position due to the lack of integrity in the life of someone else, God sees it all and He will make every crooked place straight. He keeps the records and He knows the intent and motive of every heart. He knows exactly what it will take to touch the heart of every person.

Your part is to believe God and choose to do the right thing. The more time we spend being refined by the fire of the Holy Spirit, the more we become like Jesus, and *our very words will be true as well.*

Our relationship with God must be priority in our lives. Stop living in offense and always looking for something to pick someone apart about—it is sin. Choose to walk in the love of God but don't ignore warnings. Trust the Holy Spirit and obey Him. You may sense it is no big deal, and even others may tell you that—but I can assure you that it will be a big deal if you choose to ignore the warnings from the Holy Spirit.

The judgment that will ultimately come upon the world is the result of the world casually treating Him as no big deal and not taking life in God seriously. God sent His Only Son that we might have life. He gave His best. Are you giving your best?

God realizes we all stumble at times. We all face storms in life. Families and homes have been destroyed across this nation and across the globe. A house that does not have a good foundation has little chance of surviving. The same is true of Christians who cry out a little late to build their house on the Rock when facing a storm. Let us take heed to the Word of God that instructs us to a life of obedience:

Behold, the eye of the Lord is on those who fear Him, on those who hope for His lovingkindness, to deliver their soul from death and to keep them alive in famine. (Read Psalm 33:18–19.)

The Bible also tells us, *"This poor man cried, and the Lord heard him and saved him out of all his troubles. The angel of the Lord encamps around those who fear Him, and rescues them.*

O taste and see that the Lord is good; how blessed is the man who takes refuge in Him!

O fear the Lord, you His saints; for to those who fear Him there is no want. (See Psalm 34:6–10, KJV.)

The greatest promises in the Bible are to those who fear the Lord. When we properly fear the Lord we have nothing to fear on earth. Reflect for a minute upon John, the beloved. He sat at the same table with Jesus as Judas; yet Judas was only familiar with Him and betrayed Him. Familiarity breeds presumption and is perhaps the most tragic delusion. A commitment to know Christ and a desire to be like Him breeds an increasing revelation of just how awesome and amazing He is and will produce a life of obedience.

Knowing the truth and choosing not to live by it is a good definition of a hypocrite. In effect, Jesus describes hypocrisy as the sad state of a person who reduces himself to being an actor on a stage, because he does not know God the Father. Even though we have been bought with a price by the blood of the Lamb, He will not force us to love and serve Him. We must choose to obey through freedom. Obedience is a requirement.

People live sometimes thinking they get away with evil but the Bible informs us differently, King Solomon stated: "Because the sentence against an evil deed is not executed quickly, therefore the hearts of the sons of men among them are given fully to do evil" (Eccl. 8:11).

The fact that sometimes God does not quickly judge our sin is often misinterpreted that it does not matter to Him. This is the thinking of a heart that is darkened by sin. The fact that He does not quickly discipline is in itself a judgment that leads to further hardening of the heart.

God disciplines those He loves that fear Him. Those who love the truth will quickly obey even when it is not convenient. May the Bride of Christ arise and become stronger in watching. The tools we have been given are spiritual weapons—the truth, love, peace, and patience.

We must choose to live with eternity in mind and think first about advancing God's kingdom. People deeply matter to God. When you think first about advancing God's kingdom, living in true relationship with the King of kings and embracing your place, nothing will ever be the same.

Recovery of All

The Bible says: "And there was nothing lacking to them, neither small nor great, neither sons nor daughters, neither spoil, nor any thing that they had taken to them: David recovered all" (1 Sam. 30:19).

It is time to stand up and take back every thing that has been taken by the enemy. If you feel like you are sitting on a heap of ashes, your family is in bondage and captivity, and that those who used to be with you are stoning you, making false accusations, and have turned their backs on you, don't sit there feeling sorry for yourself. Get up, put on your garment of praise, pursue, overtake, and without fail recover all. The power of the covenant life in the person with a covenant heart will lift you up above your circumstances and seat you in heavenly places where you also realize victory rather than defeat.

Jesus has won the victory—as with David, I believe, you will recover all as well. Remember, God is no respecter of persons (see Acts 10:34). Just like David, you can return from your own personal Ziklag with far more than you lost. The secret of David's success is not in his skill or ability to fight, it is his ability to lift his eyes unto the hills from hence his help cometh—from the Lord. He lifted his eyes into the heavens and focused on Zion. Choose this day to do the same.

Someone needs to hear your testimony of encouragement. Someone needs to hear what you've been through. Don't waste another minute of your life. Don't throw any pity parties—no one will show up but the devil. Choose to live with the power of the Holy Spirit!

There is a secret place—a place of spiritual loneliness, an inner place you will feel all alone no matter what family of God is around you, a place where God brings you—the seeker. It is a place where you and God meet. What a magnificent place to be—an emptiness of heart, a loneliness of the soul, but it is just before daybreak, the light of day.

We must all present our bodies to Him as a living sacrifice. (See Romans 12:1–2.) Ask for the (Luke 11:9-13) infilling and ask for a fresh filling daily. "Ask of Me, and I shall give thee" (Ps. 2:8). God has chosen us to be His witnesses in the earth.

> "The God of our father raised up Jesus whom you murdered by hanging on a tree. Him God has exalted to His right hand *to be* Prince and Savior, to give repentance to Israel and forgiveness of sins. And we are His witnesses to these things, and *so* also *is* the Holy Spirit whom God has given to those who obey Him" (Acts 5:30–32, NKJV).

Will you present yourself today as a vessel for God's honor? Will you choose to present your marriage, life as a single, your family, your business, your finances, and all relationships to God's plan? Will you pray for America to turn back to God and start in your own home?

The Lord knows the power hidden in marriage. When we come to Jesus like the woman at the well did and apply the Scriptures to our own lives, we can have freedom from sin and shame and learn to live in hope and confidence again in every area.

Marriage and Sexualty

The Bible mentions human sexuality in terms of "waters." The Book of Proverbs provides great insight as it refers to a cistern, a well, and a fountain: "Drink waters out of thine own cistern, and running waters out of thine own well. Let thy fountains be dispersed abroad, and rivers of waters in the streets. Let them be thine own, and not strangers' with thee. Let thy fountain be blessed: and rejoice with the wife of thy youth" (Prov. 5:15–18, KJV).

In Scripture, a virgin is considered a cistern of untapped water—her pure waters are sealed until the day of her marriage. Once a virgin marries she is considered a well. The married man is considered a fountain and is depicted like a fountain being a stream of water that is driven by an eternal force—men have strong sexual drives.

When a marriage is operating in God's ways and flow together in accordance with the Bible, the union brings sexual satisfaction and blessing. Both find refreshing when they come together and experience renewal, strengthening, and reassurance of love in their spiritual union.

This is God's ordained plan. When we choose to do things God's way in marriage, we actually dip into living waters and discover we are actually drinking in the true wine of God. When we live in obedience in marriage, God releases a third source of "water" in marriage that is the river of His Spirit. The Holy Spirit is also symbolized as wine in Scripture. When we do things God's way in marriage, we come to place where we find completion to the amazing picture of the union of water of human sexuality and the spirituality supernaturally into the holy union of marriage.

What a beautiful picture or type and shadow of the church (as the Bride of Christ) and Jesus as the Bridegroom. Are you starting to see why God uses this passage to share about salvation and marriage with the woman at the well?

The blood of Jesus cleanses us from all sin and unrighteousness. Jesus also told her about a well of water springing up into everlasting life that would create in her a pure heart. His words were also implying an artesian well that brings forth an inexhaustible supply of fresh water from underneath the surface with great force.

Jesus was sharing with this woman about the Holy Spirit, the river of God. Now you can see why Satan has gone to great lengths to destroy the human race through immorality and sexual perversion while attacking marriage and family.

God's Word clearly defines the boundaries that bring protection in marriage and sex. God designed the sexual union between a man and a woman in marriage to be good and for reproduction. The world, to a large degree, has bought the lie from the pit of hell that sex is just an act or event. However, there are huge consequences to fornication, adultery, and sex of any kind outside of the covenant of marriage. (Scriptures: Genesis 1:27-28; Hebrews 13:4; Genesis 2:24-25; 1 Corinthians 6:9-10; Psalm 24:3-5, and Proverbs.)

When a person has sex outside the boundaries of marriage between a man and a woman, there are spiritual ties that are developed to that person and every person they have been with sexually as well. It opens the door to immorality, perversions of all kind, and misguided thinking. Pornography is another enemy that has infiltrated America and is clearly a trap from Satan. Thank God there is forgiveness and healing when we turn to God in repentance and prayer.

The Bible says: "He that believeth on Me, as the scripture hath said, out of his belly shall flow rivers of living water. (But this spake He of the Spirit, which that they believe on Him should receive...) (John 7:38–39, KJV).

God not only gave us the blood of Jesus to cleanse us from all sin, but He also gave us the river of the precious Holy Spirit to equip and empower us to have power over sin and the devil in this life. That is great news.

Jesus told His disciples: "But ye shall receive power, after that the Holy Ghost as come upon you" (Acts 1:8a KJV). We not only need forgiveness over sin we have in our past but power over the evil one to keep us from falling prey to temptation forevermore. We need the amazing, overcoming, overflowing power of God to flood our souls and bring refreshing from the contamination of sin in the world in order to have divine impact on the world around us.

Divine Impact

We all have divining moments in our life. Whether we realize it or not, what we walk through in this life leaves a lasting impact on our future. We must choose to turn to God. In one divine moment of impact, everything in life will change.

One moment in life—everything will change—and we will either go out in the rapture of the church as believers in Christ and many will be left behind. Another moment of divine impact is when a spark is ignited deep within our soul and we are never the same—we have a hungering and thirst for more of Jesus. We want to know Him and understand His Word.

Revival can only come where unity in the Spirit is found which is one reason Satan works so hard to bring about division and hatred. He goes to extreme lengths to stir up offense and strife because it brings destruction. Strife has the power to destroy.

We must have unity in the Spirit in our own personal life, in our marriage, and in our churches if we want to experience real revival. This will only come with real times spent on our knees in our own personal prayer closet. You can find a place and go there daily. If you are traveling, you can have quiet time in your hotel room.

On a larger scale, it is the same for churches. It is the endless hours of prayers of unseen servants spending time in prayer for the door to be open for the Holy Spirit to move without distraction. When true revival comes, God does a work in our lives. We will have a greater love and hunger for Him than ever before…a desperate hunger for more of God.

I remember faxing a prayer request to League of Prayer many years ago. It was probably twenty-three years ago or more. Looking back on it now, they may have thought I was crazy—but at the time, I didn't really care what they thought. My prayer was this:

> *"Lord, I ask you to change me and make me so much like you that others can't resist You in me. I want to be like You Lord. Help me to have Your eyes to see with, Your heart to feel with, and Your ears to hear with so I won't miss one divine appointment that you set up. Take anything that is not like You out of me and mold me and make me into the image of Jesus. I want to hear Your voice at the slightest whisper at the door of my heart. Lord, I ask You to open my eyes of spiritual understanding that I might see what You see."*

Looking back over my life, I realize the major disappointments and the great victories are all a part of my life. Victory comes with a price. God showed me that a price must be paid in order to break through the lines of the enemy.

America needs revival. Every church needs revival. When the presence of the Lord is strong, people will dance freely before the Lord, corporate businessmen will repent, drug addicts will get delivered, people prostituting their bodies will fall to their faces on the floor in repentance, and church staff will come to the altar for more of God. You see, when you know you have been forgiven much you have this incredible freedom and desire to share the love of Christ with all you encounter. You know you have been forgiven.

Marriages will be restored and people will be freed from all kinds of bondages. Has the soil of your heart been prepared in prayer for revival? Do you feel weary? Do you feel something is just not quite right? Are you angry with people disobeying God? Is it making you do crazy things?

You might not recognize revival when it sparks a flame in your heart. You might not feel a thing and suddenly everything begins to change. Don't allow the enemy of your soul to hinder your relationship with God another second.

Do you have a deep longing in your soul for more of God's presence and power in your life? Do you feel a burning desire for more of God? Do you desire more of His sweet and Holy presence? Only God can satisfy the soul that yearns for Him.

Pray with me for revival to sweep across America. Revival cannot come until the heavens are crystal clear through repentance and prayer. Lord, open the windows of heaven over America and let revival begin. *Truth gives us freedom.*

The fear of the Lord is the beginning of wisdom. Peer pressure as a teen is the fear of man as an adult. You can choose to no longer waste valuable time and energy worrying about other people, what they think about you, or what you do.

The foundation for a healthy thought life is the Bible. His Word is to take priority over all else we might choose to base decisions upon, and over our thoughts, actions, and feelings. As we choose to honor God instead of being moved by people we find ourselves enjoying life to a far greater degree, and experience power over defeat, discouragement, despair, doubt, dread, and depression.

When we choose to focus on the Truth of God's Word, we find our heart drawn closer to Him; we find strength, faith, hope, joy, and peace of heart, soul, and mind. When we encounter life challenges, we experience victory instead of being crippled emotionally as we know our life is based on what God says above all else.

There is great power in God's Word and by surrendering to the leading of the Holy Spirit. God never told us to ignore earthly wisdom and common sense, but He does want us to follow the leading of the Holy Spirit rather than being driven by the enemy through destructive tactics.

Learning to renew your mind and disciplining your own thought life by focusing on God's Word will prove the reliability of God's Word and move you to truly experiencing the love of God through trusting Him.

Remember, "As [a man] thinks within himself, so he is" (Prov. 23:7a). In times of trauma and testing, choose to fill your mind with God's Word and choose to love God with your whole being.

If you know something is wrong and don't know how to fix it, what do you do? Turn to God's Word. The Word of God has the answer for everything.

Train Your Brain: Take Every Thought Captive

Are you being taken captive by your thoughts? Are you currently experiencing crippling fear that comes when you hear threats of earthquakes, terrorist attacks, or the loss of a job? You may be experiencing fear from worrying about what might happen to your children, adults kids, spouse, family or even finances. How we battle this is by taking every thought captive.

> "Whatsoever things are true...think on these things" (Phil. 4:8, KJV).

Your face can reveal the crippling fear that the enemy uses to overtake your mind, will, and emotions and it will show on your face. God's desire is that we live an abundant life (John 10:10), yet fear has the power to rob us of joy if we don't choose to focus on Jesus and renew our minds.

James writes, "Consider it all joy, my brethren, when you encounter various trials, knowing that the testing of your faith produces endurance. And let endurance have its perfect result, that you may be perfect and complete, lacking in nothing" (James 1:2–4).

People are afraid of illness and ultimately death. Paul had a different perspective on death. In his letter to the Philippians, he says, "To die is gain" (1:21).

Learn to recognize and obey God's commands found in His Word. Learn to win over worry. "Do not be anxious for tomorrow;

for tomorrow will take care for itself. Each day has enough trouble of its own" (Matt. 6:34, NAS).

Prepare in the morning, prepare in the evening, and plan ahead. Pray, proceed by moving forward and trust God for ultimate provision. Do all you know to do for each day and keep moving forward in life—one day at a time.

I was spending time with a person in an appointment and she kept going back to speaking about what someone who worked for her had not done, focusing on the lack of excellence, and getting irritated about the person she had chosen to release.

I gently told her to bring her focus back to Jesus each time she started down that trail. That *trail* can lead to tension, rehearsing, anxiety, ill feelings, and losing your joy. (T-tension, R-rehearsing, A-anxiety, I-ill feelings, and L-losing your joy.)

It is a conscious choice that we make daily. As believers, our choice should include pressing toward God's purpose. "Press toward the goal for the prize of the upward call of God in Christ Jesus" (Phil. 3:14).

While the majority of people focus on retirement and making it their life goal, this is not God's plan. As a fellow runner-of-the-race in Christ Jesus, we must consciously choose to stay in the race and never give up. As you turn through the pages of Scripture, you certainly won't find one saint who quit. While we read about many who wanted to do so (remember Elijah, Jonah, and David?), not one of them actually did. Instead they kept pressing on toward God's purpose for their lives.

Paul's final words in Philippians 4:8: "Meditate on these things" gives us a direct command. It is not a piece of advice. Philippians 4:8 is God's command to us to redirect our focus on Him, on the truth of His Word and on the things in life that are actually real.

The Holy Spirit is within and He will help you learn as you surrender and obey the smallest of instruction. Respond in immediate obedience!

> The Bible gives us a clue as we take notice of what Paul wrote in 2 Corinthians: *For the weapons of our warfare are.. mighty in God for pulling down strongholds,*

> *casting down arguments and every high thing that exalts itself against the knowledge of God, bringing every thought into captivity to the obedience of Christ.*
> —2 Corinthians 10:4–5, NKJV

You might be wondering what the word "arguments" here might mean to us today. They are not truth, but are "high things" raised up against the knowledge of God and the truth in the Bible –the living word. All of these must be brought "into captivity to the obedience of Christ."

You will begin to recognize what is not true, when your emotions are running down a rabbit trail, and will begin to have moments of WOW where you suddenly realize what this means. It will take time and training, so don't give up in the beginning.

Taking every thought captive is work. It takes your whole heart being centered on Jesus and growing spiritually. It is a choice to focus on what is true and real, and demands energy, time, effort, and a heart that is committed to change—no matter what it takes.

Are you willing?

Pressing Onward

Second Corinthians 13:14 tells us, "The grace of the Lord Jesus Christ, and the love of God, and the communion of the Holy Ghost, be with you all. Amen." We have the privilege of a moment-by-moment communication with the Holy Spirit to lead us, guide us, and protect us from harm—an intimacy that brings us into a deeper relationship with the Lord through the person of the Holy Spirit after salvation and experiencing the love of the Father God. What a privilege.

Our choice must include focusing to the end. What do I mean by that? Let's take a look at a few in the Bible who focused to the end. Abraham responded to God's commands to move every single time. He lived in tents in the nomadic lifestyle that represented his search for "the city...whose builder and maker is God" (Heb. 11:10). Abraham pressed on without receiving the fulfillment of God's promises of land, a vast number of descendants, and great blessing (see Genesis 12:1–3 and Hebrews 11:39). He could have chosen to quit, but he desired "a better, that is, a *heavenly* country" (Hebrews 11:16). He pressed on until he died.

Moses was another who pressed on—even aged and weary. He kept on serving the Lord. He needed the help of Aaron and Hur to hold his hands up so that God would continue to bless the Israelites' efforts in battle. (See Exodus 17:8–13.) Moses could have chosen to quit but instead, he chose to get the help he needed to raise his hands heavenward.

Moses failed to obey God and trust Him for water at Meribah (see Numbers 20:7–13) and as a result, God did not allow him to cross into the Promised Land he had waited forty years to enter. Rather than quit, Moses went on and spent the rest of his days teaching the law, preparing the priests, and encouraging Joshua to lead God's people into the lands his own feet would never touch.

Samuel was called by God to be his prophet. Later the people of Israel rejected his leadership and asked him to appoint a king over them so they would be like their neighboring nations (1 Sam. 8:1–5). You will find that most people quit after being rejected, but not Samuel. Instead of quitting, he help on praying and preaching (1 Sam. 12:23), and he spent the rest of his life helping Saul, the man who took his place as the leader of the nation.

King David strongly desired to build a temple to God. But the Lord Almighty said to David, "You shall not build a house for My name, because you have shed much blood on the earth in my sight" (1 Chron. 22:8). Instead of quitting, David kept pressing on for the Lord. He spent his days planning, gathering and giving materials so that his son Solomon could build the temple. (See 1 Chronicles 22:5–19.)

Paul is another great reminder. Even in prison, Paul spent his final days writing letters to guide the church of Jesus Christ in the future. He wasn't moved by his emotions that could have roared with his impending death to shift his focus from Jesus Christ and His people. Paul kept on pressing by offering encouragement, exhortation, and comfort through his pen.

The Apostle John, while exiled to the island of Patmos in his old age, could have chosen to give up, as his service for Christ seemed to have earned him only disgrace and dishonor. Rather than giving up and quitting, he consciously chose to keep pressing on. He was blessed with "the Revelation of Jesus Christ" (Rev. 1:1) in his nineties. What does that tell us for today? No matter what age we are presently, we must consciously choose to keep pressing toward God's purpose—to the end.

Jesus Christ—God's Son knew about the cross, but He chose to press onward. He endured to the end. (Read Hebrews 12:2.) He consciously chose to be a living sacrifice to save us from our sins. His three simple words—"It is finished" (John 19:30) show us He pressed on to the end. The list of people who chose to keeping pressing on is endless.

We must consciously choose to keep pressing on and take a look in the mirror of God's Word. Born-again believers are called to love Him with all our heart, soul, and mind. This gives us purpose, depth, and a significance that gives strength to our walk with the Lord Jesus Christ.

May we seek nothing other than to follow Him to the end, to exhibit His love and light along our life's journey, and to accomplish God's will and purpose for our lives as individuals.

In order to do that we must consciously choose to focus on Jesus and remember Paul's words in Philippians 3:13–14: "Forgetting those things which are behind and reaching forward to those things which are ahead, I press toward the goal for the prize of the upward call of God in Christ Jesus." You must determine your purpose and keep your eyes on Jesus—allowing Him to inspire you along the way. You must consciously choose to lay aside whatever entangles you. Are you doing that?

To run the race unencumbered, the writer of Hebrews give us valuable insight. He exhorted us to "lay aside every weight, and the sin which so easily ensnares us" (Heb. 12:1). I know from being a runner that it is far easier to run the distance when we're not weighted down or encumbered by sin. Here are some questions that will help you determine your present running condition.

HEART CHECK

What goals are keeping your pursuit of God from being the most important daily activity in your life?

What messages or influences are drowning out God's call to you personally?

What do you need to lay aside so you can more effectively serve God?

What thought patterns, habits, or daily activities are holding you back or slowing you down in life?

Take an inventory and see what is keeping you from giving your whole heart to what God has called you to do with Him. Consciously choose to lay aside the useless, the wasteful, and the unimportant things that clutter your life and weigh you down. You will then be free to serve God in greater measure.

Conscious Choice

You must consciously choose God's purposes for your life and move toward it actively. You must consciously choose to trust the Lord in all things—even those you don't understand. You must consciously choose to think on what is true or real—about God and about your life. You must consciously choose to live one day at a time—without worry and anxiety. Renewing your mind to the Word of God will equip and empower you to navigate the maze of life with success and lasting fruit. God knows all about your life. No matter where you are or what circumstances you are facing, He is not caught by surprise about anything. The more you spend time with Him and in His Word, the more hope, encouragement, and peace you will experience within.

If you need help in an area, find the scriptures to pray that cover the problem. Begin to pray them daily. You will begin to notice change in your life over time. It is a daily battle we must consciously choose to face with the Word of God. Jesus was lead by the Holy Spirit into the wilderness where He won the battle through saying the Word. "It is written."

Jesus tells us the universal necessity of regeneration. "Jesus answered and said unto him, Verily, verily, I say unto thee, except a man be born again, he cannot see the Kingdom of God" (John 3:3).

In Charles Finney's book, *Finney's Systematic Theology* (The Complete & Newly Expanded 1878 Edition) we read his words: The moral depravity of the human race is everywhere assumed and declared in the Bible, and so universal and notorious is the fact of human selfishness, that should any man practically call it in

question—should he, in his business transactions, and in his intercourse with men, assume the contrary, he would justly subject himself to the charge of insanity. There is not a fact in the world more notorious and undeniable than this. Human moral depravity is as palpably evident as human existence. It is a fact everywhere assumed in all governments, in all the arrangements of society, and it has impressed its image, and written its name, upon every thing human.
–Charles Finney

Choosing to trust God, no matter what circumstances you are facing, is the way to overcome in life. Keep your focus on Jesus—and choose to live one day at a time. Forget the past, forgive all, focus on the present, and follow after excellence.

This is following after Joseph's example in life.

You are not a finished product- He who started a good work in you will bring it to completion. Work with God – renewing your mind and consciously choose to stay in peace, be like Christ, and make right choices on purpose.

Your connection with the Holy Spirit is the key to grasping the truth about how God sees you and values you.

You are born again by the Spirit (John 3:3-5).

The Spirit lives inside you and will be with you forever (John 14:16-17).

The Spirit teaches you what you need to know (John 14:26).

The Spirit testifies to you that you belong to God (Romans 8:16).

The Spirit guides you (Romans 8:14).

The Spirit equips you with talents, abilities, and spiritual gifts so you can live the abundant life in God, focused on Jesus and service in advancing the Kingdom of God (1 Corinthians 12:4, 11).

The Spirit prays for you when you are weak (Romans 8:26-27).

The Spirit develops his fruit in you: love, joy, peace, patience, kindness, goodness, faithfulness, gentleness, and self-control (Galatians 5:22–23).

God reminds us through Paul's writings in 1 Corinthians 1:7: "Now you have every spiritual gift you need as you eagerly wait for the return of our Lord Jesus Christ" God has given everything you need to serve him. What a wonderful Father God! You have everything you need to succeed at doing exactly what God has ordained for you to be doing.

Thank God for valuing you enough to make you competent to serve Him. Amen.

Seeing yourself as God sees you is a mind game. It is thinking differently and realizing God Himself has made you *competent* in Christ.

Renewing your mind in God's Word equips you to see what the Father sees. You will begin to see the why behind circumstances and in the lives of people and situations. The Holy Spirit reveals all hidden truth and shows us things to come. A mind renewed doesn't think like the world thinks any longer.

Pray that I'll know what to say and have the courage to say it at the right time.
—Ephesians 6:19, THE MESSAGE

The Holy Spirit will begin to speak to you and say things that may not make sense to your natural mind. He waits for you to obey Him. This is how he trains us. For example, Thursday night after I finished teaching a class at a university, Mother and I were driving home and she said she needed to stop at the grocery story to pick up three items to make a birthday cake. I told her I would go in but she told me to wait in the car.

While I sat in the car, with the car running, I lost track of time as I called one of the students and she and I were talking about the class and the love of the Father God. I began to think, "Wow, Mother has been gone a long time for three items." I got out of the car and went in to check on her and I saw her in line. She told me she had waited thirty minutes standing in line. I had sat in the car 40 minutes waiting on her with the car running.

After we got to the car, I realized I had used up much of the gas and the warning light came on so we went to purchase gas at the next station. While pumping gas the Holy Spirit said to me, "Give that man pumping gas your bookmarks." I told the Lord silently in my mind that I needed to approach him away from his car. As I was going in to pay for the gas the Holy Spirit also said to give the counter clerk some too. As I was walking in the man came walking out of the station and I knew he was a Christian. He opened the door for me and said, "Come in, ma'am." I told him thank you and asked if he liked to read. He said, "Yes, I love to read," so I asked him to wait just a minute and went back to the car to get them. I gave bookmarks to both people as the Holy Spirit directed.

This would never have happened had I not waited for forty minutes, burning up gas sitting in the car. Waiting positions us for God's purposes.

God wants us to love him with all our minds.

He wants us to imagine greater things with Him.

> *All that rings true...let this be the argument for your thoughts*
> —Philippians 4:8, KNOX BIBLE

You might be thinking..."How can I cultivate this kind of thought life that leads to loving God with all my mind?" This may be your heart's cry today, as it is mine, and we begin to wrestle with the challenge to think on what is true, not the lies of the enemy.

Following the following steps will help move you forward in training your thoughts. Secondly, you must surrender to the Holy Spirit's leading. You begin to take every thought captive.

Praying God's Word

Loving is not a feeling—it is a choice. Faith is not a feeling. Despite what you and I might be feeling right now, we choose to put our faith in God and the truth of His Word and not in our feelings. Amen! We must learn to daily pray God's Word over America now, not later.

Turn to God and cling to Him. Lean on Him. Here is how you pray God's Word: "Your Word says…" and begin praying God's Word over your own personal life and family, church, communities, and nation. Pray the truth of Romans 8:28.

Stop viewing life through negative perception, the lens of feelings, and definitely not the current circumstances. Faith looks to God and trusts Him to work out every minute detail.

Joseph saw God's purposes in His life, even through all the tragedy he walked through with his family and those who betrayed him. Learn to blaze a trail through false accusations, mistreatment, undeserved punishment, and even small misunderstandings. Learn to pray and praise. Learn to pray and not panic. Choose to be a person of purpose and pursue God with your entire being. Choose to *praise God through the storm!*

God turns even the most minor of incidents to the most horrific tragedies—for good. He doesn't cause them, but He uses them. Choose to give God your love by obeying His commands. "If you love Me, keep My commandments" (John 14:15). Our love for God is measured by our obedience.

Press through in faith – to see faith in action.

"By faith he forsook Egypt, not fearing the wrath of the king: for he endured, as seeing Him who is invisible" (Heb. 11:27, KJV).

We can see here that Moses "endured" but also that Moses' faith became a "seeing" faith. I believe that we can see more clearly with our eyes of faith than with our natural eyes when we lean on God and look to Him. We can live that way today through the same decision. We choose to look to God in all decisions in our daily lives. When we choose to forsake following after things in the world for following God, our spiritual eyes are opened to a new place.

God, please open our eyes in America that we might see what You see and know what you know.

Where Is Your Focus?

When Paul writes about "reaching forward to those things which are ahead," he is likening his life to a race and visualizing himself as a runner toward the finish line in life. His body is moving forward and his eyes fixed on the goal.

We must lean forward in Christ and keep moving forward as well. Running the race in life and living for Jesus and maturing in Him requires focus and discipline. Rest and relaxation are still part of life, but we are not to let the desire to rest and relax thwart the plan of God for our lives by focusing more on comfort than advancing God's kingdom.

If you look backward in a race, you will lose it. As a matter of fact, if you focus on the bad things in life that have happened to you, the opportunity to lose it arises as well. You may blow a gasket, get a little snippy with your spouse or neighbors, or actually blow your own witness as a follower of Christ Jesus.

Leaving the elements of the past in God's almighty hands is our best option in life. When He says to pursue that does not mean sitting in the dust complaining or ignoring real life facts. It means to go after God in hot pursuit.

We must choose to focus on the present and stop allowing the past to rob of us the present and future. When you focus on the present and future what happens next is that you will begin to recognize God's purpose for you.

Who am I?
Where did I come from?
What is my purpose?

Where am I headed?

To answer the first question, you might be a Christian woman, wife, mother, and grandmother. You might be the CEO of a corporation or a stay at home mom. You may be a man who owns his own business, a lawyer, CEO, or a car salesman.

Where did I come from? I was "in [Christ] before the foundation of the world" (Eph. 1:4).

What is my purpose or why am I here? I am here to be a servant for the Lord, to my family, and His people.

Where am I headed? Because I am born again and because of God's great love and amazing grace, I am going to heaven!

Time on earth is limited and we must choose to make the best of it. I want to use my time in advancing the Kingdom of God and enjoying the journey by staying close to Jesus. After all, it is the power of the Holy Spirit that makes things happen for the kingdom when I step out in obedience to His instructions.

We are to be thankful and live with an attitude of gratitude that He chose us to use us in the process of advancing His kingdom.

We are to focus forward and sail on in life. "Straining toward what is ahead..." (Phil. 3:13, NIV)

Joseph is a great story of a man who focused forward and who was in pursuit of God. We have valuable lessons to learn from his life as we see how Joseph lived in pursuit of God and in excellence... even when life circumstances were extremely difficult and painful. His story is found in Genesis 37-50.

Pursuit of Excellence

Joseph chose to serve God by doing his best no matter where he found himself. He was sold into slavery by his envious brothers and chose to forget his past in Israel as he moved forward to become the best slave and manager of Potiphar's household until he was unjustly imprisoned.

We see Joseph made the same choices again. He pursued excellence by forgetting the lifestyle he had been accustomed in Potiphar's palace and kept moving forward to become the best manager of the prisoners. When he was finally released from prison, he chose again to become the best in a government position, a divine privilege and setup by God that positioned him to feed his father, brothers, and their families as they arrived in Egypt during the famine. His life reveals one of excellence every step of the way.

Joseph moved from surviving to thriving. We were born to thrive in Jesus Christ. We were not born to merely exist in life. Difficult circumstances can make it tough to pursue excellence as we serve God. On the other hand, circumstances that are too comfortable can have the same effect if we are not careful. Anyone can become a person who exists rather than one who actually serves God. Being content with where we are in life can prohibit our assignment from God.

No matter if we find ourselves in a life of comfort or one like Joseph (in extreme circumstances), we must choose to focus on God's purpose for us and move forward, pressing for the prize. Each of us must choose to pursue God's will for us and be strengthened by Him.

Our mind-set must be "One thing I do: forgetting what lies behind and reaching forward to what lies ahead, I press on toward the goal for the prize of the upward call of God in Christ Jesus" (Phil. 3:13–14, NASB).

Joseph chose to overcome in every place. He knew God was with Him. He moved from surviving to thriving and was used to save his own family and a nation.

City Gates

What is the significance of a city gate in the Bible? Besides being a part of protection against invaders, city gates were places of central activity in biblical times. It was at the city gates that important business transactions were made, court was convened, and public announcements were made. The Bible tells us that wisdom also sits at the gates.

To control the gates of one's enemies was to conquer the city. Part of Abraham's blessing from the Lord was the promise that "your offspring shall possess the gate of his enemies" (Gen. 22:17).

When Jesus promised to build His church, He said, "The gates of Hades will not overcome it" (Matt. 16:18). An understanding of the biblical implications of "gates" helps us understand Jesus' words. Since the gates were a place where rulers met and counsel was given, Jesus was saying that all the evil plans of Satan himself would never defeat the church.

When churches operate while advancing the Kingdom of God, we make an impact on our communities. Martin Luther King, Jr. once said, "Human progress is neither automatic nor inevitable… every step toward the goal of justice requires sacrifice, suffering, and struggle; the tireless exertions and passionate concern of dedicated individuals."

It is God's desire and plan that every individual move from knowing about Him to knowing Him personally and fulfilling his or her role in His kingdom. When we see churches reaching outward into the community in greater measure, we will experience revival across America. When we turn back to God as a nation in repentance, God will heal our land.

You can make a difference. No matter how few in number, we can make a difference. We can impact the people in the marketplace by sharing our hope in Jesus through sharing our testimonies of God's goodness and our faith in Him.

Jesus told His disciples, "Occupy till I come" (Luke 19:13, KJV). He is saying the same thing to us today. Be about the Father's business—souls! We are to make disciples, not just add names to the roll. Let me warn you right here, it won't be a walk in the park. When you begin to make an impact in the lives of others, look out. As a matter of fact, if you are doing anything with God now and are not being bothered by the enemy, you might want to check out your walk. Make sure of your direction.

Jesus wants us to be disciples. Basically this means we are a learned student of the Word. We move out and teach others by example and fan the flame in them. The ultimate goal of discipleship is to be transformed into the image or likeness of Jesus Christ (Romans 8:29), and then moving out and sharing Him with others.

As believers, we must not be ashamed of the Gospel of Jesus Christ. We must move from receiving to sharing the Good News in the marketplace and city gates! Will you join me?

The Bible says, *"The one who breaks open will come up before them; They will break out, Pass through the gate, And go out by it; Their king will pass before them, With the Lord at their head"* (Micah 2:13, NKJV).

The one who breaks open is also a messianic title, meaning "deliverer," and adding to the comforting assurance of return from exile the hope of one who will be a shepherd-king to all who recognize His caring authority. (See Micah 2:13, SPIRIT-FILLED LIFE BIBLE NKJV, Nelson.)

When we come under the authority of our shepherd-king—LORD JESUS—He is our deliverer. When we choose to honor Him and seek His wisdom, it is a picture of being swept off our feet by Jesus, the Bridegroom, to carry us over the threshold of the gate. An example would be when a groom carries his bride over the threshold of their new home.

At every new gate, there is a threshold where the enemy has two demonic structures. One is to stop us and block us from our destiny. The other is a life destroying force that comes to restrict each of us to suck the very life out of us. The old root word is symbolic of a python snake—but is not spelled that way. A python snake squeezes its prey to death. It is an assignment from hell to bring about destruction and death.

The Bible tells us that wisdom sits at the gates. (See Proverbs 8:3.) We are to seek God and find wisdom from Him. At the threshold, we must choose to overcome whatever God is revealing to us at the time. This can be a tight or restricted place where we have to trust God.

I will never forget a drive to Kiawah Island one Sunday afternoon. I was driving our Expedition and had turned the navigation system on for the trip. Mother and I were stopping at a store to make a quick purchase for the trip before heading out. There are two major interstates we take for the trip and really didn't need the navigation system on until we were coming close to the area, but I chose to turn it on at the beginning of the trip. What happened next is quite amazing!

The car's system advised me to make a legal u-turn on Interstate 77, so thinking God was giving me a warning, I called my husband to ask if he needed me for something or if he had left something in the vehicle I was driving that he needed. I told him about the system coming on and advising to make a legal u-turn. He said, "No," and we went onward to Dillard's at the local mall.

I wasn't in the store for even ten minutes. I ran in to purchase makeup and came right back out. Mother had waited in the car. We got back out on I-77 again and my husband called to ask where we were. He told me I had a set of keys that he needed and asked if I would turn around. We turned around and met him to give him the keys and off we went again headed for our destination. I knew the Holy Spirit was warning me for Dan but it took a few minutes for Dan to figure out what it was he needed.

Listen to what happened next. We drove onward for two hours listening to a CD series I had owned for 19 years and had never heard until that day. It was about the Breaker Anointing and Micah 2:13 and the gates. The minister was explaining what I have shared with you. We continued on into Columbia and just as we made the turn onto the next highway we came to a complete stop.

We finally started moving about fifteen minutes later and we came up to an exit ramp. I told Mother I believed I would take an alternate route and follow the navigation system through the country roads.

When we topped the hill we saw miles and miles of stopped traffic ahead and learned there had been a major accident with fatalities. It was apparent to me that the Holy Spirit turned us around. He saved us from perhaps even being in the accident. He kept us from potential harm and destruction.

We went through the country roads and made it just before Kiawah Island. I decided to stop at a small country store to make sure of the path we were on because it didn't look familiar and the lady told me she had never heard of Kiawah Island that worked inside.

Let me tell you something right here. She was five minutes from the main road that leads directly into Kiawah Island. People are near you that don't know about Jesus. People are in the city gates that don't know about the Good News of Jesus Christ! Are you willing to have Jesus—the Bridegroom—sweep you across the threshold to be used greatly by Him?

Are you willing to turn around and go back for the lost? Are you willing to pray for America to turn back to God? Are you willing to renew your mind in the Word of God for wisdom?

A renewed mind recognizes God's hand at work. We must choose to fix our heart and mind on God, while keeping a vigilant, steady focus on Him. We must daily ask God to rid our minds of all that interferes with our time together with Him.

Intimacy is where we find wisdom and strategy to overcome. I can't tell you strongly enough how important a time with God is on a daily basis. You will find strength to overcome and joy to run your race.

As we run our race, there are many voices that cry out to abandon the effort of spending time with Jesus. The world draws us away from following Jesus and offers tempting rewards for choosing the way of the world. The enemy tries to get us to feel pressure to be like others, and to make us feel like we are not good enough or valuable. The flesh cries out to have fun and not to think about eternity. The world doesn't understand the Christian race and the prize that awaits us as followers of Christ Jesus. Neither does the world acknowledge the cause of Christ Jesus or value the commitment His cause requires and the death and resurrection of Jesus.

Never give up on anyone – make a list and pray the names of the lost – asking God and thanking Him for salvation. Pharaoh was a great and powerful man who got into a place of great need; the butler risked his life for an audience with the king to tell him what he knew about Joseph. That is all we are called to do…tell others about Jesus. That opens the door for them to respond.

Pressing Onward Comes From a Deep Fire Within that is Birthed Through Intimacy With God

Without first quieting our hearts (our minds and mouths), we will never realize the longing we have in our hearts that actually crave deeper intimacy with God. Learn to practice and attitude of gratitude and stay in the position of a heart of praise. Praising raises you above your circumstances.

> *I press on toward the goal for the prize of the upward call of God in Christ Jesus.*
> —Philippians 3:14

Don't wait until you are proficient to create goals. Step forward and set goals. You only get what you set as a goal. Goals are our destiny, our future, and our source of actually doing what God has put in our hearts to do in life. The Lord may put a desire in your heart to run for political office or some other area, but you may run from it due to fear of exposure to your family and kids. Instead of running from the desire, turn to God and seek His wisdom and strategy.

The Bible gives us great instruction: *"Write the vision and make it plain on tablets, that he may run who reads it"* (Hab. 2:2, NKJV). When we write the vision God gives us down on paper, we can set goals. Goals fan the flame or ignite us to move forward. Goals fan the flames that have nearly gone out with unbelief. Unbelief goes out by prayer and fasting.

The primary reason we are to set goals is to have a clearly defined desire written down so we can see it. People fail to set and achieve goals because of fear. The fear of not accomplishing something can be devastating and discouraging. I personally believe that not attempting to do what God has put in your heart and not setting the goals is far more dangerous. God tells us a man who vacillates will receive nothing from the Lord. I would rather step forward and take that next step and miss it partly than sit back and do nothing. How about you?

Fear is emotionally draining and takes a toll on our strength and joy. The writer of Proverbs knew something about not getting something done when he wrote, "Hope deferred makes the heart sick" (Prov. 13:12). Not knowing what to do and feeling hopeless in a situation creates pain in the mind and body. Our bodies tell us that pain is to be avoided at all costs. However, pain is a clue something is wrong.

Pain is something we must choose to take "captive to the obedience of Christ" (2 Cor. 10:5) and say, "I *will* do this and not be stopped. I will succeed because "I can do all things through Christ who strengthens me" (Phil. 4:13).

Another reason people fail to set and achieve goals is due to irresponsibility. In life, you are ultimately responsible for your own destiny. Don't blame others. That is a mark of immaturity.

Another reason of failure is lack of knowledge. We must have set in our minds to move forward and know how to actually accomplish the task. Choose to learn and take advantage of every book, seminar, or teaching series you can find. Read and listen over and over till you get it in you. Choose to have bulldog faith and tenacity to move forward. One thing you must always remember is this; there is always more to learn.

Another reason for failure is when you don't believe, through doubt, unbelief, lack of confidence, or low self-worth. This can be paralyzing to any person. We must stand upon God's Word and not budge off of it. I believe we should not budge off God's Word and bridge the gap to God. Choose to say, "It is written" as Jesus did in the wilderness. Choose to believe the Scriptures that say, "I can do

Pressing Onward Comes From a Deep Fire Within . . .

all things through Him [Christ] who strengthens me" (Phil. 4:13), and "all things are possible" (Matt. 19:26).

Because of Jesus, we can believe. God sent His Only Son to die for you and me so that we might have life and life abundantly. Stop allowing the tactics of the enemy to thwart your destiny and choose to take every thought captive to the obedience of Christ.

If you are afraid to do something that you sense God has put in your heart, do it anyway. It is okay to feel fear and be afraid of your own inadequacy. Give it a try and trust God. When we choose to surrender to the leading of the Holy Spirit as believers in Christ, it is the job of the Holy Spirit to lead and guide us. Get up and take the next step. Choose to daily renew your mind and march forward.

Have you ever heard that you can only eat an elephant one bite at a time? Set goals and take the first step as soon as possible. I was driving to the Belmont area and chose to stop by a furniture store where God had set up a divine appointment. I met a man who shared a miracle story of God's intervention in his life. He asked if I had time to hear it and I stood there and listened as what he shared was vitally important to him and a testimony to the saving grace of God Almighty.

He told me how he had been in a small explosion and was mad at God many years ago. He was angry with God and then he was in a larger explosion some time after that. He shared how the explosion blew the entire side of a building off as he stood there with no soot to be found on him as he was supernaturally protected.

The firemen were amazed. They asked where he had been standing. As they looked at the spot, it was as if there was a bubble of protection, a round circle around him that provided protection and saved his life. That was totally God! God is totally concerned about you and America. We must take the next step to pray for America that she might come back under that same protection.

As we started the drive home from the store, we passed by a new billboard—*take the next step!* Wow! Then as we got back out on the interstate, traffic came to a sudden stop. We waited and finally started to move, only to learn of an accident where we might have been had we not stopped at the furniture store due to the prompting of the Holy Spirit where I heard the man's testimony of God's divine intervention!

You may feel like there is a fire around you now, or that you are in the middle of a fiery furnace, but I assure you that God is with you. Learn to break down large goals into bite-size goals for easier accomplishment. Decide on a goal and take the next step. You may have a desire to build a new business, preach the gospel, start your own church, or learn to gain control of your anger. Regardless of the type of goal, you will learn that when you see small steps being completed it will give you more self-confidence and the tenacity to keep moving forward.

Step out in belief and faith in God. Belief led Abraham Lincoln to endure years of political loss and defeat, a presidency ravaged by civil war, and to unify the nation and end slavery. All the years of loss did not stop him. He kept getting back up and moving forward.

Belief gave Thomas Edison the tenacity to work through over 100,000 experiments on one idea before he successfully created the incandescent light bulb and illuminated the world.

Belief in God illuminated one man – David – to step up and face a taunting giant named Goliath who threw the entire army of Israel into being paralyzed through fear of the enemy. One teenage shepherd boy dared to step forward and took five smooth stones and a sling and hit the giant in the head – cut his head off with his own sword and defeated an entire army in a single day!

The single greatest act of love ever displayed is that of Jesus Christ. Thousands of people have lost their lives rather than deny their belief in Jesus Christ as Lord. Belief was the motivator behind the greatest act of love known to all mankind.

Motivation fans a flame and ignites faith and belief to move forward. It is a fire within, a deep passion that won't burn out. Someone has to step up and fan the flame in the people who have become so discouraged and distressed through life circumstances and distractions! Will you join me today? Start in your own home and family. It will bring hope to your heart.

What motivates you? A person is motivated by his belief in something. It may be a dream, an assignment, a person, another person's vision, or a new idea. A person who is motivated and energized by his or her belief is unstoppable with God. If one teenage shepherd boy can defeat a taunting giant, what can we do with our belief in God?

Make a plan, set goals, and trust God to bring the people to assist. For every goal you set you will need specific people with specific skills who can be responsible. Choose to connect and network with other people. There are no lone rangers. When you dare to believe and step out, you will be amazed at how God will move on your behalf to connect you with people from different places just for the vision and purpose He has planned and has put in your heart. Stay connected. Remember, the only thing that never changes in life is God. Change is constant.

Therefore we do not lose heart, but though our outer man is decaying, yet our inner man is being renewed day by day. (See 2 Cor. 4:16, NAS.) Renew means "to renovate, refurbish, and refurnish."

Spiritual growth is a necessity. We are not meant to stay as babies. Seek God daily and you will grow.

Our daily prayer must be, "Lord, let me hear you at the slightest whisper at the door of my heart. May I live so close to you that I can feel your heart beat and Your wisdom will rule my mind continually."

Bless the Lord, O my soul; and all that is within me, bless His holy name. Bless the Lord, O my soul, and forget none of His benefits... Who satisfies your years with good things, so that your youth is renewed like the eagle. (See Psalm 103:1–2, 5.)

Physical Renewal is a Necessity

I studied the eagle many years ago and one thing I learned is quite fascinating. The eagle soars to extreme heights where it sits alone and pulls out all its feathers and talons and scrapes off its beak on the rocks. It finds a safe ledge to do this. The body of the eagle will be more vulnerable but will come back stronger than before. Is it any wonder the U.S. national emblem is the bald eagle?

In our lives, we must choose to take care of ourselves physically as well. Proper diet, exercise, adequate sleep, rest, and also recreation are necessary for physical health and longevity.

Peace with God and the peace of God in our hearts create a joy of intimacy with Christ that has beneficial effect upon the body and mind. Staying our mind on God leads to spiritual growth, development, a preservation of physical and mental power—even in the midst of adversity.

We grow through choosing to turn to God in challenges. Challenges come when we start to build. We learn to put on the mind of Christ and think like He thinks. *We are not tolerant and open-minded. We know who we are in Christ and whose we are.*

The body is the temple of the Holy Spirit—the place where He indwells. Christ promotes the best interest of the physical body and mind as well as inward peace. The enemy attacks when we are down and don't feel the best. No matter what we may be facing, we can have peace within and new strength that comes from being born again. You can have a new attitude. You can have hope for yourself, family, and America once again.

God's Word tells us what we are called to do: *"You are my witnesses," declares the Lord, "and my servant whom I have chosen, so that you may know and believe me and understand that I am he. Before me no god was formed, nor will there be one after me"* (Isa. 43:10. NIV). We are chosen by God to go out into a dark and troubled world, fully aware that we already possess all it takes to bring hope, create change, and live completely for Christ—because of the finished work on the cross of Jesus Christ.

It doesn't matter how many wrong turns we have taken, or how painful life experiences may be, there is hope in Jesus! I have often heard that time heals all wounds. I don't believe that at all. It is what we do with our time that can bring healing. When we turn to God as individuals, and choose to grow from our mistakes and the wrongs that come against us in life, we actually grow and are equipped and empowered to help others.

God promises that the plans He has for you are for good and not evil, to give you a future and a hope. Why not turn to God right now, rather than being weighed down by what is happing across the globe, and ask God to bring revival in your own heart. May revival sweep across this nation like lights being turned on in every home in every city and in every state across America!

Let us break free from the past and learn to thrive in God again as one nation under God. The Bible says:

> *I waited patiently for the Lord; he turned to me and heard my cry. He lifted me out of the slimy pit, out of the mud and mire; he set my feet on a rock and gave me a firm place to stand. He put a new song in my mouth, a hymn of praise to God. Many will see and fear the Lord and put their trust in Him.*
> —Psalm 40:1–3, NIV

America needs to be lifted up out of the slimy pit, out of the mud and mire, and learn to live in God again! Ask God to take hold of your thinking and to expand His influence in your heart. It doesn't matter what you have or don't have—we must learn to rely on God's ways and not our own! It doesn't matter if you feel qualified or not to do what God has called you to do with Him—God calls us and we are qualified by Him! God will begin to demonstrate what happens when we step out and take the baton like my little dog Beau who tossed his baton shaped bone with hearts on both ends! God is calling out to His people to step into His divine plan for advancing His kingdom!

Personality Issues and Renewal

Prayer changes everything – most of all you. You can choose a new attitude. Personalities differ but all people have an innate desire to know their life matters. We all have different gifts and talents. God is at work on all of us—because none of us have arrived.

I had a dear associate tell me that praying in the Holy Spirit will actually change your personality. He said he has clients who come in and take a personality test and if they will pray at least an hour a day in the Holy Spirit, their personality will change and show on the next test.

> *But now you also, put them all aside: anger, wrath, malice, slander, and abusive speech from your mouth. Do not lie to one another, since you laid aside the old self with its evil practices, and have put on the new self who is being renewed to a true knowledge according to the image of the One who created him—a renewal in which there is no distinction between Greek and Jew, circumcised and uncircumcised, barbarian, Scythian, slave and freeman, but Christ is all, and in all. And so, as those who have been chosen by God, holy and beloved, put on a heart of compassion, kindness, humility, gentleness, and patience.*
> —Colossians 3:8–12

> *That in reference to your former manner of life, you lay aside the old self, which is being corrupted in*

> *accordance with the lusts of deceit, and that you be renewed in the spirit of your mind, and you put on the new self, which in the likeness of God has been created in righteousness and holiness of the truth. Therefore, laying aside all falsehood, speak truth... be angry, and yet do not sin; do not let the sun go down on your anger...Let him who steals steal no longer...Let no unwholesome word proceed from your mouth, but only such a word as is good for edification according to the need of the moment... And do not grieve the Holy Spirit of God...Let bitterness and wrath and anger and clamor and slander be put away from you, along with malice. And be kind to one another, tenderhearted, forgiving each other...*
> —Ephesians 4:22–26, 28–32

These verses refer to the soul of mankind—the self, the heart of man—which is comprised of the emotions and personality of man. The soul is made up of the mind, will and emotions and it lives in a house—your body.

Our personality and soul is affected positively when we choose to renew ourselves through spending quality time with God. The presence of God in our lives brings about change. It doesn't mean you won't ever have a day where you don't face a trial or tribulation; it simply means you can overcome.

When we discover our purpose and begin to take steps to achieve that destiny, our lives actually take on new meaning and perspective because we begin to see what God is revealing to us—who God intended us to be.

We finally move forward to step into the destiny and the very reason we were created. With this divine revelation comes growth in confidence, self-esteem rises, and courage and tenacity increase. Everything rises because of the resurrection power of Jesus Christ. We are in a leadership crisis here in America. Husbands are afraid to lead. Women are suffering abuse. Babies are being aborted. Marriage is being attacked and the foundation of America is crumbling before our eyes. We have a spiritual problem in America. We need hearts for God.

Hearts Ablaze for God

What I want you to take notice of in particular are the following: The Bible says that we are to "put on a heart" of compassion, humility, gentleness, kindness, and patience (Col. 3:12), as well as we are to "put on the new self" be getting rid of that which is ungodly (Eph. 4:24). These are emotional concepts, thought patterns, and social concepts. Pay attention to choices in relationships and our perceptions of life.

While studying and digging into the Word I learned something profound about Ephesians 4:23: ""the spirit of your mind." The word *spirit* and the word *mind* both have the meaning of "purpose." When we move from living our lives in selfish desires to the will of God for our lives, our focus changes. Our purpose for living is to complete our destiny in God, not for living for self and our own personal will.

We find a new reason for living and it empowers us to live out God's purpose instead of our own will. Knowing your God-given purpose will actually dictate who you are in every area of your life; even your personality and emotions.

Simply put, it means you choose to focus on something different and walk away from the old. This is what Christian living is all about. When you choose to renew your mind you actually renew your very reason for living and your living turns to match your destiny.

Stand up and outlive your life in purpose. It is time for husbands to stand up and be the priest of their homes, gathering the family around and reading God's Word together. Find a great devotional and spend time talking about God.

People must stand up on God's Word and stop being afraid to offend others. Great leaders move forward and lead. Be a leader in your home and arise in God's purpose.

You will live destiny minded and eternity will be your focus. God turn America back to you and advancing your kingdom again.

> *I urge you therefore, brethren, by the mercies of God, to present your bodies a living and holy sacrifice, acceptable to God, which is your spiritual service of worship. And do not be conformed to this world, but be transformed by the renewing of your mind, that you may prove what the will of God is, that which is good and acceptable and perfect. For through the grace given to me I say to every man among you not to think more highly of himself than he ought to think; but to think so as to have sound judgment, as God has allotted to each a measure of faith.*
> —Romans 12:1–3

Transformation means metamorphosis, such as a caterpillar coming out of its cocoon and changing into a beautiful butterfly. We too, become something totally different. We even look different and act different to those around us when we fall in love with Jesus.

Once you recognize Jesus Christ is the only begotten Son of God who sacrificed His life for you and you receive Him as Lord and Savior, everything changes. To move forward in salvation, you start the journey or process. Everything about you changes, the way you think, act, and live. You move to thinking eternity-minded and are more interested in souls and advancing the Kingdom of God than anything else.

God promises that when you begin to renew your mind, you will be transformed. Thinking changes! Be careful what you think about! Think and believe that *with* God nothing is impossible. As a matter of fact, cut the word impossible out of your dictionary and out of your mind.

Let's look at a First Corinthians 2:16 for a moment. The Bible says, "We have the mind of Christ." What does that mean? It means that His thoughts, His words, and His ways *can* become ours in this life. Stay with me and dare to believe God

When we step into life by the Spirit of God and believe God's Word, His Word, His ways, and His thoughts will become a part of our daily life. For example, your plan may be to give a Christian book to the governor as you go to a planned event. When you arrive, you sense the Lord is telling you to give it to someone else. That is listening and obeying God. It is hearing the voice of God.

You and I have the ability to tap into the power of God and we can walk in His ways and hear what He is saying to us to attain victory in life. You can make the choice to stop making excuses and make a difference in your personal life and in America. You can learn how to live supernaturally through the power of a transformed mind by taking the next step in spiritual growth. Pay close attention to the following story and you will believe.

We got a new puppy that I chose to name Prince Christmas Beau—we call him "Beau." He was afraid to go up the stairs until one night my husband carried him to the top stair and put his feet on the bottom and front paws on the top landing. Then Dan gave him a little push and he went running into the bedroom.

The very next morning, Beau ran up four little outdoor steps into the back door. Later in the day, he tried to come up from the bottom of the stairs. I noticed when he got to the fourth step he turned back to look and rolled down three stairs onto the hardwood floors. He was fine, but he took a little tumble.

The third day, Beau ran up both flights of stairs without looking backward. I think he did it afraid and chose to run the entire course! He made it and so can you. Don't be afraid to take your next step. We all face opposition. Everyone has it! Even if you stayed at home, watched the news all day, and did much of nothing, you would not eliminate opposition in your life. Sitting on the sofa doing nothing will make you grow fat and lazy, not to mention unattractive to your spouse. This can also create severe marriage problems.

As long as you choose to sit on the sidelines, you won't do anything very exciting but will find yourself becoming critical of those who do. Your children will imitate you and grow up to be unproductive with no incentive and internal passion for life.

Life brings problems no matter if we are doing great things or hiding out on the sidelines. Do you want problems from doing nothing or do you want challenges that face anyone as result of stepping out to do what appears impossible to man, but is possible with God? All things are possible with God.

I don't know about you, but I have chosen to stand up for God, stand upon His Word, and do all He has put in my heart to do with Him. The Bible tells us to *"be strong and of a good courage: for unto this people shalt thou divide for an inheritance the land, which I sware unto their fathers to give them"* (Josh. 1:6, KJV).

In the midst of instability in this nation, God's Word is still true for us today! We must choose to be God-correct and stop being concerned about being politically correct. We must choose to run everything by the Word of God.

> *Blessed is the people of whom this is true; blessed is the people whose God is the Lord.*
> —Psalm 144:15, NIV

Crisis and Courage

When Joshua became the new leader of Israel, the nation was also in a leadership crisis. Moses had been dead for thirty days and the people were wondering who on earth was going to lead them. They wondered if God would speak to them. In the midst of their leadership crisis and great instability, the word of the Lord came to Joshua, calling him to arise into the position of leadership for which had been training for many years. Crisis and courage were both on display—so we can see even for today.

Choose to return to God and stand upon His Word. Believe God for greater things. I believe the best is yet to come. Believe and receive. God has greater things for us to do with Him in this last hour. Be the best man or woman you can be. Be the best husband or wife. Be the best wherever you find yourself and choose to step out in faith and courage while trusting God.

Dare to believe God. Don't wait till it is too late. As a Christian, God has greater things for us to do with Him. Don't wait until you arrive in heaven to find decorative boxes with beautiful bows of gifts that were intended for you to be used here on earth to advance the Kingdom of God. God is calling us to arise. Dare to believe and take your next step with courage. Have faith in God.

God has greater things for America as a nation. There are souls at stake here and across the globe.

This is our two-minute warning.

Will you choose to return to God?

Won By One

Even in the midst of such change, chaos, and unrest across America and the nations, we can still be reminded of our God-given purpose because of the Resurrection of Jesus Christ. We serve the only God who was crucified and raised from the dead.

Jesus wants us to be reminded that we have a purpose here on earth. It is to advance the Kingdom of God. We get up, step out, and begin to share the love of God personally and live out of God's Word in the marketplace. We must continue to do ministry, come together in unity, and respond as Jesus would in every situation. As an individual you may ask, "How can I make a difference?" We must choose to stand up and seek God and pray for America to turn back to God as a nation.

You may have failed at something personally, but that doesn't make you a failure. You may have fled the scene and abandoned your family, betrayed a friend, family member, or business partner, but there is hope for you and the people of this nation when we turn to Jesus and repent. Failure doesn't defeat your purpose in life.

The disciples scattered and fled the scene on the night of Jesus' betrayal. Nobody stood up for Christ Jesus when His life was in danger. Those closest to Him fled for safety in fear. You can choose to take a stand and be won by one. You can be won by one moment with Jesus. One moment with Jesus changes everything. One encounter with the Son of God, experiencing His power and presence changes everything, most of all you. One person can make a difference. Then we connect with others and take a stand.

You can choose to turn adversity into advocacy and add a verse to your life today. You can choose to build and advance God's kingdom, or you can sit back on the sidelines and watch life pass you by. Choose today with resolve, a firm commitment in honoring God above all else, to be won by One—the Son of God! We in turn go out and love people, pointing them to Jesus.

One moment with Jesus changes everything. Will you turn to God and pray for your family? Will you choose to commit your family and business to God? Will you do everything as unto the Lord? Will you turn back to God for America, one by one?

When we resolve to take a stand and commit everything to God and seek Him above all else, we find out that God knows best how to connect us in divine alignment. Out of the alignment with the right people we discover our assignment here on earth and are empowered by the Holy Spirit with God's anointing power from on high to live it out to the world.

We are endued with God's power and we live with a fresh revelation of God's amazing love for us! When we care about what matters to God, He takes notice! We also need to be aware and prepared for attacks that come when we step out and move forward in faith to do all God has called us to do with Him. We choose to dedicate and commit all to Him. We do business on purpose for God, doing good and promoting good in the community.

Satan never attacks a retreating army—keep moving forward in God!

God's light exposes darkness. Truth wins over lies. Anytime you mix light and darkness in any room, the light always shines forth. Our part is to wait upon the Lord and use our God-given authority to break free, realizing we will experience attack but we are not *under* attack. Jesus was crucified, buried, raised from the dead, and is seated at the right hand of the Father, interceding for us that our faith will not fail. The Bible says we are seated in heavenly places with Christ Jesus, (Read Ephesians 2:6.) We must keep our eyes fixed on Jesus by living out of His Word and running everything through His Word by prayer. We will experience attacks, but because of our position *in Christ*, we are never *under* those attacks.

The Midnight Hour

We fight the good fight of faith through spending time in prayer and waiting upon the Lord. We take time to be still and inquire of the Lord. Like David in 1 Samuel, we can use the same principles outlined for us today. David and those with him were in despair and wept till there was nothing left. (See 1 Samuel 30.) Their families taken captive and homes burned—they were in despair. The men that were with David wanted to blame David and stone him.

But David chose to encourage himself in the Lord and called for Abiathar the priest and chose to worship! Extreme worship represents a heart for God! Whenever someone despises worship, they actually are in a dangerous place of barrenness that is also a rejection of the very reason we live! (You can see this in Matthew 26:8 when the costly anointment was poured over Jesus. The disciples were upset.) We learn that extreme worship exposes religion in everyone and forces us to make a decision to enter into relationship with Jesus or not.

We can choose to celebrate, honor, and worship Jesus by living with a thankful heart. We can choose to live by faith and thank God before the answer comes to our prayers. We must choose to become people who worship, regardless of our circumstances, and we will see change and will become fruitful beyond natural reason.

Will you choose to turn to God and live by faith in His Son Jesus? Will you submit and surrender to His ways? Will you choose to surrender so that the presence of God will point you to a world in need of Jesus? When you turn to God and obey Him, the Holy Spirit will empower you to do what your natural mind may think is impossible. Though the circumstances of life seem bleak, Jesus is alive.

After the disciples scattered and fled for their lives, they waited in Jerusalem. Jesus rose from the dead and revealed Himself to Mary and then to the disciples. "Thomas, one of the twelve, was not with the disciples when Jesus came. So the other disciples told him, 'We have seen the Lord!' But he said to them, 'Unless I see the nail marks in his hands and put my finger where the nails were, and put my hand into his side, I will not believe.' A week later his disciples were in the house again, and Thomas was with them. Though the doors were locked, Jesus came and stood with them and said, 'Peace be with you!' Then he said to Thomas, 'Put your finger here; see my hands.

Reach out your hand and put it into my side. Stop doubting and believe.' Thomas said to him, 'My Lord and my God!' Then Jesus told him, 'Because you have seen me, you have believed; blessed are those who have not seen and yet have believed'" (John 20:24–29, NIV, author's paraphrase).

This should give us all great hope. We can give our doubts and fears to Jesus. That same resurrection power raises us up today. Because He lives, we are strengthened and receive hope to believe for our families and nation.

Resurrection power also reconciles and restores relationships. See how Jesus made sure Peter knew he was in right standing with Him after Peter denied Jesus three times. Let's take a look at Scripture. The Bible says "And many other signs truly did Jesus in the presence of his disciples, which are not written in this book: But these are written, that ye might believe that Jesus is the Christ, the Son of God; and that believing ye might have life through his name" (John 20:30–31, KJV). In the next chapter, Jesus aids His disciples in a great catch of fish, and Peter's love for Jesus is affirmed.

"After these things Jesus shewed himself again to the disciples at the sea of Tiberias; and on this wise shewed he himself. There were together Simon Peter, and Thomas called Didymus, and Nathanael of Cana in Galilea, and two other of his disciples. Simon Peter saith unto them, I go a fishing. They say unto him, We also go with thee. They went forth, and entered into a ship immediately: and that night they caught nothing. But when the morning was now come, Jesus stood on the shore: but the disciples knew not that it was Jesus. Then Jesus saith unto them, CHILDREN, HAVE YE ANY MEAT? They answered him, No. And he said unto them, CAST THE NET ON THE RIGHT SIDE OF THE SHIP, AND YE SHALL FIND. They cast therefore, and now they were not able to draw it for the multitude of fishes. Therefore the disciple whom Jesus loved saith unto Peter, It is the LORD. Now when Simon Peter heard that it was the LORD, he girt his fisher's coat unto him, and did cast himself into the sea. And the other disciples came in a little ship; (for it was not far from land, but as it were two hundred cubits,) dragging the net with fishes. As soon as they were come to land, they saw a fire of coals there, and fish laid thereon, and bread. Jesus saith unto them, BRING OF THE FISH

The Midnight Hour

WHICH YE HAVE NOW CAUGHT. Simon Peter went up, and drew the net to land full of great fishes, and hundred and fifty and three: and for all there were so many, yet was not the net broken. Jesus said unto then, COME AND DINE" (John 21:1–12, KJV Rainbow Study Bible, author's emphasis and paraphrase).

After the disciples had dined with Jesus, pay close attention to the details prior to and after the meal. The disciples had realized it was Jesus standing on the shore. They had made it through the night and had caught no fish. When it was morning again, they obeyed His word and the multitude of fishes were caught and the net was not broken.

What we learn from this is that we must choose to be in relationship with Jesus and move away from religion. We must learn to fellowship and dine with Him. We do this through reading, praying, and obeying His Word.

Out of relationship comes empowerment and purpose. We have a desire to please the Father God and be a witness to others. We live with eternity in mind and heart. We must choose to obey God, do business for God, and obey the Great Commission. Jesus calls us into the marketplace. As a matter of fact, Jesus was born in a manger, not in a church. He is calling us to live out of His great love that empowers us to live on purpose for God—personally, in business, and in the community and political realms to whatever sphere of influence we find ourselves.

Next in Scripture we see Jesus goes on to ask Simon Peter three questions. The three times Jesus asked Peter if he loved him was the same number that Peter denied Jesus in His betrayal. Jesus was restoring Peter and reconciling relationship, and telling him what to do next. Let's read this passage in the NIV Bible:

> *When they had finished eating, Jesus said to Simon Peter, "Simon son of John, do you love me more than these?" "Yes, Lord," he said, "You know that I love you." Jesus said, "Feed my lambs." Again Jesus said, "Simon son of John, do you love me?" He answered, "Yes, Lord, you know that I love you." Jesus said, "Take care of my sheep." The third time he said to him,*

> *"Simon son of John, do you love me?" Peter was hurt because Jesus asked him the third time, "Do you love me?" He said, "Lord, you know all these things; you know that I love you." Jesus said, "Feed my sheep.*
> —John 21:15–17, NIV

Jesus focused on His love for Peter and his purpose here on earth. The same holds true for us today. Peter's failures did not forfeit his purpose. Failure doesn't make any of us failures.

No matter what mistakes we have made or what someone else did that has affected us, the blood of Jesus still covers. We are called as the Body of Christ to affect the world for God.

God sees us through His Son—the precious blood of Jesus—that covers us completely. We must learn to see others through the cross of Jesus, through the blood, and through the pain Jesus suffered for us. People are hurting and afraid. People are searching for answers and need hope. Jesus is the answer!

Turning back to God is the answer. Turning to look for others in need of help is the answer. The church of Jesus Christ shall arise and impact the world. We must learn to affect the world through God's love and not be infected by the world and the world system.

Allow me to share one final story that brought tears to my eyes when I heard a pastor recount it.

In 1989 an 8.2 magnitude earthquake almost flattened Armenia, killing more than thirty thousand people in less than four minutes. There was utter devastation. A father left his wife at home and rushed to the school where his son was supposed to be, only to discover the building was destroyed.

After the initial shock, he remembered the promise he had made to his son: "No matter what, I'll always be there for you!" And tears began to fill his eyes. As he looked at the pile of debris that once was the school, it looked hopeless, but he remembered his pledge to his son.

He concentrated on where he walked his son to class at school each morning. Remembering his son's classroom location, he rushed there and started digging through the rubble. As he was digging, other parents arrived clutching their hearts and saying: "My son!" "My daughter!" Other parents tried to pull him from the rubble, saying, "It's too late!"

"They're dead!"

"You can't help!"

To each parent he responded, "Are you going to help me now?" and proceeded to dig for his son, stone by stone.

The fire chief showed up and tried to pull him off of the school's debris, to which this Armenian father asked, "Are you going to help me now?"

The police came and said, "You're angry, distraught, and it's over. You're endangering others. " And again he replied, "Are you going to help me now?"

But no one helped.

Courageously, he proceeded alone because he needed to know for himself: "Is my boy alive or is he dead?"

He dug for hours, for more than a day and into a second day when, in the 38th hour, he heard his son's voice. He screamed his son's name, "*Armand!*" and heard his son reply, "Dad!?! It's me! Dad! I told the other kids not to worry. I told 'em if you were alive you'd save me and them, too. And you promised, 'No matter what, I'll always be there for you!' You did it, Dad!"

"What's going on in there? How is it?" the father asked.

"There are fourteen of us left out of thirty-three, Dad. We're scared, hungry, thirsty, and thankful you're here. When the building collapsed, it made a wedge, like a triangle, and it saved us."

"Come on out, boy!"

"No, Dad! Let the other kids out first, 'cause I know you'll get me! No matter what, I know you'll be there for me!"

> *Be strong and courageous. Do not be afraid or terrified because of them, for the Lord your God goes with you; he will never leave you nor forsake you.*
> —Deuteronomy 31:5

The promise of our Father God still stands for us today. Will you turn back to God? Will you turn to God for America? After listening to this story while driving along the road back to my sister's home in

John's Island, I saw a father and son walking beside the lake carrying their fishing poles. The son turned to wave at me and the tears began to flow. I waved to him as we passed by and pulled in the driveway. I couldn't help but see how God was and is saying the same to us today—will you turn? Will you fish for souls? Will you go after the lost, hurting, and broken? Will you turn back to God for America and stand with Jesus?

Jesus left heaven and came to earth for you and me! He is calling out to us today to turn back to Him individually and as a nation.

Conclusion

America must get back to the basics and learn what walking is all about again. America must turn back to God. Will you choose to walk with Him?

Our walk with God includes walking, attacks, loving God and loving people, and the Kingdom of God! We are called to outlive our life in this world! We are to be about the Father's business—advancing the Kingdom of God!

We are living in the end of time—the Last Days. The alarms are sounding and we cannot continue to hit the snooze button and ignore the dangerous times that are in our face! The Bible says:

> *And from the time John the Baptist began preaching until now, the Kingdom of Heaven has been forcefully advancing, and violent people are attacking it.*
> —Matthew 11:12

The enemy is attacking Christianity—the inward presence of God suffers violence at the hands of Satan, but the violent take it by force. "By the grace of God, we are to keep authority over our bodies making them subject to the higher power—to God's mighty provision for sinful humanity"
—Smith Wigglesworth

Will you stand up for God? Will you pray and make a difference in this nation? Will you choose to turn back to God and have faith in Him again? We must choose to come under the ultimate authority again—God's rule—the Bible.

If we will repent and return, God will hear us and heal our land. If we want God to bless America, then we must first bless God by honoring Him and His Word.

The Bible tells us that we cannot serve two masters. We either love God or hate Him. God makes it clear and precise that we cannot have the world and have Him at the same time. (See 1 John 2:15–17.) He must be Lord of all of life. We have to arise and make a daily commitment to God above all else, as individuals, families, as the church, and as a nation!

The Bible says, "The LORD is not slack concerning His promise, as some count slackness, but is longsuffering toward us, not willing that any should perish but that all should come to repentance" (2 Pet. 3:9, NKJV). God is calling us to turn back to Him and to turn aside for the lost at any cost.

With the worldly deception, religious deception, wars and rumors of wars, and Jesus' command to us not to be troubled (or panic), nation (ethnic groups) rising against nation, kingdom (political systems) rising against kingdom, famine (scarcity-deficit-economic crisis-shortage of food), pestilence (plagues and diseases for which there is no easy cure), we know we are nearing the culmination of the end of the age. The Bible says: "And this gospel of the kingdom will be preached in all the world as a witness to all the nations, and then the end will come" (Matt. 24:14, NKJV). Never in the history of the world have we had the resources to spread the gospel like now—radio, satellite, internet—and the gospel is now available to all the inhabited places of the world.

The Bible also warns us of scoffers and mockers who would ask: "Where is this promise of His coming?" (See 2 Peter 3:1–6.) He is coming back my friends. Take time to turn aside for the lost!

The local church must return to God and become a house of prayer. The leadership must call for regular, unified times of prayer to keep the focus on our total dependency upon God! The church must call a solemn assembly where political leaders return to God's principles for government. (Read Romans 13:1–7.) We are not to be divided to the point where we are unwilling to speak truth because of party.

When we return to God and His kingdom agenda, we will see the fire of revival once again, in every man, woman and child across this land. It will sweep across America, from the White House to the marketplace, and individual communities once again. Will you pray for God to ignite your heart to be on fire for Him? Let us rise up together with hearts ablaze for Jesus and souls. You can make a deep impact and change the course of destiny in your personal family and nation.

The Call to Evangelism

America seems to be in great despair with a battle raging, but I believe God has already sent revival fires that are springing up all around. Revival is about to spark a flame in the people of this nation. God is faithful to His Word.

Many churches are already in place and stepping in when crisis has occurred in various cities to bring healing to the people. People are paying attention and taking notice of how God's people respond.

God is always faithful—people are not always faithful. Don't think that God can't use you as an individual to take a stand. Take a look at the life of Joseph. He was a man that honored God and the Lord prospered him everywhere he was in life. From the family to the pit, from the pit to the palace, God was with Him. His brothers were opportunists and they grew jealous over their own brother's calling in life with God. Their jealousy drove them to plot murder but they settled for selling their own brother off to a caravan of traders.

In the pit Joseph had to make a choice; in Potiphar's house he chose to flee sexual temptation, in the prison being falsely accused he shared his gifts (dreams and interpretation), and in the palace he shared his resources. The story ended with forgiveness and sustaining the people of nations, and our story only ends well with forgiveness and doing what God has put in our hearts to do with Him.

American must move from opportunism to evangelism if she is to be a nation that gives glory to God! Rather than being like Joseph's brothers, why not be on the lookout for lost souls? Joseph's brothers that wanted to get rid of him for selfish gain certainly fit this description of an opportunist. Their character was not so great.

The Midnight Hour

Let's look back at the Bible for a few minutes. Recall with me that God accompanied His call to Abraham with core promises. Those promises are still in operation today. (See Genesis 12:2–3.) First, God would multiply his descendants into a great nation. Second, God would bless him and third, God would make his name great, meaning he would be worthy of renown. Fourth, Abraham would be a blessing that pertains to future generations of his family, and to all the generations of the earth. God would bless those who blessed Abraham and curse those who cursed him.

Take notice that the Book of Genesis also traces the partial fulfillment through the chosen line of Abraham's descendants, Isaac, Jacob, and Jacob's sons. Among them all, it is in the life of Joseph that God most directly fulfills His promise through the people of Abraham. People from "all the world" were sustained through the food system that Joseph established and managed (see Gen. 41:57). Joseph discovered and recognized his mission, then chose to move forward and articulated the purpose of his life aligned with God's plans and purpose: "the saving of many lives" (Gen. 50:20, NIV).

Joseph believed God had destined him for greatness from a young age (Gen. 37:5-11). God has a plan and a purpose for every person on the planet. It is our choice if we choose it or not!

God assured Joseph through dreams that he would rise to a position of leadership over his family. Joseph recognized the dreams as God's way of leading him while his brother rose up in envy. His brothers must have thought the dreams were further manifestations of the favorite position Joseph enjoyed as his father's favorite son. Joseph's brothers obviously didn't understand what was happening, and perhaps neither did Joseph. (This is a parallel to the Father God sending His Son Jesus to redeem all mankind and sustain us with the Bread of Life—the Word of God.)

Was it wrong that this position fostered envy rather than cooperation? As a result of the brothers' perception, evil rose up in their hearts and they plotted a murder scheme. They were much like the elder brother in the story of the Prodigal Son. They had everything in their Father's house, but chose to devise a scheme in their minds and hearts. Rather than murder, they settled for selling Joseph to a caravan of traders bearing goods from Canaan on their way to Egypt.

The merchants sold Joseph to Potiphar, a "captain of the guard" who was an "officer of Pharaoh" (Gen. 37:36; 39:1). Joseph had a wide range of fiduciary responsibilities in the master's house and was quickly promoted to be steward and "put him in charge of over all that he had" (Gen. 39:4). After time passed, Potiphar's wife became sexually interested in Joseph (Gen. 39:7) — nothing more than a scandal to take Joseph out of his destiny in God. He was falsely accused and thrown into prison. Joseph's godliness did not rescue him from being falsely accused nor did it rescue him from being falsely imprisoned. We must remember that God defends the weak and we must take a stand as evangelism is like emergency surgery. Souls are at stake in America and across the globe.

Joseph's story and life provides an example for us, that even when falsely accused and mistreated, we are to carry on the work that God has put before us and trust God to make all right in the end.

Think with me for a minute about the parallels. Joseph's brothers became jealous of the call on their own brother's life — and resorted to plotting murder, but changed their mind to selling him off (like Judas did with Jesus).

In the Bible we find Barnabus was a great encourager and a giver. God was using him in such a great way that Ananias and Sapphira wanted to be like Barnabus, however, they resorted to lying and keeping funds back for themselves — rather than being totally honest about the sell of their land.

Deliberate deception (Acts 5:1-2) starts with a connective (but) connected with something before. What was the reason here? They saw what Barnabus did prior and wanted to do the same but without the same heart and motive. We can see in Acts 4:36-37, the account of when Barnabus sold land and laid the offering at the apostle's feet. What Ananias and Sapphira did was opposite. Barnabus sold his property and gave all.

Ananias and Sapphira created deception — sin was the deceit, hypocrisy, and lying to the Holy Spirit. They really didn't have to give anything but because they were consumed with appearance and pretended to have given all, lied to the Holy Spirit and died.

We must choose to die to the flesh as well. False appearances, trying to be like someone else, envy, jealousy, and all other forms of competition must cease.

If Satan can't conquer us in one area, he will try another. If he can't conquer you he will try to deceive you from within. Their actions were fueled by hypocrisy and greed. They had a love for money. Judas had a similar problem as revealed in Scripture. He seemingly cared more for money than he did people.

Ananias and Sapphira fell dead and were buried. They needed a heart examination. Mercy triumphs over judgment—and the church began to grow in number. God added to the church.

We must remember "there will be no mercy for those who have not shown mercy to others. But if you have been merciful, God will be merciful when he judges you" (James 2:13, NLT). Are we showing mercy and grace to others? Ask yourself that question. When we show mercy and grace to others, we reveal the love of God to others and He adds to His church—the body of believers in Jesus Christ.

We all need to maintain a heart examination on a daily basis and have our eyes checked regularly in the natural. What are we seeing around us? Real evangelism takes places when we see what God sees and realize that all people have potential in God, even if they don't see it themselves.

People have broken images and are in need of affirmation and acceptance. We must choose to love people and show our concern without making them feel condemnation. The world is experiencing an identity crisis. No matter what a man or woman does on the outside, it will never fix or heal the problem on the inside that can only be touched by God.

Shame causes people to cover and hide. Striving for position causes people to lie, steal, and manipulate circumstances to achieve their ambition. False perception is a lie from the pit of hell. Evil and disobedience cause broken relationships and the list goes onward.

Jesus came and died for all mankind. The story ends well. How will your story end? Will you turn back to God for America and all mankind? Will you turn to God in prayer for all? God wants healing to sweep across this land.

The Call to Evangelism

Joseph had forgiven his brothers long before they arrived in Egypt. He was focused on rebuilding his family and moved forward with a heart of forgiveness. You can read about forgiveness for the family in Genesis 49:33–50:9 and Genesis 50:14–26.

Forgiveness opens the door to salvation and going home to be with the Lord. The last chapter of Genesis ends with forgiveness. After a four-generation drama series of deception, discouragement, and disappointment, the story ends with forgiveness and healing. How will your story end?

This story sets the stage for nation building and introduces the theme of forgiveness. God can be trusted, even though life is full of misfortune, treachery, deception, betrayal, suffering, and disappointment. Have you moved to fully trusting God, no matter what you or someone you love is going through, to continue in leading others to Christ through your witness? Your daily walk is your witness.

Do you find mixture in your walk? Do you love people to their face and find yourself being ruthless and ridiculing when they are not present? Do you have an eternity mindset? Do you really love what God loves? Do you hate what God hates? Do you love God and the people of America and across the nations?

Do you view evangelism as a lifestyle and as emergency surgery? You must! Jesus came to make us fishers of men. Will you join me? Do you live like Jesus may come in the next two minutes? Evangelism is the heartbeat of God the Father. He gave His Son to redeem all mankind. What will you give?

Evangelism must be the natural outflow of a thankful heart. Check out your attitude toward God and others. How we treat others is how we are treating Jesus.

If you are willing to be used by God, He will use you anywhere and anytime to bring souls into His Kingdom. Are you ready to be the hands and feet of Jesus in your city and community? (You can read the following later: Mark 16:15; Matthew 28:19–20; Romans 10:10–17; Matthew 9:37–38; 1 Corinthians 9:22; Isaiah 6:8; 1 Peter 3:15; Romans 1:16; Mark 16:15–16; Acts 1:8; 2 Timothy 4:5; Colossians 4:2–6; Luke 19:10; Mark 16:16; Matthew 28:18–20; 1 Corinthians 1:17; 2 Timothy 2:15; Acts 2:38; and Proverbs 11:30.) "The fruit of the righteous is a tree of life, and whoever captures souls is wise" (ESV). These are just a few of the scriptures on evangelism.

Keep in mind that the Holy Spirit dwelling in us is far more powerful than any force of darkness in the world (1 John 4:4). No Christian should ever fear anything the devil puts in the way, from a demonic book or artifact to the wayward actions of a son or daughter, to the violence across America. Turn to God, stand firm upon the Word of God, and trust Him for the outcome.

Good always triumphs. If you don't believe me, look at the all the hero figures kids are seeing today. The Bible shows us who wins for today and forever. It is never easy to watch ungodly activity and unbiblical belief grow in popularity throughout like we are witnessing today in our culture and media, nor is it ever comfortable to take a stand against such problems of evil. In order to make a difference, you must arrive to the place of losing the fear of man—what others may think.

Nevertheless, Christians are commanded by Scripture to "preach the word" and always be prepared to impart the truth to others (2 Tim. 4:2). Just as important as truth is the manner in which we impart truth. The apostle Peter says it should be done with gentleness and reverence (1 Pet. 3:15). We are not called to condemn people and tell them how wrong they are when they come to us for help—we are to love them and show them the way. If it had not been for the grace of God, need I say more at this point? We have all failed and will most likely fail again in some manner. Get back up, shake off the dust, and keep moving forward with trust in God and be patient with yourself and others. Everyone is on a journey of growth.

Paul tells us that the spreading of the gospel involves great patience with leaning toward a view of instruction (2 Tim. 4:2). This is really how Jesus is revealed to others—through God's love. Jesus said that proof of a genuine believer is inextricably linked to how love is shown (John 13:35). Ephesians 4:15 gives clear instruction to speak the truth in love.

We are to show respect to others. Honor is not seen much today in many circles. We must learn to communicate concern rather than condemnation. We must not resort to mockery and making fun of people nor calling down fire and brimstone. The quickest way to

The Call to Evangelism

shut doors and destroy communication is by making someone feel attacked. When anyone feels attacked, emotions are about to rise up and will inevitably create distance. In Second Timothy 2:24–26, Paul teaches that every ministering encounter is to be permeated with kindness and gentleness.

Criticizing someone's point of view shuts the door as well. Rather than criticizing, ask questions or say something like, "You have made an interesting point, but have you thought of it this way?"

Remember the enemy is not people, but forces of darkness operating behind and through people. The true enemies are evil spiritual forces of darkness seeking to overshadow godly values and virtues with evil practices, immorality, and occult myths. This is really no great surprise. God warned believers long ago. Scripture tells us there would appear many deceitful spirits and doctrines of demons to draw people away from truth (1 Tim. 4:1).

As believers, we must have our facts straight and not repeat anything we have heard, assuming it to be truth. There is always something we don't know in every situation. Like Joseph, being falsely accused and wrongly imprisoned—we know that today life is still not always fair. Be careful not to judge others, but pray for the family of God and obey God's Word.

We cannot ignore the biblical instruction to put on "the armor of God" (Eph. 6:10–17). It is *only* through God's power and His strength that any of us will be able to stand against the evil and spiritual forces of darkness influencing our culture here in America and across the world.

With the belt of truth (Eph. 6:14) as a believer in Christ, being born from above gives us belief within, and we will be able to actively pursue the task of presenting boldness and humility, the warning that life is short, eternity is forever, and we must choose. The breastplate of righteousness (6:14) will enable and empower us to stand blameless and holy in front of a world that is clearly against Christ. God's spiritual footwear, the shoes of peace (6:15), a clear symbol of readiness of spirit and a willingness to communicate the good news of the Gospel no matter what struggles may arise—and they will.

Behind the shield of faith (6:16) we will be protected from fiery darts. Thank God for the shield of faith we raise up in prayer that quenches every fiery dart from hell. When we choose to keep the Word of God in our hearts, our hearts are watered with the Word and when a fiery dart comes, it will not penetrate.

Our most powerful weapon is God's Word, the sword of the spirit (6:17), which is able to divide truth from error even in the most perplexing and confusing situations (Hebrew 4:12).

Finally, remember God is in control. Maintain a heavenly perspective (2 Cor. 4:16–18) and trust that at the end of ages Christ will be victorious over everything that has exalted itself against God (10:4–5). We can confidently face each day with God.

THE BIBLICAL TRUTH ABOUT ISIS

One of the most shocking aspects of the rise of ISIS, particularly with regard to the horrifying murders it has committed, is the pure, unadulterated hatred that has accompanied these gruesome acts. Believers are facing grave challenges today from ISIS in parts of the world. We must first and foremost arm ourselves with the knowledge that Scripture provides to combat the falsehood that comes when evil rises. The battle in which we are engaged is purely demonic and evil as pointed out in Scripture.

Paul writes, "For we do not wrestle against flesh and blood, but against principalities, against powers, against the rulers of the darkness of this age, against spiritual hosts of wickedness in the heavenly places" (Eph. 6:12).

We must acknowledge that ISIS is not well understood by the West. We must also reckon with the motivation that sanctions gruesome killings and a variety of criminal activities all in the name of a religious belief that may be as fervently cherished as that of the most convinced Christians and observant Jews. The fact that ISIS is driven by their theology is what makes them so dangerous.

Our response is that we must pray for the peace of Jerusalem. If ISIS has its way, it will stop at nothing to either destroy or take over Israel. Neither Isaiah nor Jeremiah named ISIS specifically in Scripture, but they do say enemies would surround Israel, and this is apparently coming true in alarming fashion. As the second coming of the Lord seems closer and nearly at the door as predicted future unveils before our eyes, let us pray, but also prepare our hearts for the difficult times to come by drawing close to the Lord. We must also proclaim the truth that there is salvation in no one other than Jesus the Messiah. This is true for Jewish people and non-Jews, whether they follow Hinduism, Buddhism, or Islam.

Our responsibility is to be His vessels of mercy and grace to all — to the Jew first and also to the Gentiles — including ISIS.

Take time to read Zechariah chapters 12–14 and you will come to understand that the scene is set and we seem to be on the precipice of the return of Jesus with all of the events attached to the End of the Age being unveiled before our eyes.

We must be vigilant, prayerful and more committed than ever to the Great Commission to reach the Jewish people, Arabs, and all the peoples of the earth who so desperately need to know the soon-coming Savior.

(Visit: www.chosenpeople.com for more information: Dr. Mitch Glaser, President)

Visit: www.alkarmatv.com (for all Arabic speaking people)

Recommended Reading

The Harbinger, by Rabbi Jonathan Cahn

The Mystery of the Shemitah, by Rabbi Jonathan Cahn

The Four Blood Moons, by Pastor John Hagee

Brokenness: The Forgotten Factor of Prayer, by Mickey Bonner

For Further Study

"The Treasure of David: Psalm 21": www.spurgeon.org/treasury/ps021.htm
"Revelation 6:12": http://www.biblestudytools.com/commentaries/revelation/revelation-6/revelation-6-12.html
Balanced Christian Life, by Watchman Nee

Notes

THE HEART MATTERS GREATLY

1. Dr. Mehmet Oz quote from website: www.sharecare.com, visited 4/30/15.

AMERICA IS IN SERIOUS TROUBLE

1. *Lectures On Revival*, Charles G. Finney, p. 177.
2. Ibid., p. 176.
3. Ibid., p. 180.

MINISTERING UNTO THE LORD

1. *Strong's* #8334

EVIL AND SUFFERING

1. *Sparkling Gem*, by Rick Renner. (A great devotional with in-depth teaching.)

TRAIN YOUR BRAIN

1. Charles Finney, *Finney's Systematic Theology* (The Complete & Newly Expanded 1878 Edition)

About the Author

Dr. Deborah Starczewski is the Founder and President of Star National Outreach Worldwide, Inc. (Non-Profit), and Star Ministries, Inc. (Publishing and Distributing the Word of God). She is on faculty at Life Christian University and teaches at satellite universities, as well as teaching locally and globally to equip the Body of Christ across the nations. She speaks at conferences and churches upon request.

Having personally experienced heartache, pain, and rejection, Deborah understands the challenges that often accompany everyday life. She focuses on knowing God and making Him known to others as she imparts truth from the Word of God, believing that everyone has been created by God for a divine purpose. Her message is powerful and her testimonies of God's divine intervention are miraculous! She will inspire you to seek God for yourself as she shares her wisdom and insight into the heart of God!

What matters most to Deborah is seeing lives changed by the power of the Holy Spirit, hearts healed, and destinies fulfilled for those who dare to dream and step out into God's plan for their life. She is an ordained minister, wife, mother, grandmother, author of GOD'S PRICELESS TREASURE and A LEAP OF FAITH (25 Days at the Mercy Seat), evangelist, and a prophetic voice to the nations.

Contact the Author

Dr. Deborah Starczewski

Star National Outreach Worldwide, Inc. (Non-Profit) Star Ministries, Inc. (Publishing and Distributing the Word of God)
P. O. Box 70 Cornelius, NC 28031

Email: Deborah@starministriesinc.com

www.starministriesinc.com

Other books by the author

God's Priceless Treasure: How to Overcome Challenges, Be Transformed, and Know Your Purpose and *A Leap of Faith: 25 Days at the Mercy Seat* are my first two books that are filled with modern, up-to-date miracles and relevant stories that will give you hope to believe for whatever you are currently facing in life.

Each book can be purchased through Star Ministries at: www.starministriesinc.com and are also available online through Amazon, Barnes & Noble, and Christian Book Distributors.